# ENGLISH

## Writing Frames

*Inform, explain, describe*

## Roger Machin

CW00456407

# Contents

| Unit | Page |
|------|------|
| **Introduction** | 3 |
| *Unit 1:* **Meteor strike!** <br> Text level – Writing: YEAR 7, Objectives 1 and 11 | 4 |
| *Unit 2:* **A murder setting** <br> Text level – Writing: YEAR 7, Objectives 1 and 14 | 8 |
| *Unit 3:* **Big cats** <br> Text level – Writing: YEAR 7, Objectives 2 and 11 | 12 |
| *Unit 4:* **Other worlds** <br> Text level – Writing: YEAR 7, Objectives 3 and 10 | 16 |
| *Unit 5:* **Different people** <br> Text level – Writing: YEAR 7, Objectives 3 and 14 | 20 |
| *Unit 6:* **Baby talk** <br> Text level – Writing: YEAR 7, Objectives 12 and 13 | 24 |
| *Unit 7:* **Snakebite** <br> Text level – Writing: YEAR 8, Objectives 1 and 12 | 28 |
| *Unit 8:* **Dinosaurs from the deep** <br> Text level – Writing: YEAR 8, Objectives 2 and 10 | 32 |
| *Unit 9:* **Thoughts and feelings** <br> Text level – Writing: YEAR 8, Objectives 3 and 11 | 36 |
| *Unit 10:* **Weird science** <br> Text level – Writing: YEAR 8, Objectives 3 and 11 | 40 |
| *Unit 11:* **Volcano research** <br> Text level – Writing: YEAR 8, Objectives 10 and 11 | 44 |

First published 2002 by Folens Limited.
United Kingdom: Folens Publishers, Apex Business Centre, Boscombe Road, Dunstable, LU5 4RL.
Email: folens@folens.com

Ireland: Folens Publishers, Greenhills Road, Tallaght, Dublin 24.
Email: info@folens.ie

Poland: JUKA, ul. Renesansowa 38, Warsaw 01-905.

Folens allows photocopying of pages marked 'copiable page' for educational use, providing that this use is within the confines of the purchasing institution. Copiable pages should not be declared in any return in respect of any photocopying licence.

Folens publications are protected by international copyright laws. All rights are reserved. The copyright of all materials in this publication, except where otherwise stated, remains the property of the publisher and authors. No part of this publication may be reproduced, stored in a retrieval system, or transmitted, in any form or by any means, for whatever purpose, without the written permission of Folens Limited.

Roger Machin hereby asserts his moral right to be identified as the author of this work in accordance with the Copyright, Designs and Patents Act 1988.

Editor: Sue Harmes
Layout artist: Suzanne Ward
Cover design: Martin Cross
Illustrations: Kay Dixey – Linda Rogers Associates

© 2002 Folens Limited, on behalf of the authors.
Every effort has been made to trace the copyright holders of material used in this publication. If any copyright holder has been overlooked, we should be pleased to make any necessary arrangements.

British Library Cataloguing in Publication Data. A catalogue record for this publication is available from the British Library.
ISBN 1 84303 110–8

# Introduction

The series *English Writing Frames for Ages 11–14* provides structured support, detailed plans, and a wide range of ideas for teachers charged with ensuring students' skills in English are reviewed, developed and, where necessary, newly learned.

The structure of the units is common across the series, each unit consisting of four pages and sequenced in the following order.

## Sheet 1: Teacher resource
This provides a highly structured lesson plan, featuring:

**Main objectives** – the main focus of the work, taken from the *Framework for Teaching English*

**Additional focus** – other skills or knowledge covered throughout the work

**Starter activity** – an initial task or tasks for the class, providing a focus for the work to come, reviewing skills covered previously, and so on

**Further preparation** – further tasks for the class or individual students, based on the resources provided

**Main activity** – guidance on how to use the writing frame provided

**Maximising attainment** – suggestions on how more confident or weaker students can be supported.

## Sheet 2: Source material
Original sources from a range of writers, classical and modern, in a range of forms (poems, prose, screenplay, comic strip and so on). These may be used as overhead transparencies.

## Sheet 3: Worksheet (or further source material)
Usually, a task aimed at preparing students for the main writing assignment. In some units, a different source text is provided where the focus demands it.

## Sheet 4: Writing frame
In most cases, the writing frame brings together the skills covered throughout the unit, and provides an essential template around which students can 'hang' the ideas they have worked on.

## Using the CD

There is a CD to accompany each title in the series. Each CD provides all the student resources with carefully adjusted tasks to suit on-screen work. Key features include:
- a facility for the teacher to *modify and adapt* the frames to suit his or her students
- a facility to *switch between screens*, and cut and paste key information or ideas between one screen and another
- a *'drop-down' menu of key vocabulary*, that students can access and place in their writing
- a *print out of the frames*, in which the boxes disappear, leaving only continuous prose or verse (the boxes also expand on screen so that students can add unlimited prose text, where appropriate)
- a facility to project text on to a screen or electronic whiteboard for demonstration and modelling work.

*Inform, explain, describe* consists of a wide range of source texts including material on dinosaurs, meteor strikes, volcanoes and characterisation. The teaching points address relevant objectives for Years 7 and 8 from *Text Level – Writing* in the *Framework for Teaching English*. There are cross-references on the contents page to these objectives, but teachers will see that many additional targets are also covered, too numerous to list here.

# Meteor strike!

**Main Objective**

- *To select and present information using detail, example, diagram and illustration as appropriate.*

**Additional Focus**

- *To plan, draft, edit, revise, proofread and present a text with readers and purpose in mind.*

**Starter Activity**

- Get students to tell you all they know about meteors. Discuss what happens when an object hits Earth – they might be able to tell you about the collision 65 million years ago that obliterated the dinosaurs, they may know about subsequent atmospheric darkening, and some of them may have seen the Bruce Willis film, *Armageddon*. When you have completed this initial discussion, ask students what they still do not know about meteor strikes. Get them to help you make a list on the board of at least five questions, the answers to which would make them better informed on the subject. Leave the questions up for later reference.

**Further Preparation**

- Hand out copies of the source material 'Catastrophe!' and read it through with the class. Check for understanding and make the figures more immediate by relating them to your own geographical area. It is also helpful to draw students' attention to the use of the conditional 'would', which is used here to express a realistic outcome. Establish whether the text answers the questions generated in the starter activity. If there are unanswered questions, they will probably be dealt with on the worksheet 'Strike two', page 6, which you should now give out. Discuss this new information. Most students will recognise this data as less dramatic than that given before – and they should also note the mention of a human defence capability. Help students identify groups of people (religious sects, politicians, filmmakers, space scientists, environmentalists, novelists, geologists, newspaper editors) who could use the information they have encountered. For the purposes of the next activity, make sure they include novelists on their lists. Now discuss the ways that these different groups could use the same information and ask students to complete the worksheet.

**Main Activity/ Using the Frame**

- Give out the writing frame. Explain that many famous novelists employ researchers to collect data for them. On this occasion, one of these writers has requested information for a book about a meteor collision. The prompts direct students to explain to the novelist the dramatic potential of large-, medium- and small-scale strikes in turn. Help students to select relevant information from the texts before they attempt the frame.

**Maximising Attainment**

- Ask students to write a short story version of the novel they have researched. Encourage them to use as much of the information from the source texts as they can. If students have access to good research facilities they will enjoy finding out more about the Tunguska strike in 1908. Get them to give a short presentation of their findings to the rest of the class using visual aids (diagrams, photographs, illustrations or perhaps Powerpoint) that help to convey the magnitude of the event.

# Catastrophe!

Many scientists and government leaders are concerned about the possibility of a collision with a meteor with a diameter of 0.6 mile or more. At a speed of 30 miles a second, an object that size would hit Earth with the energy of one million one-megaton hydrogen bombs, or one trillion tons of TNT. Experts say the destruction and loss of life resulting from such a collision would surpass anything humanity has ever experienced from a single event.

Flashing through Earth's atmosphere in about two seconds, the object would smash into the ground with incredible force and explode in an immense fireball. The shock wave from the blast would level virtually everything for a radius of more than 60 miles. Within much of that area, the heat of the fireball would reduce the debris to ashes and shapeless blobs of melted stone and metal. Beyond the ring of total destruction, damage from the shock wave and heat would be severe to moderate for another 600 miles.

The collision would produce a crater at least 12 miles across and several miles deep. The force of the impact would hurl molten material long distances, igniting forest fires, and eject an immense volume of dust and vaporized rock into the atmosphere. The dust and gas would spread around the planet and obscure the sun. The atmospheric effects from a 0.6-mile-meteor strike might cause widespread crop failures and starvation. So even if we had adequate warning of the collision and evacuated the areas most apt to be devastated, these secondary effects could still cause great loss of life.

But what about the more likely possibility that a meteor would hit the ocean? Unfortunately, that too would be a disaster. Although a strike far out at sea might spare cities from being flattened or burned, the collision would still do plenty of damage. After its plunge through the atmosphere, the object would plough through several miles of seawater in a fraction of a second, breaking apart from the force of the impact. Still moving at immense speed, the meteor would burrow into the sea floor and explode, creating a crater more than 6 miles in diameter and spewing material in all directions. Vast amounts of steam and vaporized rock would be thrown upward before the parted water could rush back to cover the hole in the sea floor.

The worst effect of an ocean strike might be the resulting tidal wave. The object's sudden displacement of a huge volume of water, together with the titanic blast on the sea floor, would create a tidal wave a half a mile or more in height that would surge outward at almost 600 miles an hour. Many low-lying coastal cities would be submerged.

Adapted from the *World Book* website.

# Strike two

**I.** Read this second set of facts about meteors.

- An object six miles or more in diameter strikes Earth on average once every 100 million years. Such a collision is widely believed to be responsible for the disappearance of the dinosaurs and would wipe out civilisation as we know it.

- A body with a diameter of around 0.6 of a mile (such as that described in the extract you have already read) strikes Earth once every million years on average.

- An object 100 feet or so in diameter strikes Earth on average once every 200 to 300 years. The last such collision was in Tunguska, Siberia in 1908. Such events cause devastation over hundreds of square miles but are statistically unlikely to affect populated areas.

- Scientists are now very good at tracking 'Near Earth Objects'. They are increasingly confident that they could use explosives to deflect Earth-bound objects of the sizes described above.

**2.** Explain the differences between these facts and the information you read about on the first sheet.

_____

_____

_____

**3.** Now read through both extracts again. Make a list of five different groups of people who could make use of the information you have read. Then explain how they could use the information.

**a.** _____     _____

_____

_____

**b.** _____     _____

_____

_____

**c.** _____     _____

_____

_____

**d.** _____     _____

_____

_____

**e.** _____     _____

_____

_____

Inform, explain, describe     © Folens (copiable page)

# Writing frame

If you want to write a novel about total destruction caused by an object colliding with Earth, you need to know that

Total destruction is caused not only by the strike itself, but also by

A strike such as this was responsible for

However, I don't think this would make a very good story because

You might be better concentrating on a smaller strike from an object with a diameter of 0.6 mile. If it hit land, such an object would

If it hit the sea, a meteor this size would

It could be interesting to write a story about a much smaller meteor. This is because

Whatever type of meteor strike you choose, I would advise you not to write too much about

I would concentrate on

TEACHER RESOURCE

# A murder setting

**Main Objective**

- *To describe an object, person or setting in a way that includes relevant details and is accurate and evocative.*

**Additional Focus**

- *To plan, draft, edit, revise, proofread and present a text with readers and purpose in mind.*

**Starter Activity**

- Discuss with your class the elements of a good written description. Get them to talk about:

  - interesting adjective and adverb use
  - detailed observation on the part of the writer
  - imagery – especially simile and personification
  - implication – things being suggested and hinted at rather than stated.

  Now hand out copies of the source material 'Murder scene' and read through Murder Scene One. Discuss what is so obviously lacking from this description in terms of the points raised above.

**Further Preparation**

- Read Murder Scene Two. Get students to identify as many of the writer's descriptive techniques as they can. Make sure that your discussion covers the following elements of the text:

  - The use of gloomy adjectives: 'heavy', 'oaken', 'miserable'.
  - The use of adverbs for personification: 'unhappily', 'grimly', 'sullenly'.
  - Detailed observation: the clock, the spider's web, the television.
  - Similes: the cutlery, the wine, the dead fly.
  - Implication: of disturbed dinner, of death and decay, of stabbing.

**Main Activity/ Using the Frame**

- Pass out copies of the worksheet 'Bring it to life', page 10. Look at the example of 'the door' which is presented in descriptive detail through the use of adjectives, an uncommon verb and a rather colourful simile that personifies the original subject. Get students to write their own extended sentences around the other nouns on the sheet. Encourage them to use the structure of the example: Adjective(s) + Noun + Verb + Adverb + Extended Simile. The verb must not be a form of 'be' as this will make it impossible to expand the sentence further. In some of their sentences, students should use verbs and adverbs for personification. When they have completed the sheet, give out copies of the writing frame. The second, third and fourth prompts are designed to elicit examples of adverb use, detailed observation and the use of similes. The fifth prompt requires an understanding of the word 'implication'. In their own murder scenes, students should obviously try to utilise a selection of the skills covered in this lesson. Encourage them to use some of their own sentences already generated in the worksheet.

**Maximising Attainment**

- Get students to expand either their own description or Murder Scene Two into a two- or three-scene story. Remind them to continue writing in a descriptive style and discourage them from introducing dialogue.

# Murder scene

### Murder Scene One

I walked through the kitchen door. I couldn't see the far part of the kitchen because it was round a corner. There was a table in the middle of the room and it was laid for dinner with cutlery and a bottle of wine. I heard a clock ticking and I saw a spider's web with a dead fly in it. I walked towards the far part of the kitchen and heard a sound that turned out to be coming from an untuned television. I looked down and saw blood on the floor.

### Murder Scene Two

The heavy, oaken door was ajar but needed a firm push before unwillingly creaking open. The kitchen struck me immediately as the gloomiest of chambers. Only the nearer half was visible from where I stood. The further part of the kitchen, containing the cooker and the sink, was hidden around a silent corner. The sun shone unhappily through a greasy window and I could see a few specks of dust turning mournfully in the light. The wind toyed aimlessly with the faded and worn curtains. A large wooden table stood grimly in the middle of the dark floor and one object, a carving knife, lay sullenly and alone in the centre. At either end of the table were two places laid for dinner. There was an array of silver serving cutlery. It glittered like a row of sharp, well polished teeth. The only other object on the table was an unopened bottle of red wine, the contents reflected in the miserable light of the sun like the dark blood from an old wound. As I stood regarding the scene, I became aware of the noise of a clock from somewhere behind me. Its ticking affected me as being like the pulsing of a faint heartbeat. While I paused, the ticking became louder, until it became a thudding that seemed to take me over until it was like a beating fist behind my eyes. I shook my head to rid myself of the feeling. As I did so, my eyes fixed upon a corner of the grimy wall nearest me. The room had obviously not been dusted for months and a spider's web clung like a bony, transparent hand to the damp, grey wallpaper. In its centre was an insect, trapped weeks before no doubt, a hard, solid lump of dead flesh. It seemed to stare out at me like the pupil of a coal black, wicked eye and I had to pull myself away from its evil and hypnotic gaze. I walked slowly around the table, my hand on its edge as though I were walking in the dark, and towards the far end of the room, the part of the kitchen I had not yet seen. The ticking of the clock had faded from my ears and was now replaced by what seemed to me to be the sound of rain pattering on a far away roof. As I neared the hidden part of the kitchen the sound of this unnatural rain became louder. When I turned the corner I breathed out quietly in relief. The pattering had been caused by the static from a portable television, untuned but turned on, sitting on a shelf. I switched it off.  Underfoot, I felt a slipperiness, as if I were walking on melting ice. I looked down. The vinyl floor, chipped and cracked, was wet with fresh blood.

████████████████████████████

# Bring it to life

Write extended sentences around the nouns below. The first one has been done for you as an example.

**The door**

*The heavy oak door creaked open.*

*The heavy oak door creaked wearily open like the toothless, gasping mouth of a dying old man.*

**The carpet**

_____

_____

**The moon**

_____

_____

**The photograph**

_____

_____

**The telephone**

_____

_____

**The razor**

_____

_____

**The trees**

_____

_____

Inform, explain, describe          © Folens (copiable page)

# Writing frame

I have read descriptions of two murder scenes. The first is

whilst the second contains

From Murder Scene Two, here is an example of adverb use:

This is an example of detailed observation:

Here, finally, is an example of the use of similes:

I think the implication in Murder Scene Two is that

Here is my own description of a murder scene:

# Big cats

**Main Objective**
- *To select and present information using detail, example, diagram and illustration as appropriate.*

**Additional Focus**
- *To collect, select and assemble ideas in a suitable planning format.*

**Starter Activity**
- Before the lesson begins, copy the following text on to the board or project it from the CD-ROM.

  'The tiger, more than any of the other big cats, has earned a reputation as a man-eater. In the Sundarbans Reserve in the swamp lands along the coast of the Bay of Bengal it has been reported that tigers have attacked fishermen in their boats – however, such unprovoked attacks are rare. Attacks mainly occur when humans stray into reserved areas to collect firewood or food and then, more often than not, it is by old or injured tigers unable to compete for normal prey.'

  Ask students to explain why it may be necessary sometimes to reduce texts like this to note form. Now tell them that this particular text contains 85 words. Get them to help you reduce it to around twenty words of notes, making sure the essential information is retained. An example might be: 'Tiger – man-eater? Some attacks on Indian fishermen. But **unprovoked** attacks rare. Usually by old/injured tigers in reserved areas.'

  When you have done this, discuss the techniques you have used.

**Further Preparation**
- Give out copies of the worksheet 'The leopard', on page 14. Read the notes through with students. If necessary, discuss possible answers with them. Ask them to identify any points at which illustration might complement the notes. When they are ready, let them fill in the sheet.

**Main Activity/ Using the Frame**
- Now hand out copies of the source material 'The king of beasts'. Read the text and discuss how it can be divided (using the existing paragraphs) into four separate sections, as might appear in a children's information book, for example. Now get students to suggest ways in which pictures or diagrams could be used to clarify specific elements of the passage. Finally, discuss which information is essential and should not be left out of a summary.

  Give out copies of the writing frame and allow students to convert the original text from the source material into note form using some or all of the techniques of language use, layout and illustration you have studied and discussed. Remind them to use some of the skills they identified in their study of 'The leopard'.

**Maximising Attainment**
- Ask students to convert the notes on 'The leopard' into continuous prose. In order to do this, they will need to do a brief analysis of the typical verb forms and stock phrases used (present tense, words such as 'uniform', 'offspring', etc.). When they have done this, discuss the differences between the new text and the original notes. Get them to list three situations in which note form would be appropriate and three in which prose would be more suitable.

# The king of beasts

In appearance the lion is a powerfully built, muscular cat. The fur is short and generally uniform in colour, ranging from grey/buff to reddish brown in coloration with the exception of the undersides which are often white, especially in females. The back of the ears and tip of the tail are dark brown or black. However the most distinctive feature of the male lion is its mane, a ruff of thick, long fur. The colour of the mane varies from a light brown to almost black and covers the sides of the face, neck and in some animals extends to the abdomen. The adolescent male begins to grow its mane at about 18 months and it continues to grow until the cat reaches about five years of age – throughout this period it is common for the mane to darken. A fully developed male lion can grow up to 10 feet in body length.

The lion is unusual amongst the cat species in that it lives in an organised social group called a pride. The pride can consist of as many as thirty to forty lions, the majority of which are females and their offspring along with a small number of resident males. It is common for the females within the pride to be closely related and this family bonding is often extended through communal suckling and caring for the young within the group. The territory of the pride is fixed and varies in size depending on the availability and distribution of prey. In larger territories, which can be as much as 200 square miles, prides are often split into smaller social groupings.

Hunting is also a shared process – the individual is relatively inefficient at hunting, and cannot sustain high-speed pursuit for long periods of time. Lionesses hunt by ambush, with the majority of the hunting group chasing the prey toward individuals lying in wait, who are then able to give chase over short distances before leaping on the selected animal for the kill. The lions' prey consists mainly of medium to large herd animals such as antelope, gazelle and wildebeest. Once the prey is taken, it is common for the males of the pride to eat first, even though they take no part in the hunting process. The females are next to feed followed by the cubs – it is common, when prey is scarce, that the young will often starve as a result of being last in the pecking order for food.

The lion is to be found in parts of eastern and southern Africa and is commonly protected in reserves, although hunting is still common. The Asiatic Lion, once to be found throughout India, the Middle East and Southern Asia, is today only to be found in the Gir Forest National Park in Gujarat, western India, where the population is estimated to be in the region of 290. The male of the Asian species has a less prominent mane compared to that of the African male and both sexes display a long fold of skin that runs the length of the belly which is not found on the African species.

Adapted from the *Big Cats Online* website.

# The leopard

---

**Hunting**

1.  Usually hunt at night.
2.  Females with young hunt during day.
3.  In grassland Africa – young eland, wildebeest, impala, gazelle.
4.  In forest Africa – monkeys, rats, squirrels, porcupines.
5.  Often eat prey high in trees away from packs of hyenas and lions.
6.  Can carry fully grown male antelope or young giraffe (3 times own bodyweight) up tree.
7.  Direct competition from lion (Africa) and tiger (tropical Asia).
8.  Have wider prey base than either of rivals.
9.  Can exist in areas without plentiful water – rivals cannot.
10. May hunt close to houses – prey on domestic animals, livestock and rodents.

---

**1.** How do we immediately know what these notes are about?

_____

_____

**2.** Which words do you think the dashes in notes 3 and 4 replace?

_____

_____

**3.** Which word could start each of notes 1, 5, 6, 8, 9 and 10? Why has the word been left out?

_____

_____

**4.** Write down two words that have been left out of the second half of note 6.

_____     _____

**5.** What is the point of the dashes in notes 9 and 10?

_____

_____

**6.** Write down two other ways (apart from listing by number) that these notes could have been organised.

_____

_____

_____

_____

Inform, explain, describe     © Folens (copiable page)

# Writing frame

Rewrite 'The king of beasts' in note form.

# *Unit 4*

# Other worlds

**Main Objective**

- *To organise texts in ways appropriate to their content and signpost this clearly to the reader.*

**Additional Focus**

- *To use writing to explore and develop ideas.*

**Starter Activity**

- Hand out and read copies of the source material 'A stadium in Azyga'. Establish comprehension by discussing similarities and differences between Akryman and the sports stadiums we have in our towns and cities today. Ask students which elements of Akryman they find most and least appealing. Use this opportunity to revise phrases such as 'however' or 'on the other hand'.

**Further Preparation**

- Now pass out copies of the worksheet 'Azygan organisation', page 18, and explain the following:

  ■ Summary titles convey the content of a paragraph in the fewest possible words. An appropriate summary title for the first paragraph would be 'Introduction' and for the second, 'Transportation'.

  ■ Summary phrases are quotations that summarise a section of text, in this case a paragraph. An appropriate summary phrase for the first paragraph would be 'I was asked to visit Azyga to inspect one of their sports stadiums'.

  Explain that good writers often use summary titles to plan in advance the paragraphs that will make up their text. They then help the reader by providing summary phrases that 'signpost' the content of each paragraph. This process ensures the text is well-organised and clear.

  If students need help in thinking of other areas of Azygan life on which to report, suggest the following:

  ■ hospitals
  ■ shopping malls
  ■ prisons
  ■ schools
  ■ cinemas.

  When students are ready, ask them to complete the worksheet.

**Main Activity/ Using the Frame**

- Hand out the writing frame. Spend as much time as necessary discussing the potential content of a report on an Azygan hospital, school, prison or whatever. Remind students to refer to their paragraph summary titles when they are planning and, when they are writing, to help the reader by using summary phrases.

**Maximising Attainment**

- Ask students to extend their work on the writing frame into a full six-paragraph report. They should continue to use their summary titles for the basic plan and ensure that each paragraph contains a summary phrase.

# A stadium in Azyga

Before my recent census inspection of the five 'blue group' moons I was asked by our continental parliament to make a special visit to the home planet, Azyga, to inspect one of their sports stadiums. Parliament left me to decide which stadium I would visit, believing rightly I think that sports stadiums on Azyga are similar to each other and generally far better than those we have in our planetary federation. They requested a report on my findings which I shall be submitting soon for consideration. It may well be that we can learn some important lessons from the way the Azygans do things in this area.

I visited the stadium of Akryman on Azyga's western icemass. The first thing that strikes you when you arrive is how efficiently transportation is run. The stadium is so easy to get into compared with those back home. All the roads leading up to Akryman are wide, tree-lined and clear of traffic. Even on match days, cars can drive straight into the parking areas just a short stroll from the walkways that lead into the arena. If you don't want to drive, the metro system will deliver you virtually to your seat in the stands. The train goes right underneath the stadium and escalators transfer fans to ground level in less than a minute.

Akryman itself is a triumph of modern science and engineering, unmatched by anything I have seen on Earth. The central sports area is truly multi-purpose. The pitch markings are drawn by laser-directed light so they can be changed instantly one type of sport finishes and another begins. Goal posts and nets are stored in underground housings beneath the pitch. When a game is selected on the control panel, the appropriate posts arise from the astroturf which then closes seamlessly back on top of the empty space. Needless to say, Akryman has a telescopic roof that shuts over the ground in bad weather. Despite the famed cold of the western icemass, fixtures are never cancelled.

So how does Akryman shape up once you are in the ground and watching the big game? I have to say – pretty well. Every single one of the 132 000 seats has an unobstructed view of the action. The seats use computer imaging to conform within three minutes to individual posture and each one of them has an intercom system through which fans can request information or order refreshments. The on-pitch entertainment during time outs and half times is excellent. Information and video action from other games is instantly relayed on the four megascreens at the corners of the ground.

Perhaps the most impressive thing about Akryman is the quality of customer service. The moment you enter the ground you will find yourself directed politely and efficiently to wherever you wish to go. Employees are eager to help you and more than once I felt very aware of the contrast between the courtesy I was being shown here and the rudeness shown in many stadiums in our planetary federation. I am certain this was not just because I was a visitor, since all around me I could see other fans being treated in the same way.

Is there room for any criticism? Perhaps Akryman is a little too clinical – a little too efficient. There's something about shabby old stadiums that adds to the atmosphere of the game. I remember the days before our top clubs here on Earth had videophones at every seat and I miss them. After all, we do go to these grounds to watch a game, not to have our attention distracted by things that have nothing to do with it. Nevertheless, I believe we have much to learn from the Azygans in stadium design and management as in just about everything else.

 # Azygan organisation

**1.** Make a list of six things at Akryman that particularly impressed the writer.

- _____    - _____
- _____    - _____
- _____    - _____

**2.** Give a summary title for each paragraph in as few words as possible.

- _____    - _____
- _____    - _____
- _____    - _____

**3.** Now write down one summary phrase from each paragraph.

- _____
- _____
- _____
- _____
- _____
- _____

**4.** List three other areas of life (apart from sports stadiums) that a visitor to Azyga might be asked to report back on.

_____    _____    _____

**5.** Write down paragraph summary titles for one of the areas you have listed above.

- _____
- _____
- _____
- _____
- _____
- _____

Inform, explain, describe
© Folens (copiable page)

# Writing frame

*It is important to organise texts properly for the following reasons:*

*A good way to organise texts is by*

*Writers can quickly show what is in each paragraph by*

*Here are two paragraphs from a report I have written on Azyga. They are about*

# Different people

**Main Objective**

- *To describe an object, person or setting in a way that includes relevant details and is accurate and evocative.*

**Additional Focus**

- *To use writing to explore and develop ideas.*

**Starter Activity**

- Ask students to help you make a list on the board of things that can help describe a character. They will probably come up with items such as eye and hair colour, personality traits, abilities and interests, preferences in food and music and so on. Leave your list on the board. Now give out the source material 'Ways of seeing' and read Extract One. Get them to identify the characteristics that have been used to define Anisa and compare them with the items in your original list.

**Further Preparation**

- Put students into pairs. Get them to ask each other questions that provide the kind of personal information they examined in the starter activity. When they have each collected around ten separate items of information, ask them to write a character description in the same style as the one they have just read about Anisa.

  When students have finished their descriptions ask them to read the second and third extracts from 'Ways of seeing'. Discuss ways in which they are different from both each other and the first extract. Make sure that students understand that:

  - The first extract is a fairly neutral set of facts.
  - Extracts Two and Three interpret these facts to tell a story and introduce more expressive terms ('impatiently', 'with eagerness').
  - The description in Extracts Two and Three is fuller and provides a setting for the information.

  Now give out copies of the worksheet 'Three Anisas', page 22. Most students will be able to complete the sheet without further help.

**Main Activity/ Using the Frame**

- Discuss the students' answers to the worksheet. Emphasise that similar information has been used very differently in all three extracts. Now hand out copies of the writing frame. Draw students' attention to the final prompt which asks them to develop the original description of their partner in the style of either Extract Two or Extract Three. When students are clear about what they need to do, let them complete the frame.

**Maximising Attainment**

- Get students to introduce three or four more characters into the situation they have described in the final prompt. They should use the same techniques of characterisation as before. Emphasise to them that there is no real need for any action in their 'story'. It should be made interesting not by the plot but by the way the characters are presented. The story, such as it is, can be alluded to by subtle detail.

# Ways of seeing

### Extract One

Anisa's skin is quite fair, her hair is blonde, wavy and shoulder length and her eyes are blue. She is normally quite calm but she has a very quick temper when she is upset. She doesn't smile very much, but when she does you can see that one of her upper front teeth is not quite straight. When she smiles she gets dimples in her cheeks. During the week she wears school uniform but at other times she likes to wear fairly casual clothes that aren't scruffy – T-shirt, jeans, trainers. She's quite an athletic person and she's one of the best runners in the year group. Her favourite food is pasta with any type of sauce.

### Extract Two

Anisa stood by the side of the track, waiting for the beginning of her race. She kneeled down to tie up the laces of her running shoes and her blonde hair came sweeping down over her face. She brushed it away impatiently and looked up, her blue eyes bright with eagerness to begin. Mrs Frost, the sports teacher, came across and must have made a joke, because Anisa suddenly laughed. The dimples in her cheeks abruptly appeared and then vanished. Her crooked front tooth, which some of the other girls teased her about, was also briefly exposed and then disappeared as quickly as her dimples. That tooth had a history which Anisa was not about to reveal.

### Extract Three

Anisa walked quietly into the bar, her blonde, wavy hair tumbling down onto her shoulders. The murmur of conversation faded as she looked around, her icy blue eyes electric with suspicion. All eyes were now upon her, awaiting her next move. She stood perfectly still for a moment, the clear white of her T-shirt contrasting with the darkness of her jeans and the dull light of the bar. Her slender fingers curled around the back of a chair. On her left hand, a diamond engagement ring shone out like a searchlight. When she spoke, her lips drew back to reveal a slightly misshapen front tooth, a scar, perhaps, from a past encounter. "Where is he?" she said, her voice a dangerous whisper.

# Three Anisas

**1.** Write down three things about Anisa's appearance that are mentioned in all three of the extracts.

_____   _____   _____

**2.** Explain how Anisa's teeth are made an important part of her appearance in Extracts Two and Three.

_____

_____

_____

_____

_____

_____

_____

**3.** Write down something about Anisa's appearance that is mentioned only in Extracts One and Two.

_____

_____

**4.** Explain how Anisa's eyes are described differently in each extract.

_____

_____

_____

_____

_____

_____

_____

**5.** Write down something about Anisa that is mentioned only in the first extract.

_____

_____

**6.** Make a list of three different feelings experienced by Anisa.

_____   _____   _____

**7.** Write down two things about Anisa that are mentioned only in the third extract.

_____   _____

Inform, explain, describe          © Folens (copiable page)

# Writing frame

Three things that can help us describe a character are

I wrote a character description of                    . I described

Three things used to describe Anisa are

Her eyes are described differently in each extract. In Extract One, they are

In Extract Two, they are

In the final extract they are

The main difference between the first extract and the other two is that

Here is a detailed description of                    written in the style of Extract

# Baby talk

**Main Objective**

- *To give instructions and directions which are specific, easy to follow and clearly sequenced.*

**Additional Focus**

- *To develop ideas and lines of thinking in continuous text and explain a process logically, highlighting the links between cause and effect.*

**Starter Activity**

- Write the following ten time markers on the board:

| | |
|---|---|
| then | the final thing |
| before | at this point |
| when | at this stage |
| after | the following thing |
| next | the first stage |

Explain that words and phrases like these can help make writing clearer. Spend a few minutes with the class generating sentences that contain these markers. Now write these sentences on the board:

> **After** washing a car it should be completely dried. **When** it is dry, **the final thing** you need to do is wax it.

Tell students that these sentences explain part of the *activity* or *process* of washing a car. Ask them to come up with similar sentences that explain other processes. Leave everything on the board for later reference.

**Further Preparation**

- Hand out copies of the source material 'Early communication'. Read it through and explain 'auditory stimulation' and 'language acquisition device'. Check for general comprehension and ask what kind of process is being explained in this extract. Now get students to identify some of the main features of baby communication and ask them to identify how parents can affect the development of the process. Finally ask them to identify the time markers used in the extract. They should be able to find new words and phrases such as 'now', 'already', 'from the very earliest days', 'her very first lesson'. Give out the worksheet 'A two-way process', page 26, and let students complete it without further discussion.

**Main Activity/ Using the Frame**

- Give out copies of the writing frame. Tell students that for the final prompt they will need to explain a process they know in detail. Discuss processes and activities with which your students are familiar: these will obviously differ widely from class to class. Remind them that they will make their texts clearer by using some of the time markers they encountered earlier in the lesson. Point out that the baby communication text offered advice to parents. Encourage them to do the same for readers of their own text, explaining the benefits of following the advice they give.

**Maximising Attainment**

- Ask for volunteers to present their explanations to the class. Encourage other students to ask questions that clarify and extend their understanding of the process being described. Speakers should try to answer questions as clearly and in as much detail as they can.

# Early communication

Babies need and want to communicate from the very earliest days, and even before they begin to vocalize they will listen to and try to imitate sounds. The basics of languages are built into babies' brains. A deaf infant starts to babble at the same age as a child with normal hearing, so we know that auditory stimulation is not necessary for language development. Some theorists even say we have a 'language acquisition device' somewhere in the brain that makes language inevitable.

Before your baby is six weeks old, she will have learned that if she smiles or makes sounds, you will respond. What is remarkable is that even at this early stage she realizes that she can call the shots: she smiles, you are pleased and so talk to her more, and she can keep a two-way conversation going. By smiling and talking to your baby and showing your pleasure when she responds, you are giving her her very first lesson in communication.

**Newborn**    Your baby will respond to human voices from the moment of birth, and she will try to imitate gestures and expressions. She will sense when you are talking to her and will respond with sounds and by moving her entire body.

**4–6 weeks**    She can already recognise your voice. She'll respond to your smiles and speech by gurgling, and wait for you to reply. Keep your face close to hers when you talk to her so that she can see you, and reward her sounds with more smiles and talking.

**4 months**    Your baby now has a range of sounds, including squeals and blowing between her lips. She communicates with you through laughter, so laugh and giggle a lot when you talk to her.

**6 months**    There are many signs that your baby is beginning to understand what you say. She babbles and strings sounds together. Singing to her, repeating rhymes, and speaking rhythmically will all help her to understand language and encourage early speaking.

From *Complete Baby and Childcare* by Miriam Stoppard

████████████████████████████████

# A two-way process

**1.** Make a list of six different things that show babies starting to communicate.

_____    _____    _____

_____    _____    _____

**2.** Write down six things that parents can do to encourage their baby to communicate.

_____    _____    _____

_____    _____    _____

**3.** List six phrases in the first two paragraphs that tell the reader *when* things start to happen.

_____

_____

_____

_____

_____

_____

**4.** The second half of the text is laid out so it is very clear to the reader. Explain how the writer has achieved this.

_____

_____

_____

_____

_____

_____

_____

_____

_____

_____

_____

# Writing frame

I have just read a text about

It explains how

---

Three ways that parents can help their baby communicate are by

---

The writer makes her text easier to follow by using words and phrases like

---

She also organises her text clearly by using

---

I am going to explain the process of

---

# Snakebite

**Main Objective**

● *To describe an event, process or situation, using language with an appropriate degree of formality.*

**Additional Focus**

● *To experiment with different approaches to planning, drafting, proofreading and presenting writing, taking account of the time available.*

**Starter Activity**

● Ask students to tell you about occasions in their lives on which they have been given instructions or advice. They will probably focus initially on verbal experiences with parents and teachers. Now discuss common examples of instructional writing, such as school rules, sports guides, recipes or first aid manuals. Focus their attention on the need for clarity and formality in this genre and ask them to explain how instructions and directions can be made easy to follow. Emphasise the importance of clear and authoritative language and a logical, sequenced layout.

**Further Preparation**

● Hand out copies of the source material 'Bitten!'. Focus on the layout of the text (subtitling, bullet pointing, numbering) and get students to explain how it aids clarity. Look at the word 'must' after the first bullet point and the words 'some', 'cautiously' and 'recommend' after the second. Tell students that these words signal certainty and tentativeness respectively. Look at the lead words in Section B and identify them as verbs. Explain that sentences beginning with verbs tend to be directives and are common in texts that give instructions, advice or directions. Ask students to provide examples of similar sentences. If appropriate for your class, explain that sentences that start with verbs are called imperatives. Ask students which folk remedies (tourniquets and sucking out poison by the mouth) are reflected in items four and five in Section A. Now pass out copies of the worksheet 'Snakes alive!', page 30. Students should be able to complete the sheet with little further help.

**Main Activity/ Using the Frame**

● Give out copies of the writing frame. The second prompt is directing students toward an explanation of presentational devices and the third requires a consideration of the effect of starting sentences with verbs. The fourth prompt is designed to get students to think about the effect of following instruction or advice with explanation. Explain that doing this gives weight and authority to the advice because it makes clear why it has been given in the first place. To emphasise this, show students the four points under Section C in the source material. All the points begin with a sentence giving an instruction and all are followed with at least one sentence of explanation. The final prompt requires students to produce an informative text of their own. If they are likely to be stuck for ideas, discuss some possibilities as a class before they begin. They could write about things they know, such as playing a game, or giving directions to somewhere in the school to a visitor. Alternatively, they could try doing something more imaginative, such as giving advice to air travellers in the event of a hijack. Make sure that students remember the importance of maintaining an appropriate level of formality in their language.

**Maximising Attainment**

● Get students to show each other their informative texts. The reader of the text should make a list of suggested improvements he or she thinks would make the writing clearer and more effective. The suggestions should cover improvements in both presentation and language. Each text should be read by at least one other student – ideally it will be read by two or three. The writer should then revise the original text, taking into account the suggestions that have been made.

# Bitten!

## Section A: First aid for snakebites

● The following steps must be taken:

1. Wash the bite with soap and water.
2. Immobilise the bitten area and keep it lower than the heart.
3. Get medical help.

● Some medical professionals cautiously recommend two other measures:

4. If a victim is unable to reach medical care within 30 minutes, a bandage, wrapped two to four inches above the bite, may help slow venom. The bandage should not cut off blood flow from a vein or artery. Make the band loose enough that a finger can slip under it.
5. A suction device may be placed over the bite to help draw venom out of the wound without making cuts. Suction instruments are often included in commercial snakebite kits.

## Section B: Avoiding snakebites

● Some bites, such as those inflicted when snakes are accidentally stepped on or encountered in wilderness settings, are nearly impossible to prevent. But experts say a few precautions can lower the risk of being bitten:

1. Leave snakes alone. Many people are bitten because they try to kill a snake or get a closer look at it.
2. Stay out of tall grass unless you wear thick leather boots, and remain on hiking paths as much as possible.
3. Keep hands and feet out of areas you can't see. Don't pick up rocks or firewood unless you are out of a snake's striking distance.
4. Be cautious and alert when climbing rocks.

## Section C: How NOT to treat a snake bite

1. No ice or any other type of cooling on the bite. Research has shown this to be potentially harmful.
2. No tourniquets. This cuts blood flow completely and may result in loss of the affected limb.
3. No electric shock. This method is under study and has yet to be proven effective. It could harm the victim.
4. No incisions in the wound. Such measures have not been proven useful and may cause further injury.

Adapted from text by John Henkel on the US Food and Drug Administration's website.

# Snakes alive!

**I.** How many *definite* steps should be taken in the event of a snakebite? _____

**2.** Why is it easy to see how many steps there are?

_____

**3.** Choose one word from the first bullet-pointed sentence that shows
the instructions are definite. _____

**4.** Choose three words from the second bullet-pointed sentence which show that these instructions
are *not* definite.

_____     _____     _____

**5.** What type of word begins each of the instructions in Section B? _____

**6.** Write down four sentences of your own using the lead words from Section B.

**Leave** _____

**Stay** _____

**Keep** _____

**Be** _____

**7.** Explain the effect of using these types of words to start a sentence.

_____

_____

_____

_____

_____

_____

_____

_____

_____

**8.** Write down two ways that negativity is stressed in Section C.

_____

_____

Inform, explain, describe   © Folens (copiable page)

# Writing frame

I have just read a set of instructions and advice about

These instructions are made clearer by the use of

Often the sentences begin with                              .The effect of doing this is to

Sometimes instructions are followed by                              .The reason for doing this is that

Here is my own set of instructions and advice about

# Dinosaurs from the deep

**Main Objective**

● *To organise and present information, selecting and synthesising appropriate material and guiding the reader clearly through the text.*

**Additional Focus**

● *To re-read work to anticipate the effect on the reader and revise style and structure, as well as accuracy, with this in mind.*

**Starter Activity**

● Pass out copies of the source material 'Sea monsters' and read the extract through with your students. Check that they understand the text deals with two main types of sea-dwelling reptiles, the 'ichthyosaurs' and the 'plesiosaurs'. Explain that the two families of reptiles can be distinguished from one another by features of their appearance. Ask students to tell you which elements of this text would make it inaccessible to many younger primary school children. Direct them towards a discussion of the following:

  ▪ long, unfamiliar words
  ▪ a formal style
  ▪ information overload (for example, in the paragraph about the locomotion of plesiosaurs)
  ▪ measurements that are unrelated to objects children can visualise, such as houses or cars.

**Further Preparation**

● Give out copies of the worksheet 'Sea reptiles', page 34, and ask students to complete it.

**Main Activity/ Using the Frame**

● Hand out the writing frame. Explain to students that their task is to adapt the original text so that it would be accessible and interesting to younger primary school children. Use the points above to establish guidelines for editing. If the exercise appears to be causing difficulty, give further help by offering some or all of the following advice:

  ▪ Make no distinction between types of marine reptiles.
  ▪ Remove all technical words and replace them with familiar terms like 'dinosaurs' and 'monsters'.
  ▪ Use phrases like 'I'm going to tell you all about dinosaurs from the sea' to reduce formality.
  ▪ Cut all or most of the information from the locomotion paragraph.
  ▪ A tall person measures six feet from head to foot. An average car is ten feet long. An average house including the roof is forty feet high. Use these common objects to establish a visual reference when describing some of the dinosaur dimensions.
  ▪ Do not copy whole phrases from the original text.

  Students will need to produce a draft version of the revised text before completing the frame.

**Maximising Attainment**

● Libraries and other databases such as the Internet are full of information about dinosaurs. Ask students to research interesting facts about marine dinosaurs and then adapt them so that they form part of a project designed to be read by primary age children. The project could contain diagrams and illustrations as well as the simplified text.

# Sea monsters

In 1811 the fossilised skeleton of a monster was found embedded in a rock. Scientists were confused by what they saw: the shape of the creature was that of a fish, having a large dorsal fin on the back and flippers. Other features, including a long, pointed jaw filled with teeth, seemed more like a reptile. In the end they decided this strange creature which they named an *ichthyosaur* (meaning 'fish-reptile') was definitely a reptile despite its shape.

The ichthyosaurs were a collection of related species with the same body-shape. One type, *shonisaurus*, was almost 50 feet in length. Most of the ichthyosaurs were quite a bit smaller, though, and scientists think they may have behaved much like the porpoises of today. Both porpoises (which are mammals) and ichthyosaurs have a teardrop-shaped torso body, a long snout, short fins up front for steering and a large crescent-shaped tail fin to drive them forward at speeds of up to 30mph (50kph).

Different kinds of great swimming reptiles from the days of the dinosaurs were soon found. The *plesiosaur* was an animal very unfish-like in shape. It had a rounded body with a long tail, long neck and four diamond-shaped flippers to drive it through the water. The tiny head sported a set of razor-sharp teeth.

Like the ichthyosaurs, plesiosaurs were really a class of animals with this same basic design. Within this line developed a wide variety of reptiles. One of these was the *elasmosaurus* which grew to a length of 45 feet. Elasmosaurus had an extremely long neck that allowed it to suddenly reach out and snap at a prey some twenty feet away.

One of the plesiosaurs became perhaps the greatest carnivore of all time: *liopleurodon*. It is difficult to appreciate just how big liopleurodons grew. Some ran as long as eighty feet in length and weighed as much as 100 tons. That's twenty times the weight of Tyrannosaurus Rex. The head of the biggest liopleurodons were thirteen feet long with ten foot jaws. They sported teeth twice the size of a T-rex. What did a liopleurodon eat? Anything it wanted. In the prehistoric sea it was the king of the food chain.

Plesiosaurs sailed through the water using four nearly-equal-sized flippers. No animal alive today uses this form of locomotion. For a long time scientists were puzzled as to exactly how these worked. Early theories suggested that the animals might have used their flippers like oars to 'row' themselves along. This seemed awkward, though, and scientists now believe that the flippers must have worked like a set of wings and plesiosaurs literally flew though the water by flapping their flippers up and down. Further studies suggested that the plesiosaurs had very strong muscles for the downstroke, but relatively weak ones for the upstroke. This has led some scientists to speculate that the animal would cruise through the water by pushing one set of flippers down to go forward, while the other set moved back up to get in position for the next power stroke. They may have even beat both sets downward together to get a sudden, short burst of power.

All these sea reptiles shared one characteristic. They all had lungs, not gills, like fish. That meant they had to come up to the surface for air. This is another way they are similar to seagoing mammals of today.

Adapted from text by Lee Krystek on the *Unnatural Museum* website.

# Sea reptiles

**1.** Explain what scientists found so confusing about the monster skeleton they discovered.

_____

_____

_____

_____

_____

**2.** List four features that all ichthyosaurs had in common.

_____   _____   _____   _____

**3.** List four common features of all plesiosaurs.

_____   _____   _____   _____

**4.** Write down four measurements associated with liopleurodon.

_____   _____   _____   _____

**5.** How do scientists think plesiosaurs moved through the water?

_____

_____

_____

**6.** What characteristic is shared by ichthyosaurs, plesiosaurs and modern sea mammals?

_____

_____

_____

**7.** Write down six words from the text that might confuse younger readers.

_____   _____   _____

_____   _____   _____

**8.** Which part of the text do you think would be least interesting to young readers?

_____

_____

_____

Inform, explain, describe
© Folens (copiable page)

# Writing frame

Texts written for younger children have to be

This is why I have removed words from the original text like

I have also removed

In order to make the text more interesting I have

I have also

This is my full text, written so it appeals to young children.

# Thoughts and feelings

**Main Objective**

- *To explain complex ideas and information clearly.*

**Additional Focus**

- *To use writing for thinking and learning by recording ideas as they develop to aid reflection and problem solving.*

**Starter Activity**

- Give out copies of Source material 1 'A nightmare' and read it with your students. Discuss reactions to the Matron's behaviour and then focus on the task at the bottom of the page. Tell students that responses such as 'I like it' or 'I think it's boring' are not appropriate for prompts such as these. Explain that good readers approach this kind of exercise by asking *themselves* questions about their reactions to the text. Demonstrate the kinds of questions students should ask themselves with the following example. Write these two questions on the board:

  - What does the Matron do to Tweedie?
  - What is the worst thing about the Matron?

  Ensure that students understand the difference between these two types of question. The first kind is a comprehension question that tests understanding of the text. The second is a question that demands a personal response (using the pronoun 'I') that helps the reader understand his or her reactions to the text.

**Further Preparation**

- Get students to generate five responsive questions to the text they have just read. They should answer their own questions in note form as they go along. Tell them to try to make their questions as specific as possible: 'What are my feelings about this text?' is not a helpful question because it is too general. If they are having difficulty, guide them towards the following:

  - What do I dislike about what the Matron says?
  - Do I find anything funny in this description?
  - What would I have done if I had seen this happen?
  - Do I think that children need to be treated like this?
  - Have I had similar experiences with someone more powerful than myself?

  When students have generated five questions (either their own or versions of the above) let them respond to the prompt at the bottom of the sheet.

**Main Activity/ Using the Frame**

- Now hand out copies of Source material 2 'A beating'. Read and discuss the extract and then ask students to generate at least five responsive questions to the text in the way they did before. Again, make sure they answer their own questions in note form as they go along. When they have done this, pass out copies of the writing frame. Most students will complete this frame with the minimum of additional help.

**Maximising Attainment**

- Ask volunteers to read out one or two of their original responsive questions. Other students then offer their own answers and ideas in reaction to them. This activity should demonstrate clearly that tasks addressing a reader's thoughts and feelings invite and require individual responses that will differ from student to student.

# A nightmare

In the following extract from his autobiography, *Boy*, Roald Dahl describes what happens one night in the dormitory of his boarding school when his friend, Tweedie, is caught snoring by the Matron.

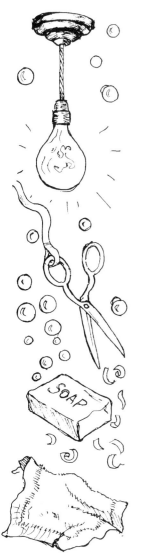

The Matron stared at Tweedie. 'Snoring is a disgusting habit,' she said. 'Only the lower classes do it. We shall have to teach him a lesson.'

She didn't switch on the light, but she advanced into the room and picked up a cake of soap from the nearest basin. The bare electric bulb in the corridor illuminated the whole dormitory in a pale creamy glow.

None of us dared to sit up in bed, but all eyes were on the Matron now, watching to see what she was going to do next. She always had a pair of scissors hanging by a white tape from her waist, and with this she began shaving thin slivers of soap into the palm of one hand. Then she went over to where the wretched Tweedie lay and very carefully she dropped these little soap-flakes into his open mouth. She had a whole handful of them and I thought she was never going to stop.

What on earth is going to happen? I wondered. Would Tweedie choke? Would he strangle? Might his throat get blocked up completely? Was she going to kill him?

The Matron stepped back a couple of paces and folded her arms across, or rather underneath, her massive chest.

Nothing happened. Tweedie kept right on snoring.

Then suddenly he began to gurgle and white bubbles appeared around his lips. The bubbles grew and grew until in the end his whole face seemed to be smothered in a bubbly foaming white soapy froth. It was a horrific sight. Then all at once, Tweedie gave a great cough and a splutter and he sat up very fast and began clawing at his face with his hands. 'Oh!' he stuttered. 'Oh! Oh! Oh! Oh no! Wh-wh-what's happening? Wh-wh-what's on my face? Somebody help me!'

The Matron threw him a face flannel and said, 'Wipe it off, Tweedie. And don't ever let me hear you snoring again. Hasn't anyone ever taught you not to go to sleep on your back?'

With that she marched out of the dormitory and slammed the door.

Now write down your thoughts and feelings about the events described in this extract.

_____

_____

_____

_____

_____

_____

_____

_____

# A beating

In this extract from *Boy*, Roald Dahl describes a caning from Mr Coombes, his headmaster at Prep School. He is being punished with some friends for putting a dead mouse in a jar of gobstoppers at a sweet shop owned by an old lady called Mrs Pratchett. She is in the headmaster's office to witness his beating – and she is enjoying every minute of it.

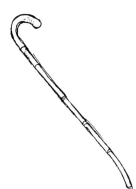

My own turn came at last. My mind was swimming and my eyes had gone all blurry as I went forward to bend over. I can remember wishing my mother would suddenly come bursting into the room shouting, 'Stop! How dare you do that to my son!' But she didn't. All I heard was Mrs Pratchett's dreadful high-pitched voice behind me screeching, 'This one's the cheekiest of the bloomin' lot, 'Eadmaster! Make sure you let 'im 'ave it good and strong!'

Mr Coombes did just that. As the first stroke landed and the pistol-crack sounded, I was thrown forward so violently that if my fingers hadn't been touching the carpet, I think I would have fallen flat on my face. As it was, I was able to catch myself on the palms of my hands and keep my balance. At first I heard only the *crack* and felt absolutely nothing at all, but a fraction of a second later the burning sting that flooded across my buttocks was so terrific that all I could do was gasp. I gave a great gushing gasp that emptied my lungs of every breath of air that was in them.

It felt, I promise you, as though someone had laid a red-hot poker against my flesh and was pressing down on it hard.

The second stroke was worse than the first and this was probably because Mr Coombes was well practised and had a splendid aim. He was able, so it seemed, to land the second one almost exactly across the narrow line where the first one had struck. It is bad enough when the cane lands on fresh skin, but when it comes down on bruised and wounded flesh, the agony is unbelievable.

The third one seemed even worse than the second. Whether or not the wily Mr Coombes had chalked the cane beforehand and had thus made an aiming mark on my grey flannel shorts after the first stroke, I do not know. I am inclined to doubt it because he must have known that this was a practice much frowned upon by Headmasters in general in those days. It was not only regarded as unsporting, it was also an admission that you were not an expert at the job.

By the time the fourth stroke was delivered, my entire backside seemed to be going up in flames.

Far away in the distance, I heard Mr Coombes' voice saying, 'Now get out.'

As I limped across the study clutching my buttocks hard with both hands, a cackling sound came from the armchair over in the corner, and then I heard the vinegary voice of Mrs Pratchett saying, 'I am very much obliged to you, 'Eadmaster, very much obliged. I don't think we is goin' to see any more stinkin' mice in my Gobstoppers from now on.'

From *Boy* by Roald Dahl

Inform, explain, describe © Folens (copiable page)

# Writing frame

The first extract I read from Boy was about

I made up some questions to ask myself about this extract. One of them was

Another was

Asking yourself questions like this is useful because

The second extract from Boy is about

Here are five questions I asked myself about the events in this extract:

These are my thoughts and feelings about the extract:

# Weird science

**Main Objective**

● *To explain complex ideas and information clearly.*

**Additional Focus**

● *To use writing for thinking and learning by recording ideas as they develop to aid reflection and problem solving.*

**Starter Activity**

● Hand out copies of the source material 'Poochie Groomer' and read it through with your students. Get them to identify where they might find this kind of text and establish that its function is to instruct and advise. Explain that this kind of writing needs to be especially clear. Now go through the text and highlight the following features:

- lead verbs (for example 'fit', 'leave', 'attach')
- time phrases (for example 'When you both feel ready', 'After a few moments', 'for about two minutes')
- technical expressions (for example 'watertight seals', 'pre-wash mode', 'combing filaments')
- typical or stock phrases ('rest assured', 'ensures', 'not recommended')
- links between cause and effect (for example the 'Poochie Pipe' enables the dog to breathe during the wash cycle).

Discuss in turn the effect of each of these features.

**Further Preparation**

● Give out copies of the worksheet 'Bright ideas', page 42. Students should be able to complete the sheet without further significant help from you.

**Main Activity/ Using the Frame**

● Discuss the way that inventions can change the quality of people's lives. Start the discussion by considering real inventions – such as the car and the telephone – and then move on to more idiosyncratic devices such as the 'Poochie Groomer'. Give students a few moments to write a list of their own potential inventions and then discuss what they have come up with. Now hand out copies of the writing frame and tell students that the main part of the exercise is to give instructions and advice on how to operate an invention of their own devising. Remind them to use the features identified in the original text. It is better if they come up with their own ideas for inventions. If they are stuck, however, suggest the following:

- a luxury burglar alarm
- a household pest exterminator
- a multifunction home tutor.

**Maximising Attainment**

● Ask students to rewrite their instructions – but this time so that they are deliberately unclear. Before they begin, discuss the features that can make for a confusing instructional text. Cover the following:

- There are few lead verbs or none at all – the focus is not on what the reader has to do.
- Time phrases are either absent or incorrect.
- There are too many difficult technical terms.
- The links between cause and effect are either missing or illogical.

# Poochie Groomer

Congratulations on your purchase! The new *Poochie Groomer* takes the effort and strain out of bathtime for man's best friend. No more bending over the bath or sink whilst your little favourite wriggles to get free – and all you get is a face full of soap and a wicked temper. *Poochie Groomer* ensures a clean dog and a happy owner every time.

It's so simple and it works like this. When you both feel ready for bathtime, play the meditation tape (supplied free with each *Poochie Groomer*) quietly about two metres away from your dog. After a few moments, you will sense him becoming completely relaxed. Put the *Poochie Pipe* in place over his nose and mouth and place the *Poochie Patches* over his eyes. Fit the *Poochie Groomer* around him, making sure all watertight seals are locked in place. When all components are correctly assembled the *Poochie Groomer* goes automatically into pre-wash mode. Your pet's body will be gently brushed by fine filaments that will comb out the dirt and grit collected in the normal daily life of any busy animal. Your dog will love the attention he is getting. Leave the hypnosis tape playing to ensure he is entirely tranquil and ready for his wash.

Attach the hose inlet to an internal tap and fill the soap dispenser with the *Poochie Suds* provided. Turn on the tap and allow the tank inside the machine to fill. The thermostat within the tank will ensure your pet's bathwater is at a perfect temperature. After approximately five minutes the water will spray into the *Poochie Groomer* from any one of eight internal shower heads. The water mixes with the *Poochie Suds* to soften and condition your pet's coarse hair. Meanwhile, the combing filaments continue to work on your dog's coat to remove any last stubborn traces of dirt. A rotating sea sponge will scrub his beard, eyebrows and other facial hair. With the *Poochie Pipe* and the *Poochie Patches* firmly in place, you can rest assured no water is getting into his delicate eyes or sensitive snout.

When the green light shows at the rear of your *Poochie Groomer* the post-wash rinse is about to begin. Purified spring water jets out of the shower heads and gives your dog an invigorating wash down. The rinse cycle lasts for about two minutes, after which time your pet will be completely free of both dirt and soap. Switch off the relaxation tape since bathtime is nearly over.

The final stage in the *Poochie Groomer* cycle is the luxury blowdry. Once all the water has drained from the machine, the shower heads convert automatically to dryers that caress your pet's body with soothing air. The combing filaments groom him as he dries. When both green lights show at the rear of the machine, your dog's grooming is complete. Open your *Poochie Groomer* and welcome out your clean, happy and sweet-smelling pet.

**Note**
Use of this product to groom rabbits, gerbils, hamsters, parrots and budgies is not recommended.

**BEFORE ...**

**AFTER ...**

# Bright ideas

**1.** Make a list of four sentences that begin with a verb.

_____

_____

_____

_____

**2.** Explain the effect of beginning sentences in this way.

_____

_____

_____

**3.** Write down four time phrases.

_____     _____

_____     _____

**4.** List four technical expressions.

_____     _____

_____     _____

**5.** List four stock/typical words or phrases

_____     _____

_____     _____

**6.** Explain the function of the following items by completing these sentences in your own words.

The fine filaments     _____

The *Poochie Patches*     _____

The *Poochie Pipe*     _____

The thermostat     _____

The shower heads     _____

The spring water     _____

# Writing frame

I have just read about an invention that

Verbs are used at the start of some of the sentences because

Time phrases are used because

The link between cause and effect is always made very clear. Here are two examples:

Now I am going to explain my own invention using the same style as the Poochie Groomer instructions.

# Volcano research

**Main Objective**

- *To explain complex ideas and information clearly.*

**Additional Focus**

- *To organise and present information, selecting and synthesising appropriate material and guiding the reader clearly through the text.*

**Starter Activity**

- Spend five minutes brainstorming the word 'volcano'. Students should be able to name some famous volcanoes and may be able to provide technical information about the way they work. They may know words like 'magma', 'crater' or 'lava'. Use this opportunity for a brief review of the source/derivations of such words. Regardless of what your class does know as a whole, establish that more information is needed for a completer knowledge. Now pass out and read the source material 'Eruption!'. Check that they understand the difference between stratovolcanoes and cinder cones (the former is made of layers whilst the latter is solid rock). They should also understand that 'pyroclastic flow' is the rapid flow down the mountainside of hot rock, gas and ash. It is more dangerous than the flow of molten lava, which is slower.

**Further Preparation**

- Hand out the worksheet 'Volcano facts', page 46. Students should now be able to complete the sheet without significant help from you. When they have done this, discuss with them how they can further expand their knowledge of volcanoes. Explain that each of them is going to take a topic area and research it in more detail. Individual students may have clear ideas about what they want to research. If they do not, suggest the following possibilities:

  - famous volcanic eruptions
  - volcanoes under the sea
  - types of volcanoes
  - current and recent eruptions
  - volcanoes in outer space.

  When they are ready, use books in the library and/or the Internet to research the chosen areas. If you have difficulty locating resources, the Geography department can probably help with text books. In order to avoid copying, insist that students use note form to record data and information as they are reading. Make sure they write down the names of their sources as they go along.

**Main Activity/ Using the Frame**

- Hand out copies of the writing frame. Remind students of the difference between stratovolcanoes and cinder cones and explain that the required diagram should be very simple. The prompt 'I discovered that …' should elicit a detailed response constructed from notes. The texts used for research should not be available to students at this stage.

**Maximising Attainment**

- Students should now, between them, have a substantial body of knowledge about this interesting subject. Get members of the class to give short verbal presentations of their findings. Encourage a tutorial format in which information is compared and discussed.

  Students can draw links between linguistic features of this text and those used in science, for example, 'absorb', 'to form', 'generated by'.

# Eruption!

Explosive volcanoes typically have a characteristic shape – tall, with a steep summit, created out of alternating layers of lava and volcanic rock fragments – known as a stratovolcano. Many of history's most famous volcanoes – Etna, Vesuvius, St. Helens, Fujiyama – are stratovolcanoes. (Very rapidly formed volcanoes, like Paricutin in Mexico, are often a type known as a cinder cone, built out of layers of ejected volcanic rock. These volcanoes are typically no more than 1000 or so feet tall, whereas stratovolcanoes can become mountains.)

Most of the damage in stratovolcano eruptions comes not from lava flow but from something known as pyroclastic flow. A pyroclastic flow is an avalanche of ground-hugging hot rock accompanied by a cloud of ash and gas that races down the slope of a volcano. The flow can reach speeds of up to 60 miles per hour, and temperatures of nearly 1 300 degrees Fahrenheit. Pyroclastic flows cause more death and destruction than any other volcanic hazard. In 1902 on the Caribbean island of Martinique, a pyroclastic flow generated by the eruption of Mt. Pelée swept into the town of St. Pierre and incinerated 29 000 people. The devastating mudflow that killed 25 000 people in Armaro, Colombia, after the 1985 eruption of Nevado del Ruiz volcano was triggered by a pyroclastic flow.

Pyroclastic flow and lava aren't the only hazards created by volcanic eruptions. Other dangers are lahars – mixtures of rock fragments and water that flood down volcanoes (mudflows are one type) – landslides, gas emissions, and ash clouds. Ash clouds are a particular problem for aircraft. They can cause engine failure, damage electrical systems, scratch the outer surface of a plane, and contaminate its interior.

The effects of a volcanic eruption can also be felt over the long term. Eruptions releasing high concentrations of sulphur-rich gas – like the eruptions of the Philippines' Mount Pinatubo, in 1991, and Mexico's El Chichón in 1982 – can alter global climate. The sulphur mixes with water vapour in the atmosphere to form clouds of sulphuric acid. The acid droplets both absorb incoming solar radiation and bounce it back into space. The result: lower temperatures. In the year after the eruption of Pinatubo, for example, global temperatures dipped by nearly a degree.

Adapted from text by Kathy Svitil on the *Savage Earth* website.

# Volcano facts

**1.** Write down the names of five volcanoes.

_____  _____  _____  _____  _____

**2.** Name two different types of volcano.

_____  _____

**3.** What three elements make up a pyroclastic flow?

_____  _____  _____

**4.** Write down two numbers associated with a pyroclastic flow.

_____  _____

**5.** List four hazards (apart from pyroclastic flow) that are associated with volcanoes.

_____  _____

_____  _____

**6.** Write down four of the effects of ash clouds on aircraft.

_____  _____

_____  _____

**7.** Name two volcanoes that have recently released sulphur-rich gas.

_____  _____

**8.** What was the global effect of the 1991 eruption in the Philippines?

_____

_____

_____

_____

_____

_____

_____

_____

# Writing frame

Two different types of volcano I have read about are

In the boxes on the right there are two simple diagrams to show the differences between them.

Some famous volcanoes are

The most dangerous thing about volcanoes is

which has caused tragedies such as

I have done some extra research on

I discovered that

The thing I found most interesting was

The exact source of my information was

# Acknowledgements and sources

**Acknowledgements**

Page 25            Extract from *Complete Baby and Childcare* by Miriam Stoppard, published by
                   Dorling Kindersley, 1995.

Pages 37 and 38
                   Two extracts from *Boy* by Roald Dahl, published by Penguin Books, 1986.


**Sources**

Page 5             'Contemplating Catastrophe' from the *World Book*™ website at:
                   http://www.worldbook.com/fun/bth/meteorites/html/catastrophe.html

Page 13            'Lion – *Panthera leo*' from the *Big Cats Online* website at:
                   http://dialspace.dial.pipex.com/town/plaza/abf90/bco/ver4.htm

Page 29            'For Goodness Snakes! Treating and Preventing Venomous Bites' by John Henkel from the
                   US Food and Drug Administration's website at:
                   http://www.fda.gov/fdac/features/995_snakes.html

Page 33            'Reptiles of the Ancient Seas' by Lee Krystek from the *Museum of Unnatural Mystery*
                   website at:
                   http://www.unmuseum.org/unmain.htm

Page 45            'Mountains of Fire' by Kathy Svitil from the *Savage Earth* website at:
                   http://www.pbs.org/wnet/savageearth/volcanoes/index.html

Pages 9, 17, 21, 41
                   Author's own invention.

# Assisting Students with Language Delays in the Classroom

## A PRACTICAL LANGUAGE PROGRAMME

Francesca Bierens

First published in 2015 by
**Speechmark Publishing Ltd**,
5 Thomas More Square, London E1W 1YW, UK
**www.speechmark.net**

© Francesca Bierens, 2015

All rights reserved. The whole of this work, including all text and illustrations, is protected by copyright. No part
of it may be copied, altered, adapted or otherwise exploited in any way without express prior permission, unless
in accordance with the provisions of the Copyright Designs and Patents Act 1988 or in order to photocopy or make
duplicating masters of those pages so indicated, without alteration and including copyright notices, for the express
purpose of instruction and examination. No parts of this work may otherwise be loaded, stored, manipulated,
reproduced, or transmitted in any form or by any means, electronic or mechanical, including photocopying and
recording, or by any information storage and retrieval system, without prior written permission from the publisher, on
behalf of the copyright owner.

Design and artwork by Moo Creative (Luton)

**002-6005**/Printed in the United Kingdom by CMP (uk) Ltd

British Library Cataloguing in Publication Data
A catalogue record for this book is available from the British Library

ISBN 978 190930 157 3

# Contents

Acknowledgements                                                                    v

## Part 1: Assisting students with language delays in the classroom: a practical language programme                                      1

Introduction                                                                        2

Chapter 1: Overview of the three-level language programme                           3

Chapter 2: Language development at a glance                                         5


## Part 2: Assisting students with language delays in the classroom to acquire 'The Preverbal Skills of Language'                          13

Introduction                                                                       14

Chapter 1: Learning to look at people – facial regard                              15

Chapter 2: Learning to attend, concentrate and anticipate                          20

Chapter 3: Learning to look around at things – visual awareness                    25

Chapter 4: Learning to listen to sounds – auditory awareness                       30

Chapter 5: Learning to copy actions – imitation of actions                         35

Chapter 6: Learning to copy sounds made – imitation of sounds                      39

Chapter 7: Learning to wait and take turns                                         44

Chapter 8: Learning awareness and control of the face and mouth muscles            49

Chapter 9: The opportunity to communicate and the desire to communicate            54

Chapter 10: Making 'The Preverbal Skills of Language' activity box                 55

Chapter 11: Making 'The Preverbal Skills of Language' activity cube                57


## Part 3: Assisting students with language delays in the classroom to acquire 'The Building Bricks of Language'                           59

Introduction                                                                       60

Chapter 1: Assisting and encouraging the development of the students' language      61

Chapter 2: Putting a name to the noun                                              65

Chapter 3: Putting verbs into action                                               75

Chapter 4: Add adjectives to put colour into words                                 84

# Contents

Chapter 5: Putting prepositions in their place     91

Chapter 6: Making sure negatives are not left out     98

Chapter 7: When we need time     105

Chapter 8: Why the cause must have an effect     111

Chapter 9: How to remember the sequence in order     118

Chapter 10: Emotions put feelings into words     125

Chapter 11: Asking questions to gain some answers     131

Chapter 12: Making 'The Building Bricks of Language' activity box     137

Chapter 13: Making 'The Building Bricks of Language' activity cubes     139

**Part 4: Assisting students with language delays in the classroom to acquire 'The Skills of Conversation'**     **145**

Introduction     146

Chapter 1: Looking politely at people and standing at an appropriate distance     147

Chapter 2: Looking carefully in order to see important things     151

Chapter 3: Listening attentively and remembering what has been heard     156

Chapter 4: Waiting, listening to others and recalling information given     160

Chapter 5: Speaking clearly     164

Chapter 6: Asking and answering conversational questions     173

Chapter 7: Making 'The Skills of Conversation' activity box     180

Chapter 8: Making 'The Skills of Conversation' activity cube     182

**References**     184

# Acknowledgements

There have been many excellent people who have assisted me in my work as a speech and language therapist over the years and more recently while working directly on this language programme.

- Thank you to the many fabulous and inspiring teachers I have worked with, especially Dianne Orevich, Juliet Jenkins, Donna Ryan, Janet Marshall, Michelle Coles, Kamila Peslova, Bridie O'Shea, Silivia Toloke, Shona McCann, Marilyn Wenge, Judi Allan, Corey Busfield and Shelley Clark, who have provided me with invaluable assistance.

- Many thanks to Diane Hankins, school Principal, for her constant support. I greatly appreciate it.

- I am indebted to all the wonderful students I have worked with who have taught me so much and from whom I am continually learning.

- I must express a very sincere and special gratitude to Donna Ryan for her unwavering enthusiasm in this language programme and for encouraging its development.

- Enormous thanks to Janet Marshall for the fun rhymes she has contributed to this programme and also for the many wonderfully clever rhymes, songs and poems she has written for her class 'speech therapy' sessions over the years.

- Thank you so much to my SLT work colleague and friend, Gail Arriola-Bagayas for her ongoing interest, assistance and support.

- I am extremely grateful to Sheena Patrick for the hours she dedicated to reviewing this programme and for her valuable suggestions. I am very thankful for her knowledge as a speech and language therapist and for her patience as a long suffering friend.

- I extend my warm thanks to Kathryn Warren and Heather Buckingham who have always provided practical support, encouragement and motivation.

- Finally, my sincere thanks to Katrina Hulme-Cross, Publisher at Speechmark Publishing and her fantastic team, especially Tom Smith, Jamie Etherington, Laura Booth and Clare Butler. I am *exceedingly* appreciative of all their support and assistance.

# Part 1

# Assisting students with language delays in the classroom: a practical language programme

# Introduction

*Assisting Students with Language Delays in the Classroom* is a language programme designed for teachers to use within the class setting. The purpose of this programme is to assist students who have speech and/or language delays to acquire the most important skills and concepts required for the development of language comprehension and functional verbal interaction. The programme is intended for school-aged children and young people from five to 18 years of age. Your speech and language therapist (SLT) will also have specific exercises and activities suited to the needs of your individual students.

The more complex linguistic features, such as verb tenses and conjunctions, have not received focused attention in this programme.

The activities in all three skill areas – 'The Preverbal Skills of Language', 'The Building Bricks of Language' and 'The Skills of Conversation' – are as practical as possible and are all purposely 'low-tech', so the majority of resources should be readily available within most classrooms or in the wider school. (You could try toy shops for items like toy windmills.)

This language programme is the result of years spent working as an SLT in classrooms, taking whole-class language sessions as well as working with small groups and individual students. Working closely with the teachers in this situation, it became clear that there was a need to create a programme that catered to the various language needs of the students and could easily be incorporated into the class programme and curriculum. The students themselves were an inspiration for many of the activities included in this programme.

I do hope that you enjoy using this programme as much as I have enjoyed creating it.

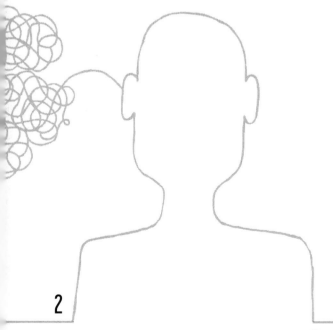

Ⓟ This page may be photocopied for instructional use only. © Francesca Bierens Speechmark Ⓢ

# Chapter 1

# Overview of the three-level language programme

This three-level language programme focuses on the most essential areas of communication:

- The Preverbal Skills of Language
- The Building Bricks of Language
- The Skills of Conversation.

Each of the three communication areas contains:

- information related to each of the language and speech skills
- activities to assist the development of each of the skills.

## The Preverbal Skills of Language

In the 'The Preverbal Skills of Language' section are exercises and activities to assist in the development of the foundation skills of language.

- Learning to look at people                        six activities
- Learning to attend, concentrate and anticipate    six activities
- Learning to look around at things                 eight activities
- Learning to listen to sounds                       six activities
- Learning to copy actions                           six activities
- Learning to copy sounds made                       six activities
- Learning to wait and take turns                    six activities
- Learning awareness and control of the face
  and mouth muscles                                  six exercises and activities

**Total number of activities: 50**

3

This page may be photocopied for instructional use only. © Francesca Bierens Speechmark

## The Building Bricks of Language

In the 'The Building Bricks of Language' section are exercises and activities to assist in the development of comprehension, vocabulary and the concepts of language.

- Putting a name to the noun       14 activities + 14 example questions

- Putting verbs into action       10 activities + 10 example questions

- Add adjectives to put colour into words       8 activities + 8 example questions

- Putting prepositions in their place       8 activities + 8 example questions

- Making sure negatives are not left out       8 activities + 8 example questions

- When we need time       8 activities + 8 example questions

- Why the cause must have an effect       8 activities + 8 example questions

- How to remember the sequence in order       8 activities + 8 example questions

- Emotions put feelings into words       8 activities + 8 example questions

- Asking questions to gain some answers       10 activities

**Total number of activities: 90**

## The Skills of Conversation

In the 'The Skills of Conversation' section are exercises and activities to assist in the development of functional, interactive conversation.

- Looking politely at people and standing at an appropriate distance       six activities

- Looking carefully in order to see the important things       six activities

- Listening attentively and remembering what has been heard       six activities

- Waiting, listening to others and recalling information given       eight activities

- Speaking clearly       eight activities

- Asking and answering conversational questions       eight activities

**Total number of activities: 42**

4

This page may be photocopied for instructional use only. © Francesca Bierens    Speechmark

# Chapter 2
# Language development at a glance

Language skills impact on every aspect of daily interaction and learning. When expecting a student to communicate, it is essential to be fully aware of the skills and knowledge required in order for the student to be able to respond correctly.

If you want a student to tell you what they are doing, they will need to have acquired 'verbs' in their verbal language in order for them to identify the appropriate action, for example, 'drawing'. If you want a student to tell you 'where' they have put an item, they will need to have acquired prepositions, for example, '*in* the box'. In order for a student to tell you 'why' they did something, they will need to have acquired more than just 'nouns' in their verbal vocabulary and be able to respond in more than single words. They will also have developed at least a basic understanding of the concept of 'cause and effect' and be independent of the need for visual cues. If you tell a student what they are *not* allowed to do, be sure that they have acquired an understanding of the concept of negatives.

The expectation is that the majority of students will eventually be able to answer and ask questions in an interactive manner and be able to establish and maintain some degree of conversation. However, in the busy classroom environment where students are constantly being asked to follow instructions and respond accurately to questions, we must make sure that they have the prerequisite skills necessary to respond appropriately, and we need to know where to start in order to teach these skills.

To assist with this, a practical framework is provided in the programme, describing the basic structure of language development. This framework illustrates what skills are required in order for effective verbal interaction to occur, the sequence in which to best teach these skills and exactly where to start to assist a student's language development.

Just because a student can talk does not automatically mean that they can communicate. In order for the student to develop functional and interactive language skills, they must acquire:
- The Preverbal Skills of L anguage
- The Building Bricks of Language
- The Skills of Conversation.

P This page may be photocopied for instructional use only. © Francesca Bierens Speechmark

'The Preverbal Skills of Language' are the foundation skills of language on which the development of effective verbal communication is dependent. If any one of these skills is not consistently present or is missing, then a student's speech and/or language development will be affected to some degree.

'The Building Bricks of Language' are the words required in order for comprehension and communication to develop. The level of verbal communication becomes richer in function, information and interest as the knowledge and use of a student's vocabulary and language concepts increases.

**Nouns** are used primarily to label a person, place or thing, for example, **'girl'**, **'supermarket'**, and **'car'**. Proper nouns can of course be used in isolation to call someone, for example, 'Toby' or with an inflection in order to ask a question, for example, 'Tammy?' (requesting, 'Is that you, Tammy?'). Nouns can also be used with an inflection to form a question, for example, 'Car?' in order to seek clarification ('Yes, it's a car.'). As adults we often use a single noun as a shortened form of a full question, for example, 'Coffee?' ('Yes, please, I'd love to have a coffee if you are making drinks.'). Despite their limitations for verbal interaction, nouns make up the vast majority of a person's vocabulary, and a good vocabulary is critical for effective communication. This, therefore, makes them the most essential concept for the development of receptive and expressive language.

**Verbs** make nouns 'do things', for example, 'girl **walk**', 'fish **swim**' and 'car **go**'. Verbs provide the most functional information for communication, for example, 'eat', 'sleep' and, second only to nouns, provide the basis of a person's vocabulary. Verbs can stand alone and communicate effectively, for example, 'Sit' and, even in isolation, they can carry vitally important information; for example: 'Stop.'

**Prepositions** add practical and useful information to the conversation; for example: 'Car go **under**.' An understanding of prepositions is important in order to follow many instructions; for example: 'Put your book in your bag.'

**Adjectives** are generally not essential in order for conversation to develop. They do, however, provide a more specific and interesting aspect to verbal language; for example: **'big, blue** car go under'. Knowledge of adjectives is often important in order to accurately carry out some instructions; for example: 'Please, get me a **big** book.'

**Negatives** tend to be taken for granted. It is frequently assumed that this concept is understood by students, and thus it is often left out of structured learning programmes. Many of the teachers I have worked with realised that they did not actively teach negatives, yet assumed that the student had acquired adequate knowledge of this concept to be able to fully understand

This page may be photocopied for instructional use only. © Francesca Bierens Speechmark

classroom statements and instructions that frequently included a negative; for example: '**Don't** put your bag on the floor.'

A student will need an understanding of **time** in order to answer even the most simple 'When' questions, such as, '**When** do we go swimming?' and '**When** do you need to bring your swimsuit to school?' Knowledge of time impacts significantly on the students' correct use of verb tenses.

**Cause and effect** is required for the student to give an accurate response to 'Why' questions. It is also essential in order for the student to develop 'problem-solving' skills.

**Sequencing and sequential memory skills** are required in order for a student to retain and recall a sequence of events or information necessary in order to answer such questions as, 'How did we make the model volcano?', 'How did we make the toasted sandwich?' and 'How do you get to the school office?'

In order for a student to respond to 'when' 'why' and 'how' questions accurately and completely, they need to be able to answer questions without the need for visual cues. They also need to be able to speak in sentences of three or more words.

**Emotions** are an important skill area to teach, as the students need to be aware of many different emotions in order to express how they are feeling and also to gain an understanding of the feelings of others.

'The Skills of Conversation' ensure the correct use of language skills and concepts in order for comfortable interaction to occur between people. The skills of social interaction also include the ability to ask and answer appropriate questions. These skills are essential in order to turn communication into interaction whether it is a child communicating or adult professionals participating in an interactive conversation.

Figure 1 – 'The Preverbal Skills of Language' – illustrates the preverbal skills of language, briefly explaining what they are and why they are important.

Figure 2 – 'The verbal language development summary' – provides a general step-by-step guide to the sequence and broad structure of language development.

When assisting language to develop, it is not a matter of teaching a skill or concept and then moving on to the next level. The acquisition of this knowledge is accumulative, so as each new language skill is acquired, it is necessary to ensure that the previous skills continue to expand and increase in consistency and complexity.

This page may be photocopied for instructional use only. © Francesca Bierens Speechmark

## Figure 1 – The Preverbal Skills of Language

The foundation skills of language

The skills required for the development of functional communication

| **Able to look at people** **(Facial regard)** | **Able to attend, concentrate and anticipate** | **Aware of sights around them** **(Visual awareness)** | **Aware of sounds around them** **(Auditory awareness)** |
|---|---|---|---|
| **What is it?** The student's ability to look at you or in your direction both spontaneously and when requested (ie when their name is called). | **What is it?** The student's ability to remain in one place and attend to an activity for a required period of time. | **What is it?** The student's ability to be aware of sights around them and to recognise this information. | **What is it?** The student's ability to be aware of sounds occurring around them and to recognise this information. |
| **Why is it important?** It is an indication that the student is attending to you. It is necessary in order for the student to imitate and learn. | **Why is it important?** Learning to attend, concentrate and anticipate are essential in order for a student to learn from the activities presented to them. | **Why is it important?** Visual awareness is important because a student must first be aware of what is going on around them before they can learn about what is around them. | **Why is it important?** Auditory awareness is important because a student must initially be aware of what is going on around them before they can learn about what is around them. |

This page may be photocopied for instructional use only. © Francesca Bierens

| Able to copy actions | Able to copy sounds made | Able to wait and take turns | An awareness and control of the face and mouth muscles |
|---|---|---|---|
| **(Motor imitation)** | **(Verbal imitation)** | | |
| **What is it?** The student's ability to copy actions that have been shown to them or that they have observed. | **What is it?** The student's ability to copy sounds that have been modelled for them or that they have heard, such as intonation patterns, transport and animal sounds, speech sounds and words. | **What is it?** The student's ability to understand the need to wait for a turn. The ability to understand that an object can be shared. The student should be able to wait for their turn or for an object to be returned without becoming distressed and remaining attentive while the other person is having a turn. | **What is it?** The student's ability to use their tongue, lips and jaw efficiently to allow them to eat effectively and to form speech sounds. |
| **Why is it important?** Imitation provides the student with the knowledge and some degree of understanding of a skill that then allows them to make their own spontaneous attempts. | **Why is it important?** Imitation provides the student with the knowledge and some degree of understanding of a skill that then allows them to make their own spontaneous attempts. | **Why is it important?** These skills provide the basis for interactive communication. Communication is a waiting, turn-taking and interactive process. | **Why is it important?** It is necessary for the tongue, lips and jaw to be working effectively in order for clear, intelligible speech to develop. The student needs to have an awareness, flexibility and control of these muscles in order to correctly form speech sounds, necessary for the development of intelligible speech. |

*(Source: author's own creation)*

Ⓟ This page may be photocopied for instructional use only. © Francesca Bierens  Speechmark Ⓢ

## Figure 2 – Verbal language development summary

**Outcome: The student will be able to communicate**

**Sequential memory skills:** This is required in order to *answer*:

**Cause and effect:** This is required in order to *answer*:

**Basic concept of time:** This is required in order to *answer*:

**Non-visual information – In order to answer these next questions, the student**

**Negatives:** These are required in order to *answer*:
**For example: 'not', 'isn't' and 'didn't'**

**Prepositions:** These are required in order to *answer*:
**Identify the location; for example, 'in', 'on' or 'under'**

**Verbs:** These are required in order to *answer*:
**Identify the action; for example, 'eating' or 'walking'**

**Nouns: Identify general people, places and objects.** These are required in order to *answer*:
**Proper nouns: Name specific people, places and objects.**

10

P This page may be photocopied for instructional use only. © Francesca Bierens

████████████████████████████████████████████

## effectively in an interactive manner.

| | |
|---|---|
| **How** did you make the salad?<br>• First we … Then … |  This is required to *ask*<br>**'Who'**, **'What'**, **'Where'**, **'How'**, **'When'** and **'Why'** questions<br>**Conversational skills.** |

| | | |
|---|---|---|
| **How** did you get there?<br>• Van • By bus | **Why** did you go?<br>• To see the planets<br>• Because we wanted to see the planets |  This is required to *ask*<br>**'Who'**, **'What'**, **'Where'**, **'How'**, **'When'** and **'Why'** questions<br>**Conversational skills** |

| | |
|---|---|
| **When** did you go?<br>• Tuesday |  This is required to *ask*<br>**'Who'**, **'What'**, **'Where'**, **'How'**, **'When'** and **'Why'** questions<br>**Conversational skills.** |

## must be able to respond to questions without the need for objects or pictures.

| | | | |
|---|---|---|---|
| **Who** is **not** swimming?<br>• Ben • Ben not swimming | **Who didn't** finish their homework?<br>• Fred • Fred didn't | **What** is **not** in the box?<br>• Book<br>• Book not in box |  This is required to ask<br>**'Who'**, **'What'** and **'Where'** questions.<br>**Conversational skills** |

| | | | |
|---|---|---|---|
| **Who** is sitting **beside** Bob?<br>• Pat<br>• Pat beside Bob | **What** is **on** the table?<br>• Book<br>• Book on table | **Where** is the book?<br>• On table<br>• On the table<br>***Acceptable verbal response must include a preposition.*** |  This is required to ask<br>**'Who'**, **'What'** and **'Where'** questions.<br>**Conversational skills** |

| | | | |
|---|---|---|---|
| **Who** is **eating**?<br>• Bob<br>• Bob eating<br>• Boy/Girl<br>*(people in pictures)* | **What** is he **doing**?<br>• Eat • Eating<br>• Eating banana<br>*Acceptable verbal response must include **a verb**.* | **Where** is boy **eating**? (picture of)<br>• Student points to or gives relevant picture.<br>*(nonverbal)* |  This is required to ask<br>**'Who'**, **'What'** and **'Where'** questions.<br>**Conversational skills** |

| | | |
|---|---|---|
| **Who** is this?<br>• Bob<br>*Acceptable verbal response must be a **name**.* | **What** is **this**?<br>• Book | **Where** is **Bob/book**?<br>• Student points to relevant person or object. *(nonverbal)* |

Source: *author's own creation with acknowledgement of Crystal, Fletcher and Garman, 1979*

**P** This page may be photocopied for instructional use only. © Francesca Bierens **Speechmark**

A student's speech and language development can be affected by a wide range of factors, so as their teacher you will need to be aware of:

- **A student's level of hearing**. Each student should have a hearing test, and this is especially the case if there are specific concerns about speech and language delays. Also be aware if the hearing in one ear is better than the other so that you know which side should be towards the teacher. Always make sure the student can see your face when you are speaking to them.

- **A student's vision**. Has the student had their vision tested? Make sure that a student with poor vision is seated in the appropriate position in class with the correct level of light available.

- **Significant medical history**. Does the student have a medical condition that may be affecting their speech and language development? Breathing issues, for example, can affect a student's ability to speak in longer sentences and can affect their voice projection.

- **Background**. English may not be the first language for some of your students, and they may not use English at all at home.

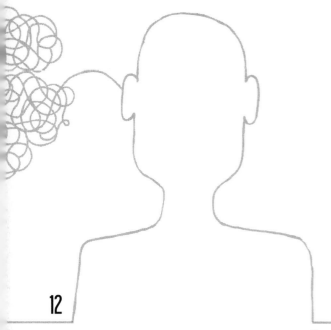

℗ This page may be photocopied for instructional use only. © Francesca Bierens  Speechmark

# Part 2

## Assisting students with language delays in the classroom to acquire 'The Preverbal Skills of Language'

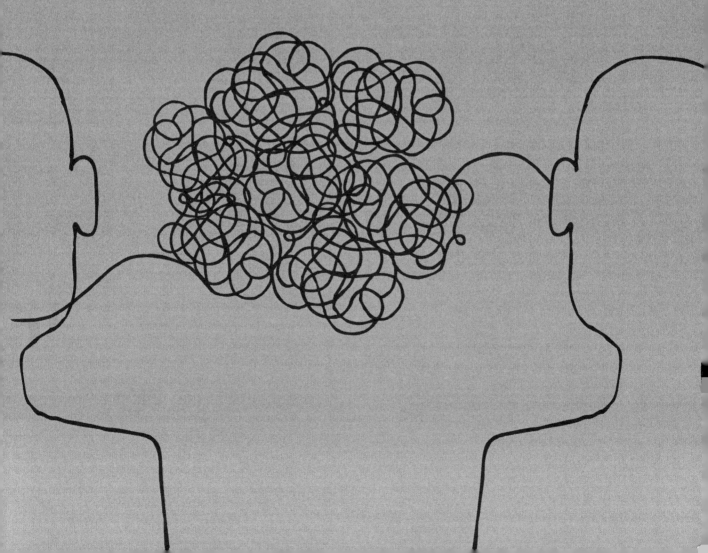

# Introduction

The development of speech and language is extremely complex. It involves a child learning to understand what is being said and developing the ability to express their own needs and wants, responding to questions and interacting verbally with others using intelligible speech. In order for all of this to occur, the child must initially acquire the 'preverbal' skills that provide the foundation and framework for the development of effective verbal communication. The preverbal skills of language are the foundation skills of language and, as such, are, in effect, the prerequisite skills of learning.

A child may acquire words but if one or more of the preverbal skills are absent or inconsistent then a child's speech and/or language development and therefore their ability to communicate will be affected to some degree.

Assisting the development of the preverbal skills of language is the place to start in order to assist a student's communication. In order for children to acquire understanding and appropriate use of language they must have practical experience. Children need to experience language before they can understand it or use it. They need to: **explore – experience – experiment – learn**.

When carrying out activities with students at this preverbal stage, it must always be kept in mind that this is the foundation level of language development. The students are a 'blank canvas', so all information must be seen as new. This is the 'feeding skills in' stage, so all activities must be modelled. The students should not be asked to do anything that has not been completely modelled. At this preverbal stage, the majority of responses are nonverbal.

Many of the activities provided can be used in more than one skill category. It is essential, however, to constantly keep in mind exactly what the goal is and precisely what you want the students to achieve. Only focus on one goal at a time. If the goal is to imitate an action then the students are not required to imitate an accompanying sound.

The bold 'student' headline is the skill or response required from the student. The rest of the activity is the procedure to teach that skill and assist the student to give the appropriate response.

Being able to interact with people is beneficial and enjoyable. So it is important that learning the skills necessary to communicate is as positive an experience for the students as possible. Therefore, keep these activities and exercises short, light-hearted and fun both for the students and for yourself.

P This page may be photocopied for instructional use only. © Francesca Bierens  Speechmark

# Chapter 1

# Learning to look at people – facial regard

| | |
|---|---|
| **What is it?** | The student's ability to look at you or in your direction both spontaneously and when requested (ie when their name is called). |
| **Why is it important?** | This skill is important because it is: <br>• an indication that the student is attending to you <br>• necessary in order for the student to learn. |
| **What can we do?** | Encourage the student to look at you or towards you as often as naturally possible. It does not have to be for long, however, get into the habit of gaining the student's attention before you ask them a question or give an instruction. |
| **Prerequisite:** | • Vision test. <br>  A vision check or screening will have told you: <br>  ❖ if the student's vision is good <br>  ❖ or, if not, to what degree the vision is affected. |

## Recommendations for encouraging students to look at people

**Ideal response.** The student puts their head up and establishes comfortable facial regard spontaneously during an activity or when their name is called.

**Acceptable response.** The student stops their current activity and slightly raises their head without looking up, to indicate awareness and/or interest.

• When speaking to the students always keep your head up and constantly look slowly around the class so that all the students can see your face.

• Some students use their 'peripheral' vision, that is, looking from the side. It is not possible for them to look at you 'face to face'. As long as the student is 'attending' in your direction, this is perfectly acceptable.

Ⓟ This page may be photocopied for instructional use only. © Francesca Bierens  Speechmark Ⓢ

- For some students, just establishing facial regard is enough of a challenge for them. They cannot maintain facial regard and also carry out an activity. In this situation keep in mind what your goal is and exactly what you want the student to be able to achieve.

- Always call the student by name *before* directing an activity towards them. This lets them know that whenever they hear their name something is about to happen and it prepares them to attend to you.

- Avoid turning this or any other activity into a battle of wills. If the student refuses to look at you, keep encouraging them to do so but never prevent them from getting the object. This will only lead to the student losing complete interest in the activity. Instead, gently call the student by their name and wait.

## Carrying out the 'Learning to look at people' activities

- Remember that when carrying out these activities your ultimate goal is to encourage the students to look at your face. The activity is merely a means of encouraging this, so always bring the activity back to your face.

- **Watch the bubbles and then look at the teacher.** When blowing the bubbles, you want the students to look back at your face after they have watched the bubbles, eager for you to blow more. So keep their attention on your face for as long as possible without losing their interest by keeping your movements slow, that is,  keep the bottle close to your face as you slowly dip the wand into the bubble mixture and then gently blow the bubbles.

- **Watch the puzzle pieces and then look at the teacher.** If you are all sitting on the floor, put the puzzle up on a small table so that you keep your head up; working with objects on the floor immediately limits your visual field so you are unable to maintain eye contact with your students.

- **Watch the puppet and then look at the teacher.** Most students tend to respond well to puppets, however, occasionally a child may find them frightening, so do introduce them cautiously. If a student does appear to be reluctant or frightened, then instead of a puppet use a small stuffed toy such as a teddy or dog.

- It is very important to be patient. Remember that your long-term aim is to encourage interaction and communication, so try to keep the activities as stress-free as possible so that the students learn that interaction is a positive experience.

P This page may be photocopied for instructional use only. © Francesca Bierens Speechmark

# Activities to encourage the students to look at the teacher

**1   The students need to:  Watch the bubbles and then look at the teacher.**

**Teacher:**

1   Hold the bottle of bubble mixture close to your face, making sure you do not cover your face.

2   Slowly put the bubble wand in the bubble mixture and gently blow the bubbles up in the air, so that the students watch the bubbles as they float past.

3   Slowly put the bubble wand back in the mixture, looking around the class at the students before repeating the action.

4   Always bring the bubble wand and mixture back to near your face and wait a couple of seconds before blowing more bubbles so that the students learn to spontaneously watch your mouth in anticipation of the action.

**2   The students need to: Watch the little piece of paper and then look at the teacher.**

**Teacher:**

1   Place a small piece of paper or tissue paper, which you have rolled into a ball, into the palm of your hand.

2   Bring your hand up to just below your mouth, making sure you do not cover your face.

3   Sit or stand directly in front of the students. Gently blow the piece of paper so that it lands in a space where the students can see it.

4   Look around at the students as you place the piece of paper back in your hand, bringing it back up to your face.

5   Repeat this activity five times so that the students learn to spontaneously watch your mouth in anticipation of the action.

**3   The students need to:  Watch the beach ball and then look at the teacher.**

**Teacher:**

1   Place a deflated, medium-sized beach ball up close to your face, making sure it does not cover your face.

2   Sit directly in front of the students and place your hands on the beach ball. Take a deep breath, looking around the class at the students, and then gently blow the beach ball up.

3   Every few seconds, stop and talk to the students about the ball getting 'bigger' and 'bigger', encouraging them to watch the ball.

4   Look at the students as you gently blow up the ball.

Ⓟ This page may be photocopied for instructional use only. © Francesca Bierens  Speechmark Ⓢ

5   When the ball is completely inflated, gently throw it up in the air, looking around the class at the students each time you catch it.

6   Always bring the ball back to near your face and hold it there for a couple of seconds before throwing it back up in the air so that the students learn to spontaneously watch your mouth in anticipation of the action.

### 4   The students need to: Watch the puzzle pieces and then look at the teacher.

**Teacher:**

1   Show the fully completed jigsaw puzzle to the class and talk about the picture or the individual pieces (depending on the type of puzzle).

2   Remove each piece of the puzzle slowly, always bringing the puzzle piece up to near your face before you put it down on the table.

3   Involve the students when completing the puzzle. Always bring the puzzle piece up to near your face and wait until the students look at you or in your direction before giving the piece to a student to place in the puzzle.

4   If a student will not look at you, either spontaneously or, when asked, hold the puzzle piece up to near their face (without getting too close) and slowly move the item around to your face so that the student 'eye follows' the object to look at you.

Note: Keep the pace slow enough to encourage the students to look at you but not moving so slowly that they lose interest or become distressed.

### 5   The students need to: Watch the puppet and then look at the teacher.

**Teacher:**

1   Hold the puppet close beside your face, making sure it does not cover your face. The puppet will help to encourage the students to look at your face while you are singing, especially when you are greeting or saying farewell to them by name.

2   Use the puppet to help sing the 'Morning Greeting' song and/or 'Home Time' song, taking turns to look at each student during the song.

3   Greet or say goodbye to each student by name (if the class size allows).

4   Always finish a song or name by bringing the puppet close beside your face and mouth and wait a few seconds before saying the next name. This will encourage the students to spontaneously watch your mouth in anticipation of the next name or song.

℗ This page may be photocopied for instructional use only. © Francesca Bierens  Speechmark Ⓢ

**6 The students need to: Watch the windmill and then look at the teacher.**

**Teacher:**

1 Hold the windmill close to your mouth, making sure not to cover your face.

2 Exaggerate breathing in while looking around the class at the students, and then gently blow the windmill.

3 Look slowly around the class at the students each time you breathe in and then blow the windmill.

4 Always bring the windmill back to your face and wait a couple of seconds before blowing it again so that the students learn to spontaneously watch your mouth in anticipation of the action.

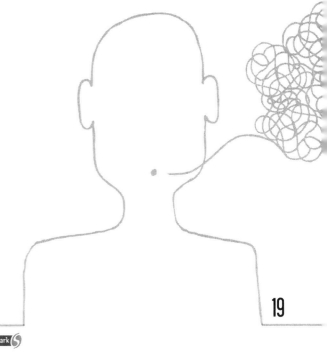

Ⓟ This page may be photocopied for instructional use only. © Francesca Bierens Speechmark ⟳

Chapter 2

# Learning to attend, concentrate and anticipate

| | |
|---|---|
| **What is it?** | The student's ability to remain in one place and attend to an activity for a required period of time, and to understand and expect that a recent experience is going to occur again. |
| **Why is it important?** | Attention, concentration and anticipation skills are essential for a student to focus long enough in order to learn from the activities being presented to them. |
| **What can we do?** | Take note of the student's level of attention to different activities. Encourage them to attend to a variety of activities that are not always of their own choosing. |
| **Prerequisites:** | • Comfort – make sure that the student has recently:<br>  ❖ had something to drink and eat<br>  ❖ been to the bathroom.<br>• Appropriate seating<br>• Minimal distractions. |

## Recommendations for encouraging students to attend, concentrate and anticipate

**Ideal response.** The student sits attentively and is completely focused on the activity presented for the duration of the session.

**Acceptable response.** The student attends intermittently throughout the activity and may fiddle with an object such as their clothes but does not disrupt the class or distract any other student.

• **When trying to establish the students' attention and maintain their interest, the manner in which you present the activity is significantly more important than the**

Ⓟ This page may be photocopied for instructional use only. © Francesca Bierens  Speechmark Ⓢ

**activity itself.** It is essential that you use your voice, varying the volume from quiet to a whisper and then to normal volume, using inflection and just enough pause time to create anticipation.

**So remember to:**
- ❖ keep it visual
- ❖ speak and move slowly and quietly and maintain eye contact with all of the students
- ❖ keep the activity varied, of a relatively short duration and use voice, volume and inflection to maintain interest.

- **Make sure that the students are correctly and comfortably seated.** Being seated at a table and chair enables the students to attend better than when seated on the floor. It also enables them to have a wider field of vision. The students should:
  - ❖ be seated in a chair that is the correct height for the table
  - ❖ have both feet placed securely on the floor or on a solid object such as a box
  - ❖ have a stable chair that does not wobble
  - ❖ be seated as upright as possible and be unable to slide forward.

- **Minimise distractions.** The room should be as quiet as naturally possible with minimal peripheral movement of people or objects, for example, curtains flapping.

- **Avoid clutter.** The students should only be presented with one activity at a time and only have the items that they require for that single task.

- **The table should be clear of pens and markers at all times**. When speaking to the students, there should be nothing on the desk to distract them. When working with pens or crayons, use only one or two.

- **Introduce one activity at a time. Put the previous activity away before introducing the next one.**

- **Avoid letting the students decide when an activity should finish.** If the students start losing interest, don't immediately stop the activity but instead hold their attention a bit longer by extending the activity for just one or two more seconds. It is not necessary to complete the activity but it is important that the decision to finish is made by the teacher.

- **Increase the length of the activity by a couple of seconds each time.** Each time the student works on the activity, slightly increase the length of time they are required to attend; for example, encourage the student to wait for an extra one or two pieces to be placed in the jigsaw puzzle or wait for one additional page of a book to be shown before finishing the activity.

21

## Carrying out the 'Learning to attend, concentrate and anticipate' activities

- **Tell a short, fun story, using visual props such as Fuzzy-Felts.** When *telling* a story, you tend to establish a closer interaction with the students than when reading a book. Consequently, a greater level of interest is established, maintaining the students' attention.

- **Put the photos into a 'photos-only' album with no written words.** 'Words' for some students are very distracting and can be stressful, as the student may feel that they are going to be required to read them. The purpose of this activity is to establish and maintain the students' interest and children are usually very motivated by photos of themselves. Remember, this is not a verbal language activity, so the students are not required to answer questions about who is in the photograph.

- **Put photos or pictures of the activity options into a bag**. Often it is when the students have finished one activity and are moving into another activity that their attention is lost and they can be distracted by other things occurring in the classroom. Making the transition stage a little more interesting and visual often assists the students to reestablish focus and understand what is expected of them.

- **In order to acquire or regain attention, do a movement activity.** Doing this exercise for a few seconds as a short break in the middle of a more concentrated task often helps to refocus the students' attention when they have lost interest and appear tired.

- **Drawing around fingers.** From my experience, this exercise is excellent for calming students and focusing their attention prior to beginning an activity.

## Activities to increase the students' attention, concentration and anticipation

**1 The students need to: Attend and remain focused.**

**Teacher:**

1 Slowly remove a whole tissue from a pocket packet while looking at the students and very slowly unfold it.

2 Hold the unfolded tissue in front of your face so that it covers your face.

3 Blow the tissue gently but with enough pressure to lift the tissue, allowing the students to see your face.

Ⓟ This page may be photocopied for instructional use only. © Francesca Bierens  Speechmark Ⓢ

4   As soon as the tissue lifts and you can see the students, smile and say 'hello' before the tissue falls, covering your face.

5   Wait a few seconds before repeating this action.

## 2   The students need to: Attend and remain focused.

### Teacher:

1   *Tell* a short, fun story, using movement, gesture, expression and a small number of visual props such as Fuzzy-Felts (of trains, people, animals, trees, etc.), magnetic objects or puppets.

2   While you are telling the story, look slowly around the class or group in order to maintain eye contact with the students.

3   Use variations in the volume of your voice and pause occasionally at critical parts of the story in order to maintain the students' interest in 'what is going to happen next'.

4   Have a fun, interesting ending to the story.

5   Stories with repetitive phrases are particularly effective for maintaining attention.

## 3   The students need to: Attend and remain focused.

### Teacher:

1   Have a small selection of class photos of students participating in class activities. Go through these photos individually, drawing the students' attention to 'who is in the photos', pointing them out to the class; for example: 'Look at this photo. Here is Bob.'

2   Also point out some of the things you can see in the photos, for example, zoo animals.

3   Make sure they are good quality, uncluttered photos that clearly show the students involved in an activity in which they have very recently participated.

4   Have one, two or three students in each photo but as much as possible have at least one photo of each student.

5   Maintain interest by slightly prolonging the time it takes to show the photographs – but be careful not to take too long.

6   Put the photos into a 'photos-only' album with no written words.

## 4   The students need to: Attend and remain focused.

### Teacher:

1   When transitioning from one activity to another or at choosing time, put photos or pictures of the activity options (eg computer, reading, and maths block corner) into a bag.

Ⓟ This page may be photocopied for instructional use only. © Francesca Bierens  Speechmark

2  Shake the bag of pictures in order to gain the students' attention. (For this activity it is not necessary to go through the photos before putting them into the bag.)

3  Slowly remove each photograph one at a time with a slight delay before showing the students.

4  Identify the photos and point to the corresponding activity, for example, book corner or computer.

5  Either give each student the photo of the activity you want them to work on or put the photos on a board for the students to make their own selection at choosing time.

**5   The students need to: Attend and remain focused.**

**Teacher:**

1  In order to acquire or regain attention, do a movement activity.

2  Stand up and tap named body parts, for example, knees, toes, shoulders and elbows.

3  Intermittently change the speed and volume of the instruction, for example, slow and then fast and loud and then quiet.

4  Model the actions with the students as you give the instructions.

5  Recite or sing the alphabet or count to 20 while clapping. Frequently change the rhythm and volume in order to keep the students' attention.

**6   The students need to: Attend and remain focused.**

**Teacher:**

1  For students who have significant difficulty attending, or are particularly restless, encourage them to place one hand on a piece of paper and then very slowly draw around their fingers.

2  Very quietly say, 'I'm drawing around your fingers: one finger, two fingers, three fingers, four fingers and your thumb.'

3  If necessary, gently place your index finger on the back of the student's hand in order to keep their hand in place.

4  Very quietly do the same thing with the other hand. Do not place the two hands on the paper together.

5  The student may then want to draw around your fingers.

24

 This page may be photocopied for instructional use only. © Francesca Bierens **Speechmark**

# Chapter 3

# Learning to look around at things – visual awareness

| | |
|---|---|
| **What is it?** | The student's ability to be aware of sights, objects and people that are present around them. |
| **Why is it important?** | This skill is important because a student must initially be aware of what is going on around them before they can learn about what is going on around them. |
| **What can we do?** | As much as possible, develop the students' awareness and interest in the world around them. |
| **Prerequisites**: | • Vision test.<br>A vision check or screening will have told you:<br>❖ if the student's vision is good<br>❖ Or, if not, to what degree the vision is affected. |

## Recommendations for encouraging students to look around at things

**Ideal response.** The student spontaneously looks at objects or activities of interest around them.

**Acceptable response.** The student looks towards an object or activity that is drawn to their attention by identifying and/or pointing.

- Developing the ability to be aware of sights occurring around them is a preverbal skill that prepares the student for the development of verbal language. In order to be able to accurately recognise and verbally identify an object or person, the student first needs to be aware of it.

- Students with language delays or disorders can be very passive. They often wait for someone – usually an adult – to bring things to their attention rather than looking for themselves. The students need to be made aware of the need to look beyond what is immediately in front of

Ⓟ This page may be photocopied for instructional use only. © Francesca Bierens Speechmark Ⓢ

them. They need to be encouraged to look around, not just directly in front of them. Encourage them to be aware of objects beside, above and behind them, such as on their neighbour's desk and on the wall. Encourage them to be aware of people nearby and further away.

- Language and communication is about being aware of what is going on around you and responding to it, for example, observing dark clouds and thinking that you will take a coat when you go out; seeing an object on the floor and deciding to walk around it; or seeing a familiar person and contemplating whether to wave at them or not.  Encourage the students to be aware of what is going on around them in all situations and environments.

- 'Pointing' is a very important skill and should be actively focused on and taught. Regularly encourage students to look at and point to objects in the distance, for example, aeroplanes that they can see out of the window as well as objects and people close to them. Point to isolated objects or people in photos and on picture cards.

## Carrying out the 'Learning to look around at things' activities

- **'Look and point to' instructions.** 'Pointing to' or 'looking at' objects on computers, iPads or even in a book has not been included in this activity at the preverbal stage. The goal is to expand the students' visual field, encouraging the students to look up and beyond the small screen or page and their immediate desk or table environment.

  Photos and photo albums are included, however, because the students need to be aware of people in all situations – beyond the classroom.

  When pointing to things, it is important to explain what you are pointing to and where the object is. It doesn't matter if the students do not understand the content of what you are saying; they will be able to follow your gaze and gesture.

- If you do have an interactive whiteboard in your classroom, they are excellent for putting photos of people up on the big screen in front of the class. The photos are then clearer and easier for the whole class to see.

This page may be photocopied for instructional use only. © Francesca Bierens

# Activities to encourage the students to look around at things

**1  The students need to: Look and point to objects inside the classroom.**

**Teacher:**

1  Have six to eight photos or pictures of large common classroom objects, for example, a door, lights, books, a computer and a bookcase.

2  Show the students each of the pictures individually and name each object.

3  Hold up each picture individually, identifying it by name game, and then show the students where the object is in the class by pointing to the corresponding item; for example: 'It's a computer' (holding up a picture of a computer to the students) and, 'There is the computer' (pointing to the object in the classroom).

4  Place the picture on or in front of the corresponding object when possible, repeating the name of the object for a third time. If it is not possible to put the picture with the object, then just point to the object and ask the students to do the same; for example: 'It's a light' (holding up a picture of the lights to the students) and then, 'Point up to the lights.'

**2  The students need to: Look and point to objects outside the classroom.**

**Teacher:**

1  Have photos or pictures of items you may see outside the classroom, for example, trees, flowers, a playground, birds, rubbish bins, and houses.

2  Show the students each of the pictures individually and name each object.

3  Go for a walk outside or look through the window.

4  Show the students where the object is by pointing to the corresponding item; for example: 'There's a bird' (pointing to a bird) and, 'There's a rubbish bin. Let's all point to the rubbish bin' (pointing to a bin).

5  Encourage the students to be visually aware of objects around them even when you have not shown them a picture; for example: 'There's a plane up in the sky. Point up to the plane.'

**3  The students need to: Look at familiar people in the classroom.**

**Teacher:**

1  Collect together photos of students and teachers.

2  Hold up each picture individually, identifying the person by name, and then show the students where that person is in the class by gesturing 'hello' to the appropriate person; for example: 'It's Pat. Let's look at Pat. Hi Pat.'

3  Place the photo on a board or in a class photo album.

27

**4   The students need to: Look at the balloon floating around the room.**

**Teacher:**

1   Blow up a balloon and gently pat it up into the air so that it floats slowly up to the ceiling.

2   The students can then watch it float around the room and can hit it back up as it begins to float down.

3   Draw the students' attention to the movement of the balloon by pointing and explaining where it is going; for example: 'Look, the balloon is floating over to the bookcase.'

4   If the risk of the balloon popping and frightening the students is too high, then do the same activity by blowing big bubbles.


**5   The students need to: Look at people and things moving outside the classroom.**

**Teacher:**

1   Go for a walk outside or look through the window of the classroom.

2   Encourage the students to be visually aware of actions occurring around them by pointing things out to them and explaining the various activities taking place; for example: 'Look, the caretaker is sweeping the path', 'Look, the students are sliding down the slide', 'Look at the cars driving past the school' and, 'Look at the builders working.'

3   Encourage the students to also be aware of very fine movements; for example: 'Look, the leaves are falling off the tree.'


**6   The students need to: Look at photos of familiar people and actions.**

**Teacher:**

1   Take photos of students and teachers from the class during class activities or events or outings, for example, a celebration of a student's birthday, a visit from fire fighters with photos of the students in the fire engine or a visit to a zoo.

2   Look at each of the photos with the students in a relaxed manner and point to and relate where the various students and teachers are, for example: 'There's Bob and Pat eating lunch at the zoo.'

3   Put photos in a small photo album with one clear photo per page. This should be a 'photos-only' album (ie no words written underneath).

Ⓟ This page may be photocopied for instructional use only. © Francesca Bierens Speechmark

**7   The students need to: Look at objects or people through a cylinder.**

**Teacher:**

1   Have different types of cylinders – short and long and thick and thin – from, for example, rolls of kitchen paper towels and wrapping paper.

2   Give each student a cylinder and model the action of looking through the cylinder. Then, still looking through the cylinder, show the students how to look at objects and people around the room. Swap cylinders and have the students look at objects and people through a different cylinder.

3   If the students have difficulty remaining focused and on task, then this may be an activity that needs to be done one cylinder at a time.

4   Model the activity by looking through a cylinder at different objects or people around the room, keeping the students' attention by naming six things that you can see. Then pass the cylinder to a student. The student then looks through the cylinder while you identify areas that they are clearly viewing; for example, 'Bob is looking at the library corner and the ceiling.' The student then passes the cylinder to the next student.

*The goal of this activity is for the students to look at objects and people in order to increase their visual awareness. They do not need to vocalise.*

**8   The students need to: Look at objects or people through different coloured paper.**

**Teacher:**

1   Have different types of transparent papers, for example, different colour cellophane paper.

2   Give each student one piece of coloured paper and model looking around the room at different objects and people. Swap papers and have students look around the room through a different coloured or textured paper.

3   If the students have difficulty remaining focused and on task, then model the activity using just one piece of paper at a time.

4   Look through a piece of coloured paper and identify objects or people that you can see around the room. After identifying six things, pass the paper to a student. The student then looks around while you identify areas that he is clearly viewing; for example, 'Bob is looking at the window and the computers.'

5   The student then passes the paper to the next student.

*The goal of this activity is for the students to look at objects and people in order to increase their visual awareness. They do not need to vocalise.*

Ⓟ This page may be photocopied for instructional use only. © Francesca Bierens Speechmark Ⓢ

Chapter 4

# Learning to listen to sounds – auditory awarenesss

| | |
|---|---|
| **What is it?** | The student's ability to hear and respond appropriately to sounds they hear. |
| **Why is it important?** | Children need to learn to listen in order to gain information from the world around them. A 'listening attitude' is crucial for the development of effective speech and language. |
| **What can we do?** | Encourage the students to 'wait and listen' when you are speaking to them. Avoid talking over the voices of other people, the sound of computers or printers and so on. Keep the students' environment as 'quiet' as possible. |
| **Prerequisite:** | • Hearing test.<br>A hearing test will have told you:<br>❖ if the student's hearing is adequate in both ears<br>❖ or, if not, what is the degree of hearing impairment and which is the better ear. |

## Recommendations for encouraging students to listen to sounds

| | |
|---|---|
| **Ideal response.** | The student spontaneously listens and shows an interest in sounds around them. |
| **Acceptable response.** | The student demonstrates an awareness of sounds drawn to their attention. |

• The acquisition and development of verbal language is predominantly auditory. Teaching children names of objects is of little sense if the student has no awareness or knowledge of

Ⓟ This page may be photocopied for instructional use only. © Francesca Bierens Speechmark Ⓢ

the object to which the word is referring. Being aware of the sights and sounds around them is essential in order for a student to make sense of language.

- The student must initially be aware of the larger, louder sounds occurring around them in order to be able to acquire the fine auditory subtleties required for the development of speech and language.

## Carrying out the 'Learning to listen to sounds' activities

- **Listen to the sounds around the classroom and listen to the sounds outside**. Although photos are excellent, they are not essential for these activities, so don't worry if you don't have access to a camera. In order to draw the students' attention to the sounds made by specific objects, just stand near an item – for example, a printer – and encourage the students to listen to the sounds it makes.

- **Listen and move to the music and listen to the song and play instruments.** Some students may be sound-sensitive, so do be cautious about introducing louder sounds or higher-frequency sounds.

- **Listen to the sounds at home.** At this stage, make your own recordings of familiar sounds rather than use the commercially available recordings, as those sounds are more difficult to identify and discriminate. They are excellent at the next skill level but, at this early stage, the goal is just for the student to be able to identify common household sounds.

- **Listen to the animal sounds**. Remember the goal of this activity is for the student to listen to the sounds being made. They do not need to imitate the sounds themselves.

- Remember to allow the students sufficient time to process the information before responding. Wait just a few extra seconds before repeating the sound.

## Activities to encourage the students to listen to sounds

**1 The students need to: Listen to the sounds around the classroom.**

**Teacher:**

1 Have photos or pictures of common classroom objects and people that make noise, for example, printers, chairs (scraping) and singers.

2 Show the students each of the pictures individually and identify each object and sound.

This page may be photocopied for instructional use only. © Francesca Bierens Speechmark

3 Hold up each picture individually, identifying it by name, and then show the students where the object is in the class by pointing to the corresponding item; for example: 'It's a printer' (holding up a picture of a printer to the students) and, 'Can you hear the printer printing?' (pointing to the object).

4 Place the picture on or in front of the corresponding object when possible, repeating the name of the object.

5 Have students listen quietly and have them identify the different sounds they hear.

## 2 The students need to: Listen to the sounds outside.

**Teacher:**

1 Have photos of some things that you may see outside that make a sound, for example, a bird, a car and some children. Talk about the sounds they make, for example, the chirping of birds, the blaring of police sirens and the laughing and shrieking of children.

2 Go for a walk around the school and tell the students to look out for things that are making a sound and then listen to that sound, for example, teachers talking and children singing.

3 Return inside and talk about sounds they may have heard.

4 Go through photos or pictures of things in the community that make familiar sounds, for example, a builder hammering and a refuse collector knocking glass bottles together.

5 Put the pictures up on a board in front of the class and have the students listen to a recording that you have made of these familiar sounds and then assist them to point to the associated picture.

## 3 The students need to: Listen and move to the changing music.

**Teacher:**

1 Have a selection of music, for example, band music, quiet music and slow music. Walk around a large area – outside if possible, but otherwise the school hall or the classroom – showing the students how to move appropriately to the speed and volume of the various pieces of music.

2 Play the loud marching music and take big steps around the room with your head up. Play quiet music and tiptoe cautiously around the room with your head down.

3 Draw the students' attention to the changes in music and relate this to the different way of walking by explaining as you move; for example: 'This is loud music, so we walk with big steps and with our head up.'

4 Gradually reduce your prompts and cues so that the students have to listen for themselves and respond appropriately to the changes in the music.

Ⓟ This page may be photocopied for instructional use only. © Francesca Bierens  Speechmark

**4   The students need to: Listen and recognise household sounds.**

**Teacher:**

1   Have photos of household things and talk about the sounds they make, for example, a telephone ringing, a bath running, a toilet flushing, a door shutting, a radio playing and a kettle boiling.

2   Identify each picture as you put it up on a large board in front of the class.

3   Make sure the pictures are well-spaced so that they can be clearly identified when pointing.

4   Play a recording you have made of six familiar, easily distinguishable sounds made for the students to listen to.

5   As each sound is heard, initially assist the students to identify it; for example: 'Listen, what's that sound? It's the telephone ringing.' Then model the action of pointing to the associated picture.

6   Gradually reduce your prompts and cues so that the students have to listen for themselves and respond appropriately.


**5   The students need to: Listen to and recognise simple animal sounds.**

**Teacher:**

1   Collect together some toy animals or animal puppets. Have no more than six.

2   Identify each animal individually and then make the associated sound; for example, 'Cow: moo.'

3   Put the toys or puppets on a table at the front of the class so they can be seen clearly by all of the students.

4   Point to the associated toy or puppet as you make each of the animal sounds.

5   Present two toys or puppets to the students and make one of the associated sounds.

6   Model the action of pointing to the correct animal.

7   Gradually reduce your prompts and cues so that the students have to listen for themselves and respond appropriately.


**6   The students need to: Listen to the song and play instruments.**

**Teacher:**

1   Sing a little song or play a recorded song.

2   Give each student a sound maker, for example, a bell, a pair of small maracas, two blocks to be hit together or a drum.

Ⓟ This page may be photocopied for instructional use only. © Francesca Bierens  Speechmark

3   Have the students participate by playing their instrument.

4   As you sing the song and/or play an instrument, draw the students' attention to the music, directing them to listen when the music starts and when it stops.

5   Gradually reduce your prompts and cues so that the students have to listen for themselves and respond appropriately.

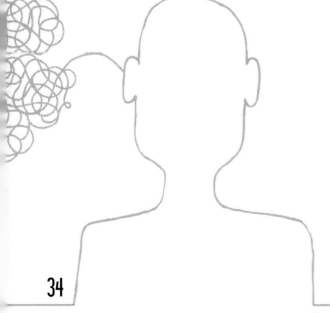

34

# Chapter 5

# Learning to copy actions – imitation of actions

| | |
|---|---|
| **What is it?** | The student's ability to copy actions that have been shown to them or that they have observed. |
| **Why is it important?** | Imitation is important because it provides the student with the knowledge and some degree of understanding of a skill that then allows them to make their own spontaneous attempts. |
| **What can we do?** | Encourage and assist students to imitate actions whenever possible. Remember that every action should always be accompanied with a vocalisation but the student does not need to imitate the vocalisation. |
| **Prerequisites:** | • Able to achieve simple 'gross motor' movements (unless the student has a physical disability that prevents this).<br>• If seated, the students should be correctly positioned at a chair and table appropriate for their height. |

## Recommendations for encouraging students to copy actions

**Ideal response.**   The student accurately imitates the action modelled.

**Acceptable response.**   The student makes an attempt to copy the action or part of the action modelled.

## Carrying out the 'Learning to copy actions' activities

• Throughout these activities, it is important to remember that the goal is imitation of the actions, so a verbal response – even if modelled – is not required. If the students are able to combine an action and vocalisation then that is excellent but it is not required.

Ⓟ This page may be photocopied for instructional use only. © Francesca Bierens  Speechmark Ⓢ

- **Copy the movement.** The students can get quite enthusiastic with this activity, so keep the actions as controlled as possible.

- **Copy the action to the song or rhyme.** Although it is ideal if the students are able to tap the body part as modelled and named, the goal for this activity is imitating the action, not body awareness. So if a student is making an attempt to imitate but is not keeping up with tapping the right body part then that is not important. If they are actively participating and making some attempts to imitate then that is excellent and should be encouraged and praised.

- **Copy the action with the finger puppet.** The students often enjoy playing with their finger puppet during this activity so tend not to watch or copy the actions modelled. So for the first song or short story, let them decide how their own puppet should move, and then, for the main story or song, they are required to imitate the action modelled by the teacher.

- **Copy drawing lines and simple shapes.** This is quite a complex activity, as there are a number of skills involved. For this activity the students have to wait and watch before copying on to paper a line or shape, which may be quite a challenge for some students. Keep lines short and simple, that is, one line across the page or one line up the page and draw only very basic shapes, for example, a circle. This should ensure that there is minimal waiting and watching time for the students. It is not essential that the lines or shapes are copied accurately. Any attempt to imitate should be praised.

  Some students will just want to do their own drawing, so it may be beneficial to let them do so after they have copied your lines or shapes.

- **Copy stacking the blocks.** This can also be a challenging activity for some students. Some students will have difficulty manipulating the blocks and others will have difficulty with their perceptual skills. These students will require assistance with actually knowing how to place a block beside or under another block. Therefore, keep the activity as easy as possible for as long as necessary by just getting the students to copy putting the blocks on top of one another.

  Keep the activity short and as light-hearted as possible. Provide as much assistance as a student requires, allowing them to complete at least the final action, for example, placing the block where you are quietly indicating that they should do so.

  This is an important skill in preparation for the development of prepositions.

  **Note:** Do this activity when the students are able to consistently imitate all other actions modelled.

Ⓟ This page may be photocopied for instructional use only. © Francesca Bierens **Speechmark** ⑤

# Activities to encourage the students to watch and copy actions modelled for them

**1  The students need to: Copy the 'pretend' action.**

**Teacher:**

1  Read or look through a big picture book that has action pictures, for example, children swimming, climbing, painting and sweeping.

2  As you read the story or talk about the pictures, draw attention to the actions shown in the pictures; for example: 'The boy is swimming. Let's all pretend to swim.'

3  Model these actions so that the students can see what you are doing and can copy your movements.

Remember that the skill being looked for is imitation of actions, so verbal response or identification of the action is not required.

**2  The students need to: Copy the dance movements.**

**Teacher:**

1  When dancing, or during a music activity, encourage the students to copy your 'moves', for example, jumping, skipping and waving arms. Keep the actions quite simple and preferably keep the movements symmetrical so that both arms are moving together.

2  Perform each action long enough for the students to be able to work out how to carry out the action. Then perhaps change from one action to another.

**3  The students need to: Copy the action to the song or rhyme.**

**Teacher:**

1  Sing the 'Head, shoulders, knees and toes' song or rhyme and model the action of tapping various parts of the body as they are named; for example: 'We're touching our knees, knees, knees; we're touching our ears, ears, ears.'

2  Occasionally, vary the speed of the rhyme so that the students sometimes have to move faster or slower. This helps to keep it interesting and also encourages the students to keep watching.

Remember that the skill being looked for is imitation of the actions, so singing the words to the song is not required.

This page may be photocopied for instructional use only. © Francesca Bierens Speechmark

### 4  The students need to: Copy the action with the finger puppet.

**Teacher:**

1   Give each student a finger puppet.

2   When telling them a story or singing a song, model an action with your finger puppet – for example, 'flying up in the sky', dancing, nodding for 'yes' or shaking side to side for 'no' – and encourage the students to imitate the action with their puppets,.

Remember that the goal is for the students to imitate the action, so verbal responses are not required.

### 5  The students need to: Copy drawing lines and simple shapes.

**Teacher:**

1   Put a large piece of paper (such as A2) on an easel or up on a wall. Obtain a large felt-tip pen or paintbrush and paint. Alternatively, prepare to use a whiteboard.

2   Make sure that each student has their own piece of paper and a large coloured pencil, felt-tip pen or finger paints.

3   Draw one thing – such as a line, a circle or a set of dots – on the paper or whiteboard.  Tell the students to copy what you have drawn.

4   Draw another thing and continue to do so, but only draw one thing at a time so that the students have adequate time to watch and then copy what you have drawn.

Only give assistance if the students need help managing their materials. The items they copy should be their own attempts.

### 6  The students need to: Copy stacking the blocks.

**Teacher:**

1   Give each student a set of approximately six blocks. Ensure you have a matching set yourself.

2   Stack the blocks on top of another, one at a time and reasonably slowly, so that the students can copy the action one block at a time.

3   When all the students can copy that action, put the blocks beside one another in a line.

Remember that the goal is for the students to imitate the action, so no verbal responses are required.

P This page may be photocopied for instructional use only. © Francesca Bierens  Speechmark

# Chapter 6
# Learning to copy sounds made – imitation of sounds

| | |
|---|---|
| **What is it?** | The student's ability to copy sounds that have been modelled for them or that they have heard, such as intonation patterns, transport and animal sounds, speech sounds and words. |
| **Why is it important?** | Imitation is important because it provides the student with the knowledge and some degree of understanding of a skill that then allows them to make their own spontaneous attempts. |
| **What can we do?** | Encourage and assist the students to imitate vocalisations whenever possible. |
| **Prerequisites:** | • Hearing test.<br>A hearing test will have told you:<br>  ❖ if the student's hearing is adequate in both ears<br>  ❖ or, if not, to what degree the hearing is impaired and which is the better ear.<br>• The Preverbal Skills<br>  ❖ **Copying actions.** Correctly making sounds is the finest of the fine motor skills. The student should therefore initially be able to imitate gross motor actions, for example, walking and crawling, and fine motor actions, that is, hand actions (unless the student has a physical disability that prevents this).<br>  ❖ Listening to sounds. The student should be aware of sounds in their environment. |

## Recommendations for encouraging students to copy sounds made

**Ideal response.** The student accurately imitates the sound modelled.

**Acceptable response.** The student makes an attempt to imitate a sound.

Ⓟ This page may be photocopied for instructional use only. © Francesca Bierens Speechmark

- Keep instructions clear and minimal.

- Avoid repeating the sound too often or too intensely in an effort to assist the student to produce a more accurate sound.

- Keep these activities fun and light-hearted.

- Praise every attempt made to imitate. There are no 'wrong' sounds at this stage.

- Remain at a comfortable distance from the student when modelling the sounds. Getting close to their face will not improve a student's ability to imitate. It is more than likely going to have the opposite effect.

- It is important that the students learn to wait until you have finished making the sound before they begin to copy. This can be very difficult for some students.

- Often children may initially have difficulty combining an action with a vocalisation. They may be able to do each separately but not together. Remember the goal is imitation of sounds, so imitation of the actions is not required.

## Carrying out the 'Learning to copy sounds made' activities

- **Copy the sound of the animal**. Animal sounds are excellent sounds to begin with, as they encourage the use of the lip and tongue muscles. They are also the early developmental speech sounds, so they are usually easier for the student to see and imitate.

- **Copy the inflection.** The use of inflection is very important, as it carries a great deal of information when conversing; for example, the rising inflection of a word changes it from a statement that merely identifies an item (eg 'ice cream') to a question (eg 'Ice cream?') that requires a response ('Oh, yes please.').

  Some students find altering inflection very difficult while others enjoy changing the inflection in sounds, words and phrases. Combining this with a motor activity, for example, standing with arms up and then crouching down, does appear to assist the students who find this skill a little challenging.

  Also vary the volume of your voice in this activity.

- **Copy the train sound.** Any attempt to imitate this sound is acceptable and should be praised.

This page may be photocopied for instructional use only. © Francesca Bierens   Speechmark

- **Copy the sounds that the objects make**. Students generally love this activity ...... as many of the words are difficult for the students to say correctly at this stage.

- **Copy saying 'pop' as they pop the bubbles.** Approximations of this word are acceptable.

- **Copy the lip sounds.** The goal for this activity is for the students to be able to make the lip sounds 'p', 'b' and 'm' by putting their lips together so that you 'can't see their teeth'.

  Demonstrate to the students that the 'b' sound is a strong voiced sound by making the dots – to be made on the page – strong and 'louder'. The 'p' is unvoiced, so make the dots quiet. Whisper the 'p'. The 'm' is a sustained sound, so draw the line to extend the sound, for example, 'mmmmmm'.

  If the students are unable to imitate these sounds correctly, it is not that important at this stage; the focus should be on establishing lip closure, that is, putting the lips together.

  Greater focus will be given to these sounds in the section on improving intelligibility of speech in the 'The Skills of Conversation' section.

## Activities to encourage the students to watch and copy sounds modelled for them

### 1 The students need to: Copy the sound of the animal.

**Teacher:**

1 Gather a selection of four to six common animals – for example, a sheep, a cow, a cat or a dog – in the form of toy animals, animal puppets or large and clear pictures.

2 Look at each animal individually, making the appropriate animal sound.

3 Slightly exaggerate and prolong each sound; for example: 'Meeooww.'

4 Pretend to be one of the animals and encourage the students to imitate the animal sound.

5 Sing 'Old McDonald Had a Farm' and hold up the appropriate animal as you model the associated animal sound, encouraging the students to copy the sound.

### 2 The students need to: Copy the inflection.

**Teacher:**

1 Model the action of climbing up the ladder of a slide; bend down with your arms reaching down, and then, as you gradually stand up, lift your arms slowly as you say, 'Up, up, up,' with a slowly rising inflection, reaching your arms up above your head.

**41**

Ⓟ This page may be photocopied for instructional use only. © Francesca Bierens

2   Slowly 'go down the slide', gradually lowering your arms and bending back down to the ground as you say, 'Dooooown' with a downward inflection. Do this two to three times. Encourage the students to copy the rising and falling inflections of the words.

3   Draw lines on the board to demonstrate a rising and falling inflection, for example, draw 'mountains' by drawing a line up the page with a rising inflection, that is, 'uuuuup', and then a downward line as you go 'doooown' the mountain. Do this slowly initially, for example, 'uuuuuup' with one long, slow moving line going up and then 'dooown' with one slow moving line going down. Then make the 'mountains' shorter and increase the speed of the inflection; for example: 'Uuup down … uuup doown.'

### 3   The students need to: Copy the train sound.

**Teacher:**

1   Using blocks, make a 'train' by placing the blocks side by side.

2   Slowly push the 'train' along a desk or a table or on the floor and simultaneously model the sounds of a train moving; for example: 'Ch-ch-ch-ch. Toot toot!' Always make sure your head is up so that the students can see your face and see how you are making the sound – so only go on the floor if the students are also sitting on the floor.

3   After modelling this sound approximately five times, if appropriate, have the students make their own block train from three or four blocks and encourage them to imitate the modelled sound.

### 4   The students need to: Copy the sounds that the objects make.

**Teacher:**

1   Collect together photos and/or pictures of objects that have noises easily associated with them, such as an ambulance, a fire engine and a computer keyboard.

2   Identify each of the objects individually and make the associated sound as you look at each object; for example, 'A hammer: bang.' Always make sure that your head is up so that the students can see your face and see how you are making the sound.

3   Encourage the students to imitate the sounds.

Praise all attempts to imitate as many students will only be able to achieve an approximation of the sounds or words and this is perfectly acceptable at this stage.

Ⓟ This page may be photocopied for instructional use only. © Francesca Bierens   Speechmark Ⓢ

**5 The students need to: Copy saying the sound 'p' or word 'pop' as they pop the bubbles.**

**Teacher:**

1 Blow bubbles and, as they float down, gently and slowly pop each bubble one at a time with your index finger, clearly modelling the word, 'pop'.

2 Go around the group and blow the bubbles near each student so that they all have an opportunity to reach a bubble nearby and pop it. As you blow the bubbles, clearly model the word 'pop' and encourage the students to imitate the word as they pop the bubbles. As much as is practical, make sure that the students are watching you as you blow the bubbles.

**6 The students need to: Copy the lip sounds 'p', 'b' and 'm', individually.**

**Teacher:**

1 Draw dots and lines on a large piece of paper or on a whiteboard so that all the students can see the images. Accompany each action with a vocalisation.

   a) Put strong dots on the page, modelling the sounds 'b … b … b'.

   b) Put light dots on the page, whispering 'p … p … p'.

   c) Draw long lines across the page, modelling the sounds 'mmm … mmm … mmm'.

   d) Make sure that you are facing the students so that they can see your face and can see how the sound is made. Gesture the action of strong or light dots and lines.

2 Encourage the students to imitate the sounds patterned.

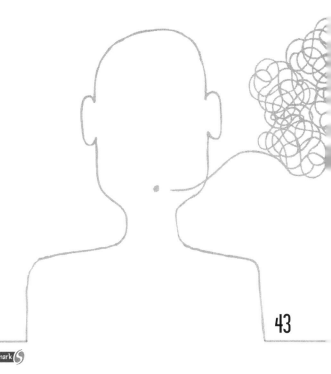

Ⓟ This page may be photocopied for instructional use only. © Francesca Bierens  Speechmark Ⓢ

## Chapter 7
# Learning to wait and take turns

| | |
|---|---|
| **What is it?** | The student's ability to understand that an object or activity or person's attention can be shared. |
| **Why is it important?** | Waiting and turn taking provide the basis for interactive communication. Communication is a waiting, turn-taking and interactive process. |
| **What can we do?** | As often as possible provide students with situations where they have to wait their turn or share an object or activity with another student or adult. |
| **Prerequisite:** | • The Preverbal Skill:<br>  ❖ Attention, concentration and anticipation skills. The student will have acquired adequate attention skills to work in a group. |

## Recommendations for encouraging students to wait and take turns

| | |
|---|---|
| **Ideal response.** | The student will be able to wait for the object to be given to them. They will wait for their turn within the activity without becoming distressed and will remain attentive while another person is having a turn. |
| **Acceptable response.** | The student will be able to wait briefly, without becoming distressed, for one or two other students to have their turn with an object or activity or for the teacher to be able to attend very briefly to one other student before giving them attention. |

• Keep the 'waiting time' for the student short, especially the students who find this skill the most difficult. Let another student have a brief turn before returning the activity or object to the waiting student. Gradually lengthen the time required to wait, for example, two students have their turn before the waiting student or attend to another student for slightly longer before responding to the waiting student.

Ⓟ This page may be photocopied for instructional use only. © Francesca Bierens Speechmark

Remove other distractions as much as possible.

- When appropriate in your class programme and depending on the other students, for students who always want to go first, gradually lengthen their waiting time for an activity, for example, second, and then first again, and then third, and then first again.

- Accompany turn-taking activities with the phrases 'your turn', 'my turn' and, for example, 'Bob's turn' and extend your hand towards a student or indicate yourself with the palm of your hand as you do so.

  Waiting and turn taking are very useful skills for the students to acquire, as they make it easier when teaching verbal imitation skills because the students are able to wait and listen when it is your turn and then imitate when it is their turn.

## Carrying out the 'Learning to wait and take turns' activities

- **Wait for your turn with the ball.** Sometimes just having the students sitting on the floor and remaining on task can be a challenge but with guidance and perseverance the students will eventually be able to achieve this skill.

- **Wait for your turn with the pen.** Make sure the students are all able to hear and see what is going on when it is not their turn. Keep them involved by telling them what the other student is doing; for example: 'Bob is drawing a round shape ... a circle. Fabulous, Bob.' Include them all in your eye contact while the other student is completing the task.

- **Wait for your turn to 'drum' on the ball.** It is sometimes beneficial for the teacher to have their own ball in order to model appropriate actions, as the students can often get quite excited with this activity.

- **Wait for your turn for a favourite activity.** Tell the students when they will be taking their turns, especially those who always want to go first and find waiting for their turn very difficult; for example, 'Bob, it's your turn with the computer now. Then it will be your turn, Pat.'

- **Wait for your turn with the obstacle course**. Assist the student to see exactly when they will have their turn by putting them in a line either standing or sitting in their chairs.

This page may be photocopied for instructional use only. © Francesca Bierens Speechmark

# Activities to encourage the students to wait patiently for their turn

**1 The students need to: Wait for their turn with the ball.**

**Teacher:**

1   Sit on the floor, with the students sitting a short distance away.

2   Before rolling a ball to each student, say their name to make sure they are ready and watching to catch the ball; for example, 'Bob, I'm rolling the ball to you.' The student then rolls the ball back to you.

3   After the first turn for each student, just call the student's name as you roll the ball to them. Roll the ball in a random manner with each student having to wait until their name is called before they get the ball. Roll the ball at various speeds, sometimes fast, sometimes slow. The students can return the ball to the teacher at the speed they wish.

4   After each student has had at least two turns receiving the ball, a student is chosen to be the 'teacher' and has a turn to roll the ball to each student.

If you are outside or in a large hall, you can throw or bounce the ball to the students.


**2 The students need to: Wait for their turn with the pen.**

**Teacher:**

1   Draw a shape on a large sheet of paper pinned to the wall.

2   Give the pen to a student to imitate your drawing, add to your drawing or do a drawing of their own choice on the same page. Keep the 'waiting time' for the students short, so each student can only draw one shape before passing the pen to another student. Frequently model phrases like 'Bob's turn', 'my turn' and 'Pat's turn' as appropriate.

3   At the end of the activity, hang the 'picture' up on the wall as a combined class artwork.


**3 The students need to: Wait for their turn to 'drum' on the ball.**

**Teacher:**

1   During music sessions, sing a song or play some music. Have a large physio ball (Swiss ball) or very large beach ball, which the students can take turns using as a drum.

2   While the rest of the class are participating by singing or clapping, one student can 'drum on the ball' for a song or part of the song before passing it on to the next student when directed.

Have the students sit in chairs in a circle away from their desks or tables so that the ball can easily be rolled and 'drummed' from one student to another.

Ⓟ This page may be photocopied for instructional use only. © Francesca Bierens  Speechmark

**4  The students need to: Wait for their turn to do an action.**

**Teacher:**

1  In the group sessions, stand in front of the students and model actions – for example, putting your hands on your head or standing on one foot – one at a time, which the students have to copy.

2  After modelling two actions, the teacher then points to one student who has a turn to model two different actions that the other students have to copy.

3  After modelling two actions, the student then points to another student who has a turn to model two actions.

Doing this activity to music tends to keep it moving at a faster pace and is more fun for the students.

**5  The students need to: Wait for their turn to do a favourite activity.**

**Teacher:**

1  Have a selection of favourite activities set up around the classroom, for example, playing on a computer, doing a jigsaw puzzle, reading a book and painting a picture.

2  Take photos of each of these activities, matching the number of photos with the number of students in the class.  The number of photos taken of each activity should correspond with the total number of students who can participate in that activity at any one time, for example, six photos of book corner.

3  Either give each student a photo of the activity you want them to go to or put the photos in a bag or box and give each student a turn to take an image out of the container without looking.

4  Set up a timer, for example, an hourglass. When the time allotted has expired, the students change activities. Enough time must be allowed to ensure the students are able to finish what they are doing, for example, looking through a picture book.

**6  The students need to: Wait for their turn on the obstacle course.**

**Teacher:**

1  Make up a simple obstacle course of approximately six obstacles in the classroom, the hall or outside. Appropriate obstacles would be, for example, a hoop for the students to stand in, a blanket to climb under, a table to go around or a large box to climb through.

2  Put photos or symbols of each of these six activities on a board beside the students.

3  Either have the students wait in a line or sit on their chairs in a line.

Ⓟ This page may be photocopied for instructional use only. © Francesca Bierens  Speechmark Ⓢ

4   Each student has a turn to choose three of the photos from the board – corresponding to a selection of three obstacles – and gives them to the teacher.

5   The student then completes the three-step obstacle course they have selected, with as much assistance as they require.

6   When the student has completed the course they return to the back of the line or sit back on their chair.

7   If possible, allow the students to have a couple of turns with this activity.

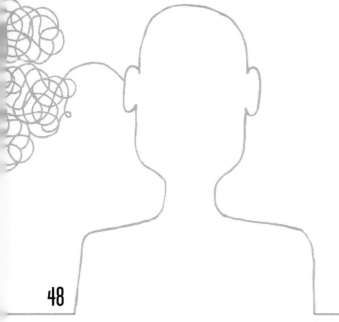

P This page may be photocopied for instructional use only. © Francesca Bierens  Speechmark

# Chapter 8

# Learning awareness and control of the face and mouth muscles

| | |
|---|---|
| **What is it?** | The student's ability to use their tongue, lips and jaw efficiently to allow them to eat effectively and accurately form speech sounds. |
| **Why is it important?** | It is necessary for the tongue, lips and jaw to be working effectively in order for clear, intelligible speech to develop.<br>The student needs to have an awareness, flexibility and control of these muscles in order to correctly form speech sounds, necessary for the development of intelligible speech. |
| **What can we do?** | Encourage and assist the student to imitate these exercises. However, it is important that these are kept indirect and fun. If the student is having difficulties with the exercise and becomes upset, stop immediately, make light of the situation and talk about something else. |
| **Prerequisites:** | • The Preverbal Skills<br> ❖ Facial regard – be able to look at your face<br> ❖ **Copying actions.** Speech sounds are the finest of the fine motor skills. The student should initially be able to imitate 'gross motor' actions e.g. walking, creeping and crawling and fine motor activities, for example, clapping and hand actions (unless the student has a physical disability that prevents this). |

## Recommendations for assisting students to develop awareness and control of the face and mouth muscles

**Ideal response.** The student is able to successfully carry out the exercise.

**Acceptable response.** The student makes any attempt to carry out the exercise.

49

Ⓟ This page may be photocopied for instructional use only. © Francesca Bierens Speechmark Ⓢ

- We use the same muscles to eat as we do to speak, so developing efficient eating skills is necessary for the development of intelligible speech.

  Encourage the students to drink from a cup rather than a sports bottle or spouted lid mug. This is particularly important if the student tends to be a bit dribbly or places the tongue well forward in their mouth when they vocalise.

  **Priority note**. If the student will not drink from anything other than a bottle, then naturally ensuring the student takes sufficient fluids is the priority.
  Sports bottles and lids on mugs have their place – particularly when you are on outings – but limit their use when possible.

## Carrying out the 'Learning awareness and control of the face and mouth muscles' activities

- Keep these activities and exercises short and fun. Do not prolong an exercise hoping the student will eventually be able to successfully achieve the skill. If the student has difficulty with them then always finish with an activity that is fun and easy for the student to achieve. Never finish with failure.

- Ensure that the students are either standing or sitting upright and comfortably when carrying out these exercises. This will make a difference to their breath control.

- **Move the tongue**. For many students, moving their tongue upwards or side to side is very difficult. Praise all attempts and keep this activity short and light-hearted. Avoid singling out a student to repeat this exercise if they are unable to carry out this exercise and avoid getting the students to carry out this exercise more than a couple of times each session.

- **Blow the object**. Many students will have difficulty blowing, so use an object where minimal air is required to make it move. Some windmills will move with minimal breath. Sitting beside the student and blowing gently to assist the object to move can be motivating for them.

- **Put the lips together**. The goal for this activity is for the students to be able to put their lips together so that you can't see their teeth. Many of the students will find this difficult because they are unable to breathe through their nose so will not be able to maintain lip closure for more than a couple of seconds. So begin this exercise requiring only a few seconds for lip closure and gradually increase as appropriate.

- **Move the lips**. The priority for this exercise is for the students to change the position of their lips so there is some variation with the placement of these simple vowels.

P This page may be photocopied for instructional use only. © Francesca Bierens Speechmark

- **Find the sticker.** Some children do not like anything touching their face or head. These children may be 'tactile defensive'. If this is the case, begin activities on the hands, for example, putting stickers on the hands, until the student becomes more tolerant. A mirror may initially be beneficial, however, as soon as possible, remove the mirror so that the student can find the stickers without visual prompts.

## Activities to assist the students to develop awareness and control of their face and mouth muscles

### 1 The students need to: Move their tongue.

**Teacher:**

1  During structured class sessions such as morning greetings or news-time when you have the attention of the whole class, stand or sit in front of the students and model the tongue exercise.

2  Encouraging the students to imitate you, model lifting the tongue up to 'touch' the nose and down to 'touch' the chin; move it to either side of the mouth to 'touch' the ears and then around in a circle around the lip line.

3  Pretend to lick food off your top lip, and then slowly from around the lips.

Keep this activity short and light-hearted. Praise all attempts, as this can be a difficult exercise for many of the students.

### 2 The students need to: Blow, to make the object move.

**Teacher:**

1  During morning circle time or during another structured class session, do some blowing exercises.

2  Have a small windmill and gently blow to make it spin around. Do this a couple of times to show the students what they need to do.

3  Hold the windmill in front of each student's mouth and model the action of blowing.

4  Some students will be able to blow effectively to make the windmill spin around; however, some students will have difficulty. Assist those students by sitting beside them and gently blowing to help the windmill to move.

5  Also blow a ping-pong ball across a table to another student who should then blow it back.

Keep this activity short and light-hearted and praise all attempts.

Ⓟ This page may be photocopied for instructional use only. © Francesca Bierens  Speechmark Ⓢ

**3   The students need to: Put their lips together and keep them together for five seconds.**

**Teacher:**

1   Model the action of putting lips together and tell the students to put their lips together.

2   Maintain the 'mmmm' sound for a count of five seconds, holding up your hand so that the students can see as you count the seconds off on your fingers.

3   Repeat this exercise and increase the time to 10 seconds.

4   Draw an imaginary line in the air, walking across the classroom to see if the students can keep their lips together for that length of time.

Keep this activity short and light-hearted and praise all attempts.


**4   The students need to: Move their lips to form simple vowel sounds.**

**Teacher:**

1   Make exaggerated vowel sounds – 'ah', 'ee' and 'oo' – in order to achieve variation in lip movements.

2   Practise these sounds one at a time, for example, 'ah' and then 'ee' and then 'oo'.

3   Prompt the students to achieve good lip variation when making these sounds by modelling the 'ah' by saying 'good open mouth', modelling the 'ee' by saying, 'smiley mouth' and modelling the 'oo' with round lip sounds, drawing the students' attention to the shape of your mouth.

4   Do this five times with each sound.

5   When the students are able to achieve these sounds or an approximation, combine the sounds into a three-sound sequence, that is, 'ah – ee – oo'.

6   Do this sound sequence exercise five times, for example, 'ah – ee – oo' and then 'ee – ah – oo' and then 'oo – ee – ah' and then 'ah – oo – ee' and then 'oo – ah – ee'. Encourage good lip variation with each vowel.

Keep this activity short and light-hearted and praise all attempts.


**5   The students need to: Feel and find the sticker on their hands and face.**

**Teacher:**

1   Have coloured stickers and start by placing these on the students' hands and fingers. Then tell them to remove the stickers one at a time.

2   For those who can tolerate it, place one sticker on each student's face, for example, on their nose, chin or cheeks. Have them remove the stickers after five seconds.

℗ This page may be photocopied for instructional use only. © Francesca Bierens   Speechmark Ⓢ

3   Place two or three stickers on the students' faces of those who are tolerating this. Have them remove them after five seconds.

4   Some students may have difficulty finding some of the stickers, particularly those on the chin. A mirror may initially be beneficial to assist the students to find the stickers; however, as soon as possible, remove the mirror so that the student can find the stickers without visual prompts.

For the students who cannot tolerate having stickers on their face, keep the activity just on their hands.

Keep this activity short and light-hearted.

### 6   The students need to: Exercise the muscles on their face.

### Teacher:

1   Prepare to have a fun 'exercise your facial muscles' activity with the class. Talk about what you will be doing, and then model a slightly exaggerated action, for example, a very happy or sad facial expression.

2   Pretend to wash your face and brush your teeth.

3   Pretend to bite and chew an apple, taking one big bite out of the apple at a time. Chew, chew, chew, making sure the jaw moves from side to side, and then swallow.

4   Pretend to lick an ice cream.

5   Encourage the students to watch and copy or create their own related action or expression.

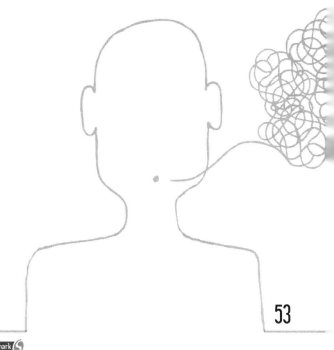

Ⓟ This page may be photocopied for instructional use only. © Francesca Bierens  Speechmark Ⓢ

Chapter 9

# The opportunity to communicate and the desire to communicate

The desire to communicate and the opportunity to communicate are extremely important skills that must be kept in mind constantly.

## Desire to communicate

In order for functional language to occur, the student must see communication as a desirable thing. You cannot teach a student to have a 'desire to communicate' but you can develop an environment where communication is positive and motivating. So be excited about teaching language. A teacher who demonstrates excitement and enthusiasm is more likely to inspire and motivate their students. In order for a student to develop functional interactive communication they must want to communicate.

Make sure there is some time in the day for the student to attend to the activity that they enjoy or find particularly motivating. This will increase their desire to communicate. Take time to listen to what they are saying during this activity.

## Opportunity to communicate

In order to encourage functional communication it is essential that every opportunity is provided for a student to communicate. Routine and structure are very important; however, within that structure there must be regular opportunities for a student to be able to initiate communication, make requests, make choices and express themselves.

P This page may be photocopied for instructional use only. © Francesca Bierens  Speechmark

# Chapter 10

# Making 'The Preverbal Skills of Language' activity box

Learning awareness and control of the face and mouth muscles

Learning to wait and take turns

Learning to copy sounds made

Learning to copy actions

Learning to listen to sounds

Learning to look around at things

Learning to attend, concentrate and anticipate

Learning to look at people

## Box One

### ACTIVITIES TO TEACH THE PREVERBAL SKILLS OF LANGUAGE

**The foundation skills of language**

**The skills required before all the talk**

Creating a 'Preverbal Skills of Language' activity box (Figure 3) gives you immediate access to the skill and activities required. It is also easy for the students to access the activity cards for each appropriate skill when necessary.

Ⓟ This page may be photocopied for instructional use only. © Francesca Bierens  Speechmark Ⓢ

**Procedure:**

1   Buy or make a box that can fit a standard photo-sized card.

2   Make up the 'Preverbal Skills of Language' headings and use as dividers in the box.

3   Colour-code the skill headings for quick and easy recognition by both teacher and students.

4   Copy and paste each activity on to a card and place it in the appropriate skill section.

5   Place the 'Preverbal Skills of Language' activity box in a very visible and readily accessible location in the classroom.

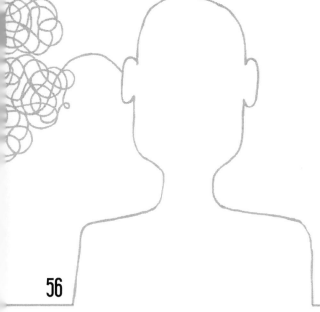

Ⓟ This page may be photocopied for instructional use only. © Francesca Bierens Speechmark Ⓢ

# Chapter 11

# Making 'The Preverbal Skills of Language' activity cube

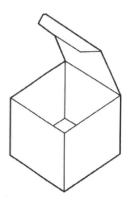

## Six-sided cube with a preverbal skill either written or illustrated on each side

The Preverbal Skills of Language cube (Figure 4) has a preverbal skill either written or illustrated on each side. This cube can be used as a dice to select a skill. The teacher rolls the dice or the students take turns to roll the dice to determine which skill they are going to practise. The teacher or a student then selects an activity from the appropriate section of the 'Preverbal Skills of Language' activity box:

- Learning to look at people

- Learning to look around at things

- Learning to listen to sounds

- Learning to copy actions

- Learning to copy sounds made

- Learning to wait and take turns

- Learning awareness and control of the face and mouth muscles

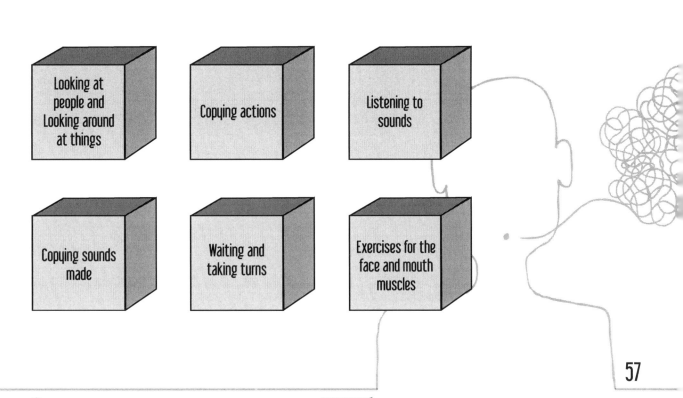

57

Ⓟ This page may be photocopied for instructional use only. © Francesca Bierens  Speechmark Ⓢ

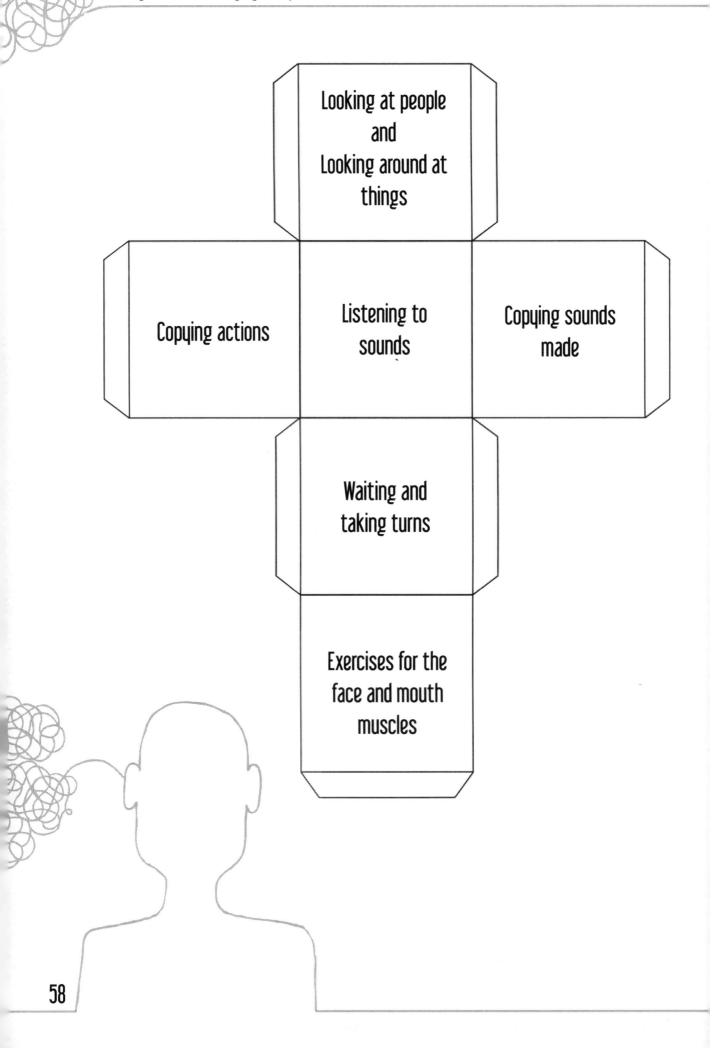

# Part 3

# Assisting students with language delays in the classroom to acquire 'The Building Bricks of Language'

# Introduction

**The Building Bricks of Language** are the vocabulary and concepts essential for the development of comprehension and communication.

All activities are 'low-tech' and require minimal preparation and resources, so they should be able to be carried out at any time in any classroom. Technology can be fabulous as a teaching tool, however, it is not readily available in all classrooms, nor is it always the most appropriate tool or resource to use in all situations. The majority of resources recommended in this programme should be available within the classroom or school and the activities can be easily adapted to become a very short activity to include in circle time or expanded to become a full language programme activity.

Photos are recommended throughout the programme, as these are extremely beneficial and very motivating because they are relevant to the student. They do need to be uncluttered, good-quality photos. The majority of activities can, however, be easily carried out without the need for photos. Remember to always gain permission from the students' families before taking photos of the students, even though the photos are solely for usze in the classroom programme.

Reading books to the students is an important part of language development, but you should regularly 'tell' them a story using puppets or props such as Fuzzy-Felts or magnetic figures and plenty of expression. This tends to encourage a closer connection with the students and increases their interest and attention.

**Example questions** are provided as models and do not always include examples of all 'wh' questions possible at that skill level.

**Example question: 'Where'**. At the 'noun', 'verb' and 'adjective' level, visual prompts such as people, objects or photos must be provided for the student to look at and point to in order to answer the question. A verbal response is not required.

All the **Activities, Procedures to teach the skills** and **Example questions** provided are a guide only. Please adapt them to suit the abilities and interests of your students and your classroom programme.

Ⓟ This page may be photocopied for instructional use only. © Francesca Bierens **Speechmark**

# Chapter 1

# Assisting and encouraging the development of the students' language

In order to assist the students' speech and language development, it is essential to remember:

- **In order to get language out, you need to put words in**. So before expecting the student to use language, you must feed the language in, using all methods to assist the student to understand, that is, visuals such as gesture, signing, facial expressions and pictures and, of course, accompanying words.

- Always focus on achieving comprehension before requiring a verbal response. The student must have the necessary knowledge in order to follow the instruction or answer the question. Students need to demonstrate consistent understanding of a concept before they can use it in their functional verbal language.

- Asking a question is always a 'test' situation for a student, no matter how casual the question. If you ask a student a question that you expect them to answer correctly, for example, 'What did you do last night?' then there must be evidence that they have the skills to do so. Is the student able to recall the information without the assistance of visual prompts such as photos? Do they have the vocabulary to provide that information?

  Before asking a question, be sure that the student has had the opportunity to learn the necessary words required to respond correctly. Asking a question is the method of determining if the student has acquired the relevant language knowledge. It is not a teaching method.

- The students' responses to questions are likely to be significantly shorter than their spontaneous language. When speaking spontaneously, the students use words that they know in order to talk about a topic of their choice. When responding to questions, however, the student needs to process the question asked of them and then provide an answer that requires words that they may or may not know or have difficulty recalling or pronouncing, on a topic that they may not be interested in or familiar with.

Ⓟ This page may be photocopied for instructional use only. © Francesca Bierens Speechmark

- If a student has difficulty answering a question and visual prompts such as photos are not available, provide assistance by giving them a choice of two answers; for example: 'Who visited our class on Monday? Was it a fire fighter or a police officer?'

- Language must be functional, meaningful and memorable. In order to encourage students to use language in a communicative manner, teach words in conjunction with a relevant and meaningful activity. The student is then more likely to see its purpose and retain the information.

- Allow the student time throughout the day or week to focus on activities or topics that are of particular interest to them. As they are motivated by this subject, they are more inclined to remember words that are related to this activity and this will assist in building up their vocabulary. The student may also have acquired an adequate vocabulary related to this activity that can be further developed and then expanded to other topics.

## Six reasons why students to do not respond to instructions or questions

1  They don't understand the question.

2  They don't know the answer.

3  They don't have the necessary words in their vocabulary required to give the answer.

4  They can't say the word because it is too difficult to pronounce.

5  They lack the confidence – they are too scared to try in case they fail.

6  They are just not interested in *that* topic.

## Three things to check if the student is not making progress

1  **Review all the preverbal skills of language**. If the student has successfully achieved all the preverbal skills and if the environment is appropriate then move on to reviewing the level you are working on.

2  **Review the level you are working on in the language programme**.
   - The skill you are working on may be too difficult for the student. Have they acquired the prerequisite skills and knowledge required to achieve that goal? Gradually go back step by step to earlier language levels until you reach the point at which the student achieves success. Remain at this level until the student demonstrates clear understanding and achieves consistent success. Then gradually move up to the next level.

P This page may be photocopied for instructional use only. © Francesca Bierens  Speechmark

- The skill you are working on may be too easy and boring for the student. Take a chance and choose a more challenging activity one or two steps in advance of where you are currently working. If they are unable to do this, however, then provide as much assistance as required in order for them to succeed and then go back to the more appropriate level.

- The student may have acquired 'splinter skills' rather than having reached the developmental level where that language skill would usually be present. Gradually go back step by step to earlier language levels until you reach the point at which the student achieves more consistent success.

3 **If the language programme appears to be appropriate, then review your presentation of the information**.
  - **Check that you:**
    - ❖ have a patient relationship with the student
    - ❖ are using words you know that the student understands
    - ❖ are presenting the information at the correct speed and allowing sufficient time for the student to process the information and respond appropriately
    - ❖ are presenting the correct amount of information at a time.
  - **Check that the student:**
    - ❖ understands what you want them to do.
  - **Also consider:**
    - ❖ the motivation factor of the topic and activities, as the student may have very specific areas of skill interest
    - ❖ the student's current personal or family circumstances
    - ❖ the student's current health issues.

# Five points to remember when carrying out the language programme

1 **Be aware of the knowledge a student requires in order for them to accurately follow an instruction or answer a question**. Make sure that they have this knowledge if you expect them to respond correctly.

2 **Allow additional processing time**. A student is more likely to give a response or carry out an instruction when you allow them that extra bit of processing time. Waiting quietly for their response can make all the difference.

3 **Keep in mind the importance and value of modelling the response**. This is an excellent method of providing the students with the correct response and assisting language expansion. The students can gain great confidence when responses are quietly modelled with them. It

Ⓟ This page may be photocopied for instructional use only. © Francesca Bierens **Speechmark** Ⓢ

should not be underestimated. Students can, however, only retain and accurately repeat a sequence of words with meaning when those words are already in their vocabulary.

4   **Always keep in mind the students' desire to communicate and opportunity to communicate**. Within the classroom programme provide an environment and as many situations as possible in which the students want to participate and have the opportunity to communicate. As often as possible, in order to increase a student's desire to communicate, ensure that there is some time in the day for students to attend to activities that they find particularly motivating.

5   **When speaking to the students, use enough words to convey information and encourage their response but avoid using too many words that tend to overwhelm and limit their responses**.

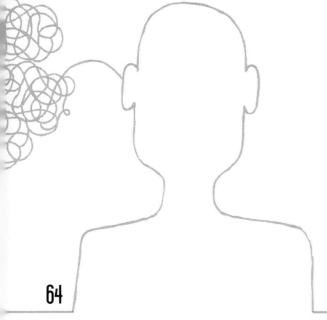

ⓟ This page may be photocopied for instructional use only. © Francesca Bierens  Speechmark

# Chapter 2
# Putting a name to the noun

| What is a proper noun and a noun? | 'Common nouns' identify general people, places and things, for example, 'boy', 'river' and 'magazine'. |
|---|---|
| | 'Proper nouns' name specific people, places and things, for example, 'Harold', 'London' and 'Waikato River'. |
| Prerequisite: | • The Preverbal Skills of Language. |

## Important points to remember when teaching 'proper nouns and nouns'

**Nouns provide the basis of a person's vocabulary and therefore they continue to develop throughout life**. Nouns are used primarily to label a person, place or thing. Proper nouns can be used in isolation referring to someone, or with an inflection in order to form a question; for example: 'Jamie?'

Nouns can also be used with an inflection to form a question, for example, 'Book?' in order to seek clarification (required response, 'Yes, it's a book.').

Nouns make up the vast majority of a person's vocabulary and a good vocabulary is critical for effective communication. This makes them the most essential concept for the development of receptive and expressive language.

- **Developmentally, a child acquires nouns for people, places and objects that they see regularly, are important and of interest to them and easy to say.** (Gleason, 1996, p.122)

- **It is important never to assume that a student has acquired a certain level of vocabulary just because they are verbal and have reached a certain age**. If you are going to give instructions or ask questions and expect the correct response, it is essential to determine whether or not the student has the necessary vocabulary. Often a student's ability to share information or answer a question has stalled simply because they did not know the

Ⓟ This page may be photocopied for instructional use only. © Francesca Bierens Speechmark Ⓢ

word. It is like taking a student into a room of strangers and asking them to name each person when asked, 'Who is this?' Then when they are naturally unable to do so, a report is written stating that they are 'unable to answer "who" questions' when in fact they were just unable to name those particular people. The student may have words, just not the right words required to answer your question.

- **Asking a question is the method of determining if the student has acquired the relevant language skill**. It is not a teaching method (ie requiring students to name picture cards). Therefore, do not ask a question until you have provided the student with the opportunity to gain the appropriate information required to answer.

- **Activities – Example question: 'Where'. At this level, visual prompts such as people, objects or photos must be provided for the student to look at and point to. A verbal response is not required**.

## Activities – Putting a name to the noun

**Name our classmates and teacher**

*Photo album*

1   Have a class photo board and/or make up a small class photo album of all of the students in the class. Have one clear photo per page.
2   Write the name of the student or teacher beneath the photo.
3   Daily, or if not then regularly, identify each student in the photo and see who is at school that day.

*Greet and farewell students by name*

1   Greet each student by name during the 'Good morning' session. The student named then responds to the teacher's greeting, using the teacher's name.
2   In the morning, each student gives their name and greets the class.
3   As often as possible throughout the term, allow each student to have a turn greeting each student by name.
4   Farewell each student by name during the 'Goodbye' session at the end of the day, which is initially modelled by the teacher. The student named then responds to the teacher's farewell, using the teacher's name.

Remember to include teachers and support staff in the greetings and farewells.

*Examples of 'who, what, where' questions*

❖ Who is this? (Indicate a student.)
❖ Who is at school?

Ⓟ This page may be photocopied for instructional use only. © Francesca Bierens

❖ Who is your teacher?

❖ Where is (name a student)?

❖ Where is your teacher?

Nonverbal responses: The student responds by pointing.

**Name the things we use in the classroom**

1   Place a selection of frequently used classroom items on a table in front of the students, for example, a pencil, a pair of scissors, a glue stick, some paper and some books.

2   Have a set of matching photos of these objects.

3   Name each object as you point it out to the students.

4   After each object has been clearly identified, have the students point to each object when it is named.

5   The students take turns to match the photo to the object.

6   Show photos of larger items that you regularly use in class – for example, computers, printers and paints – or areas corresponding to activities that you regularly engage in in class – such as, the music corner and library corner. Have the students point out these items or areas.

7   Play the 'wh' question cube activity using the photos on the board as prompts for the students to point to and to assist with their verbal responses.

8   Put the photo of each object in a small photo album with one photo per page and the label written underneath.

9   This then becomes a classroom dictionary that can be referred to regularly.

*Examples of 'who, what, where' questions*

❖ Who has the picture of the (blocks)?

❖ What is this? (Show object.) What is this? (Show photo.)

❖ Where is the (computer)?

• Give one of the named photos to each student or have each student choose a photo to hold.

  ❖ Who has the picture of the (paints)?

  ❖ What does (name a student) have a picture of?

Nonverbal responses: The student responds by pointing.

**Name the things we see in our classroom**

1   Take photos of the most common items of furniture to be found in the classroom that are a regular part of the classroom routine, for example, cupboards, doors, desks and bookshelves.

2   Show and name each photo to the students and have students point to the location of the item. Place the photo on a board so that it can be seen clearly by the students.

3   Play the 'wh' question cube activity using the photos on the board as prompts for the students

Ⓟ This page may be photocopied for instructional use only. © Francesca Bierens  Speechmark Ⓢ

to point to and to assist with their verbal responses.

4   Put the photo of each object in a small photo album with one photo per page and the label written underneath.

5   Acting as a classroom dictionary, make frequent reference to the album.

*Examples of 'who, what, where' questions*

❖ Where are the bookshelves?

❖ Where is the cupboard?

❖ What is this? (Show picture.)

❖ What is this? (Indicate item.)

• Give each student one of the named pictures or they can choose a photo.

   ❖ Who has the picture of the (bookshelves)?

   ❖ Who has the picture of the (desks)?

   ❖ What does (named student) have a picture of?

Nonverbal responses: The student responds by pointing to the photos on the board or the objects.

**Name the people we see in our school**

1   Take photos of the important people at your school, that is, the head teacher, the secretary, the caretaker, the librarian and the school nurse.

2   Name the person in each photo.

3   Go around the school and, where practical, meet these people.

4   Place the photos in a small photo album with one photo per page and the person's name and job label written underneath, for example, Mrs King, the head teacher; Miss Keys, the caretaker; and Mrs Booker, the librarian.

5   Acting as a classroom dictionary of the people whose names the students need to know, refer to it regularly or as needed.

*Examples of 'who, what, where' questions*

❖ Who is this? (Show picture.)

❖ Who is the librarian?

❖ What is Miss Keys's job?

❖ Where is the (school nurse)?

❖ Where is (Mrs King – head teacher)?

Nonverbal responses: The student responds by pointing to the photos.

Ⓟ This page may be photocopied for instructional use only. © Francesca Bierens   Speechmark Ⓢ

## Name the places we see in our school

1   Walk around the school and identify the common locations of interest that the students frequently see and use, for example, the playground, the school office, the bathrooms and the sick bay. Take photos of each of these places.

2   In the classroom, show each photo to the students, identifying each place by name.

3   Place the photos on a board so that they can be seen clearly by the students.

4   Play the 'wh' question cube activity using the photos on the board as prompts for the students to point to and to assist with their verbal responses.

5   Place the photos of each item in a small photo album with one photo per page and the label written underneath.

6   Acting as a classroom dictionary of places in the school, make reference to the album when required.

*Examples of 'who, what, where' questions*

❖  What is this? (Show picture of places.)

❖  Where is the (sick bay)?

Nonverbal responses: The student responds by pointing to the photos.

## Name the things we buy when we go shopping

1   Go through supermarket leaflets and flyers with the students and assist them to cut out items.

2   Make a number of copies of each item.

3   Name each item – for example, apples, shoes, toys and DVDs – as you put each picture on the board.

4   Place the copies of the items on the board.

5   Have the students identify which items they would like to buy, by either pointing to the picture or naming the object. Put their picture in a 'to buy' section of the board.

6   Always model or repeat the word regardless of whether the student has pointed or named the object.

7   Go through and name the items that you would all buy at the shops.

8   Play the 'wh' question cube activity using the pictures on the board as prompts for the students to point to and to assist with their verbal responses.

9   The students can then make up their own shopping lists by putting these pictures into their scrapbooks. Label the items underneath the pictures.

10  Also keep copies of these pictures in a class box to be used again for the 'verb' activity.

*Examples of 'who, what, where' questions*

❖  Who wanted the 'book'?

❖  Who wanted the 'chocolate'?

This page may be photocopied for instructional use only. © Francesca Bierens  Speechmark

❖ What is this? (Point to pictures.)
❖ Where is the (DVD)?
❖ Where is the (hat)?

Nonverbal responses: The student responds by pointing to the photos.

**Name the familiar things in picture books**
1   After an initial read or look through a book, go back through the book slowly and label one or two objects in each picture, for example, 'dog' and 'table'.
2   Point to the pictures as you name them.
3   Encourage the students to point to the object as you repeat the name.
4   Play the 'wh' question cube activity using the pictures in the book for the students to point to and to assist with their verbal responses.

*Examples of 'who, what, where' questions*
❖ What is this? (Point to an object in picture.)
❖ Where is the (dinosaur)?
❖ Where is the (bird)?

Nonverbal responses: The student responds by pointing to the photos.

**Name the unfamiliar people in photos or books**
1   Go through clear, individual pictures of unfamiliar people, and identify the people in the book, that is, the man, the girl, the boy and the lady.
2   Point to the person, stressing the word, for example, the **'boy'**.
3   Go through and identify the people in six pictures. Then point to the person, and identify them again with a slight delay to allow the students an opportunity to identify the person if they wish; for example: 'The … **girl**.' Only wait a couple of seconds and then either provide the information or confirm the students' response.

*Examples of 'who, what, where' questions*
❖ Who is this? (Point to a person in the picture.)
❖ Where is the (girl)?
❖ Where is the (man)?

Nonverbal responses: The student responds by pointing to the photos.

**Name the people in our community**
1   Gather together pictures of various people in the community, for example, a fire fighter, a police officer, a librarian, a doctor and a dentist.

Ⓟ This page may be photocopied for instructional use only. © Francesca Bierens   Speechmark Ⓢ

2   Go through these pictures with the students and name the profession of the person in the picture.

3   If you know specific people in your community and have their photos (possibly from the local newspaper), then identify the person by name, for example, 'Miss Blooms, the florist' and 'Mr Good, the community police officer'.

4   Have students recognise and point to the relevant person in the picture when their profession is named.

5   Have students recognise and point to the relevant person in the picture when their profession is named from a choice of two pictures presented.

6   If practical, visit some of these people in the community and, if you have photos, put these in a small photo album with one photo per page and their names and jobs written underneath.

7   This then becomes a classroom dictionary of people you know in your community.

*Examples of 'who, what, where' questions*
❖   Who is this? (Point to a person in the picture, for example, a bus driver.)
❖   Who is this? (Point to a person in the photo; for example: 'Mr Good, the community police officer'.)
❖   Where is the (fire fighter)?
❖   Where is (Mrs Reid, the librarian)?

Nonverbal responses: The student responds by pointing to the photos.

**Name the places in our community**
1   Have pictures or photos of popular places in your community, for example, the local swimming pool and the local play park.

2   Go through these pictures or photos with the students and name each place.

3   Put the images on the board so that they can be clearly seen by all of the students.

4   Place a large piece of paper beside the board and draw any additional places that the students may mention, for example, the cinema complex and the recreation ground.

5   Play the 'wh' question cube activity using the photos on the board as prompts for the students to point to and to assist with their verbal responses.

6   Put the images in the small photo album with one photo per page and the label written underneath to be used as a classroom dictionary of things to do in the community.

*Examples of 'who, what, where' questions*
❖   What is this? (Show picture of park.)
❖   What is this? (Show picture of places, for example, the swimming pool.)
❖   Where is the (playground)?
❖   Where is the park?

Nonverbal responses: The student responds by pointing to the photos.

Ⓟ This page may be photocopied for instructional use only. © Francesca Bierens  Speechmark Ⓢ

### Name the people, places and objects in a story

1   Tell a story using visual prompts such as Fuzzy-Felts or /magnetic pieces of objects and people, for example, a train, some trees, a boy, a girl and a lady. Identify each of the individual items as you remove them from the box and put them on a felt board or magnetic board beside you. As you tell the story, a student has to place the appropriate felt or magnetic figure from the small board on to the big storytelling board when directed. Parts of the story should be along the lines of, for example: 'The **girl** got off the **train** with her **mother**. They went to the **playground**. The playground had a **swing** and a **slide**.'

2   At the end of the story, identify the important items that were present in the story by pointing to and naming the objects on the large storytelling board.

3   Play the 'wh' question cube activity using the Fuzzy-Felts on the board as prompts for the students to point to and to assist with their verbal responses.

*Examples of 'who, what, where' questions*

❖ Who (got off the train)?

❖ What was (at the playground)?

❖ Where is the (train)?

❖ Where is the girl?

❖ Where is the mother?

❖ Where did they go?

Nonverbal responses: The student responds by pointing to the Fuzzy-Felt pictures.

### Name the people and things we have in our house

1   If possible, have photos of each of the student's family, that is, their mum, their dad, their brothers, their sisters, their grandparents, their aunts, their uncles and their pets.

2   As appropriate, go through each student's photos with the class.

3   Make up a small photo album for each student with the name of each family member. This can be referred to when a student talks about family events.

4   Using a book or large poster picture, identify the various rooms in a typical house, for example, a bedroom, a kitchen and a bathroom.

5   Using picture cards, photos or images cut out from supermarket flyers or leaflets, identify and name items that you may find at home, for example, a television, a bed, some books and some DVDs.

6   Put the images up on a board for the students to see. Assist students to identify a couple of the items that they have in their home.

7   Play the 'wh' question cube activity using the pictures on the board as prompts for the students to point to and to assist with their verbal responses.

Ⓟ This page may be photocopied for instructional use only. © Francesca Bierens   Speechmark Ⓢ

*Examples of 'who, what, where' questions*

- ❖ Who has a (table) in their house?
- ❖ What is this room? (Point to a room in the 'house' picture.)
- ❖ What is this? (Point to a picture of a household item, for example, a bed.)
- ❖ Where is the bedroom? (Direct students' attention to pictures of only two or three rooms so choices are limited.)

Verbal responses: Family photos:

- ❖ Who has a dog called (named dog)?
- ❖ Who has a sister called (named sister)?

Nonverbal responses: The student responds by pointing to the photos or person.

## Name the parts of the body

1. Have each student lie on a large piece of paper and have an adult draw around them.
2. Have the students draw in their own hair, eyes, ears, nose and mouth. Assist the students to carry out this activity as necessary.
3. Together with the students, identify the different basic body parts on the pictures and on themselves.
4. Label the basic body parts on the paper.
5. Put the pictures up on the wall.

*Examples of 'who, what, where' questions*

- ❖ Who is this? (Point to one of the pictures.)
- ❖ What is this? (Point to the (shoulder) on a picture.)
- ❖ What is this? (Point to the (toes) on a picture.)
- ❖ Where is your chin?
- ❖ Where is your nose?
- ❖ Where is your neck?

Nonverbal responses: The student responds by identifying on the picture and on themselves.

## Name the things, people and places in our topic study or field trip

1. At the beginning of a topic, for example, 'volcanoes', talk about the things you are going to study, using pictures, photos and books to demonstrate these to the students.
2. On a large piece of paper, draw a simple diagram of the volcano and write up the key words around this picture that will be used often throughout that study, for example, 'volcanoes', 'lava' and 'rocks'.
3. Use the large piece of paper as a big chart 'word list' and put it up on the wall so that it becomes a reference for the students throughout the course of that topic study.

This page may be photocopied for instructional use only. © Francesca Bierens Speechmark

4   Before going on a field trip, for example, a visit to a zoo, on a large piece of paper write up the key words of animals, things and people you expect to see, for example, lions, tigers, picnic tables and zookeepers.

5   When you return from the field trip, go through the photos and assist the students to recall information about the trip by identifying people, animals and so forth. Add any additional information to the first word list.

6   Use the large piece of paper as a big chart 'word list' and put it up on the wall with the photos of the trip so that it becomes a reference for the students to assist them when talking about or writing about the trip.

*Examples of 'who, what, where' questions*

❖ Who did we meet?
❖ Who went to the zoo?
❖ What did we see?
❖ What is this? (Point to animal in photo.)
❖ Where did we go?
❖ Where is the zoo keeper?

Nonverbal responses: The student responds by pointing to the photos.

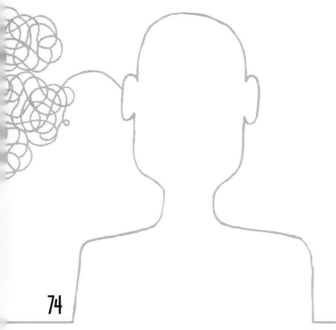

74

Ⓟ This page may be photocopied for instructional use only. © Francesca Bierens Speechmark

# Chapter 3
# Putting verbs into action

| | |
|---|---|
| **What is a verb?** | A **verb** is an action word, for example, 'run' or 'drink'. |
| **Prerequisites:** | • The Preverbal Skills of Language<br>• Nouns. |

## Important points to remember when teaching 'verbs'

• Verbs provide functional information so are therefore very important for communication.

• Teaching the function of objects by putting a word to the action provides the transition from nouns to verbs.

• Students often use 'nouns' to answer a 'verb' question when they do not know the appropriate verb, for example, responding with '**book**', instead of '**reading**' when asked, '**What is Bob doing**?'

The following are important to assist the student to respond correctly:
• Always correct the response in a confirming manner, stressing the verb; for example: 'He is **reading** the book.'
• Then repeat the question; for example: 'What is Bob doing?'
• Then model the answer back with the student; for example: 'He is **reading** the book.'

Giving a 'noun' response when a 'verb' is required is not the correct answer, so it is important that the student is provided with the accurate response. The student has, however, still given a response and it is associated with the question asked, so avoid using the word 'no' or saying, 'That's wrong.' We always want the students to feel encouraged to answer even if they don't know the correct words. So provide them with the correct information in a confirming manner and then ask the question again in order to assist them to give the correct response.

Ⓟ This page may be photocopied for instructional use only. © Francesca Bierens Speechmark Ⓢ

# When making up and using a 'photo book' for each of the students

- Use photos taken during class activities or events. Also include any photos sent from home.

- Before making up the book, look through each individual photo with the student first. If the student is verbal and talks about the picture, use the word(s) they provide (even if it is a single word) whenever possible when writing your single sentence.

- When working with the photo book, allow the student to look through the book first.

- Then have the student read the sentence written on each page – assisting when necessary. Remember that it is not a reading exercise, so praise the student for reading well – regardless of how well they read.

- Repeat the sentences yourself using a confirming manner, pointing to the appropriate object and action in the photo as you read.

- For students who are unable to read, read the sentences slowly yourself.
  - ❖ Wait longer at the key words (nouns and verbs) for the student to vocalise before reading these words yourself.
  - ❖ Point to the appropriate object and action in the photo as you read.

- Ask the student the questions written on each page.

- If the student responds using a single word (eg Question: 'What are you doing?'; Response: '**Kicking**.') then expand the answer, stressing the key words (eg 'That's right, you're **kicking the ball**.')

- If the student answers a question using the **noun** instead of a **verb** (eg Question: 'What is he doing?'; Response: '**Banana**.'), then confirm the answer stressing the key words (eg 'He's **eating a banana**.')

- Then repeat the question, in order to determine if the student will respond using the more expanded language.

- Take time reading each page and allow the student time to process the question and respond verbally.

Ⓟ This page may be photocopied for instructional use only. © Francesca Bierens Speechmark Ⓢ

# Activities – Putting verbs into action

## What we all do in our classroom

1  Have clear picture cards of people carrying out various activities. Look at each picture with the students and identify the appropriate` action; for example: 'The man is **eating**, eating an apple.' Demonstrate the action using gesture.

2  Then present the students with two pictures and assist the students to point to the correct action when named and gestured.

3  Take photos of your students involved in various activities in class, for example, writing, playing instruments and drawing.

4  Take photos of the teacher involved in various activities in class, for example, reading to the students and writing on the board.

5  Look through these photos with the students, identifying the actions; for example: 'Bob is **writing**'; 'Penny is **drawing**'; 'Everyone is **singing**'; 'The teacher is **reading**'; and 'The teacher is **writing** on the board'.

6  Put the photos on the board so that they can be seen them clearly by all the students.

7  Play the 'wh' question cube activity using the pictures on the board as prompts for the students to point to and to assist with their verbal responses or present only two pictures at a time.

8  Put these photos into a small photo album, one picture per page, with a short simple noun-verb sentence structure written underneath; for example: 'Bob is reading.'

9  This then becomes your dictionary of verbs related directly to your students.

*Examples of 'who, what, where' questions*
❖ Who is (cutting paper)?
❖ Who is (reading)?
❖ What is Penny doing?
❖ What is your teacher doing?
❖ Where is (singing)?

Nonverbal responses: The student responds by pointing to the photos.

## What we do with things in the classroom

1  Place a selection of frequently used classroom items – for example, a pencil, a pair of scissors, a ruler, a computer and some books – on a table in front of the students,. Also have the matching photos of these objects and additional photos from the 'noun' activity (see the relevant 'Noun' activity – 'Name the things we see in the classroom', that is, doors, bookshelves and so on.

2  Name each item in the photos as you put them on the board.

3  Name each object as you put it on the table, demonstrating and identifying its function; for

Ⓟ This page may be photocopied for instructional use only. © Francesca Bierens  Speechmark Ⓢ

example: 'We **cut** with scissors'; 'We **draw** with a pencil'; 'We **hang** our schoolbags on the bag hooks'; 'We **open** windows'; and 'We **close** doors'.

4   Then using the photos of the objects, have the students point to the appropriate picture when the function is gestured and identified (eg 'We paint with a …') from a choice of two photos presented, for example, a paintbrush and a glue stick.

5   Play the 'wh' question cube activity using the pictures on the board as prompts for the students to point to and to assist with their verbal responses.

6   Put the photos of each object back in the small photo album, with one photo per page with the label written underneath. Beneath the label, add the function of the object.

*Examples of 'who, what, where' questions*

❖   What do we cut with?

❖   What do we paint with?

❖   What do we draw lines with?

❖   Where is the paintbrush?

❖   Where do we hang our school bags?

❖   Where do we find books to read?

• Give each student one of the named photos or have each student choose a photo to hold.

   ❖   Who has the thing we (paint with)?

Nonverbal responses: The student responds by pointing to the photos or pictures.

**What people do in our school**

1   Have the photos of the important people in the school (see the relevant 'Noun' activity: 'Name the people we see in our school').

2   Identify and name each person in the photo; for example: 'This is the head teacher, Mrs King.'

3   Visit these people around the school, see what they do and take photos of where they work; for example: 'Mrs Booker is a librarian. Look … she works with books and computers'; 'Miss Keys is the caretaker. Look … she fixes things and keeps the school safe and tidy.'

4   Return to class and identify each person in the photos and talk about what they do.

5   On a large board, have one photo column of these people and another column of their place of work, naming each as you place the photos.

6   Assist the students to match them up by drawing a line from the person to the office; for example: 'Mrs Greeter – receptionist … front office.'

7   Play the 'wh' question cube activity using the pictures on the board as prompts for the students to point to and to assist with their verbal responses.

8   Return the photos to the small photo albums with each person's name, job and location written underneath to use as a reference.

This page may be photocopied for instructional use only. © Francesca Bierens  Speechmark

*Examples of 'who, what, where' questions*
- ❖ Who is the (head teacher)?
- ❖ Who is this? (Show photo.)
- ❖ Who works in the sick bay?
- ❖ Who works with books and computers?
- ❖ What does Mrs King do?
- ❖ Where is the (school nurse)?
- ❖ Where is (Mrs Greeter – receptionist)?
- ❖ Where is the person who looks after you if you are sick? (School nurse.)
- ❖ Where does Miss Keys work?

Nonverbal responses: The student responds by pointing to the photos.

## What we do with everyday things – categories

1  Have a selection of common object picture cards, with at least two pictures from four categories, for example, food, clothes, transport and musical instruments.
2  Show each picture to the students, name each object and identify its function, also demonstrating the function of the object by gesture; for example: 'We can eat an apple'; 'We wear shoes'; 'We travel in a bus'; or 'We play a guitar'.
3  Have students recognise and point to the picture when named and then from a choice of two pictures presented.
4  Place each photo on a board after it has been named so that it can be seen clearly by the students. Place each photo in a line across the top of a board.
5  When you have at least one picture from each category, after naming the object and demonstrating its function, talk about things that 'go together' and name the four categories.
6  Ask the students to decide where the next picture should go. Place the picture below the first picture in that category.
7  Remove the pictures from the board and have the students help to stick each picture into a scrapbook, putting them into the correct categories. This then becomes a classroom dictionary that can be regularly added to and referred to frequently.

*Examples of 'who, what, where' questions*
- ❖ What can we wear?
- ❖ What is this? (Point to picture.)
- ❖ What can we eat?
- ❖ What can we travel in?
- ❖ Where is the (apple)?
- ❖ Where is the thing we (travel in)?

- • Give each student one of the named photos or have each student choose a photo to hold.
  - ❖ Who has the thing we can (wear)?

Nonverbal responses: The student responds by pointing to the photos.

Ⓟ This page may be photocopied for instructional use only. © Francesca Bierens  Speechmark Ⓢ

**What people in our community do**

1   Have pictures of various people in the community, for example, a fire officer, a police officer and a librarian.

2   Go through these pictures with the students and name the profession of the person in each picture.

3   If you know specific people in your community and have their photos (see the relevant 'Noun' activity: 'Names of people in our community'), then identify the person by name; for example: 'Mrs Reid, the librarian' and 'Dr Wells, the doctor'.

4   If possible, visit with these people in the community and see what they do; for example: 'Miss Blooms **sells** flowers'; 'Mr Waters, the fire fighter, **puts out** fires'; 'Mrs Reid lets us **borrow** books'; 'Dr Wells **examines** us when we are sick'; and 'Mr Wheeler **drives** the bus'.

5   Return to class and identify each person in the photos and talk about what they do.

6   Have students recognise and point to the relevant person in the picture when their profession is identified from a choice of two pictures presented.

7   Play the 'wh' question cube activity using the pictures on the board as prompts for the students to point to and to assist with their verbal responses.

8   Put the photos of these people in the community back into the small photo album with one photo per page and their names and jobs written underneath.

9   This then becomes a classroom dictionary of people you know in your community and what they do.

*Examples of 'who, what, where' questions*

❖ Who puts out fires?

❖ Who examines us when we are sick?

❖ Who is this? (Point to a person in the picture, for example, a doctor.)

❖ Who lets us borrow books?

❖ What does Mr Wheeler do? (Bus driver.)

❖ Where is (Miss Blooms)?

Nonverbal responses: The student responds by pointing to the photos.

**What people and animals in stories can do**

1   Tell a story, using visual prompts such as finger puppets or toys.

2   Give each student one or two different items. As you tell the story, the students must move their puppet or toy appropriately, for example, 'making the birds fly' or 'making the horse gallop'.

3   As you tell the story, stress the action and demonstrate by gesturing so that the students can imitate; for example: 'The bird was **flying** and the fish was **jumping** out of the water' or 'The girl was **eating** a piece of birthday cake and saw the rocket **blast off**'.

℗ This page may be photocopied for instructional use only. © Francesca Bierens  Speechmark

4   At the end of the story, assist the students to identify the actions carried out by their toy by using gesture to prompt their recall.

5   Play the 'wh' question cube activity using the toys and puppets as prompts for the students to point to and to assist with their verbal responses.

*Examples of 'who, what, where' questions*

❖ Who was (hiding)?

❖ Who swam and swam and swam?

❖ What blasted off?

❖ What did the rabbit do?

❖ What did the girl eat?

❖ What did the girl see?

❖ Where is the (horse)?

Nonverbal responses: The student responds by pointing to the toys or puppets.

**What we do in our house**

1   Have pictures of people carrying out a variety of actions, for example, talking, eating and sleeping.

2   Go through these pictures with the students, identifying each action and using gesture to demonstrate it.

3   Using pictures as prompts, assist students to take turns telling the rest of the group what they do at home, for example, **sleep**, **play** with toys, **play** on the computer, **eat**, **drink**, **brush** their teeth, **read** books, **ride** their bike, **jump** on trampoline and **watch** DVDs.

4   Using any photos you may have of each student's family, talk about what each person at home likes to do; for example: 'Granddad watches television'; 'Aunty cooks'; 'My brother plays on the computer' and 'Our dog chases balls'.

5   Put the pictures of people carrying out actions up on a board.

6   Play the 'wh' question cube activity using the pictures on the board as prompts for the students to point to and to assist with their verbal responses.

*Examples of 'who, what, where' questions*

❖ Who reads books at home?

❖ What do you like to do at home?

❖ What is the man doing? (Point to picture.)

❖ Where is the girl drawing a picture?

❖ Where is the lady cooking?

❖ Where is the boy eating?

Nonverbal responses: The student responds by pointing to the photos.

Ⓟ This page may be photocopied for instructional use only. © Francesca Bierens **Speechmark** Ⓢ

**What we can do at fun places in our community**

1   Have pictures or photos of popular places in your community, for example, the local swimming pool and the local play park.

2   Go through these images with the students and name each place and then put them on the board so that they can be clearly seen by all the students.

3   Place a large piece of paper beside the board and draw any additional places that the students may mention, for example, a cinema complex and the recreation ground.

4   Identify each place and talk about what you would do there; for example: 'What do we do at the swimming pool? … We swim'; 'What do we do at the playground? … We swing and slide and climb'; and 'What do we do at the movies? … We laugh and eat popcorn'.

5   Play the 'wh' question cube activity using the photos on the board as prompts for the students to point to and to assist with their verbal responses.

6   Put the images in the small photo album with one photo per page and the label written underneath to be used as a classroom dictionary of things to do in the community.

*Examples of 'who, what, where' questions*

❖   What can you do at the movie theatre?

❖   What can you do at the zoo?

❖   Where is the (swimming pool)?

❖   Where can we go to play on the swings and slide?

•   Give each student one of the named photos or have each student choose a photo to hold.
    ❖   Who has the place you can go swimming?
    ❖   Who has the place you can feed the ducks and have a picnic?

Nonverbal responses: The student responds by pointing to the photos.

**What we can make our bodies do**

1   Move around the classroom or, if possible, outside. Model different movements and identify the actions; for example; 'We are jumping'; 'We are creeping'; and 'We are walking' .

2   Each student can then take turns to initiate an action for the rest of the class to copy and for you to identify; for example: 'Penny is clapping.'

3   Model the correct response and then direct the question to the students. Pause. Then either provide the correct response or confirm the students' responses; for example: 'Bob is hopping. What is Bob doing? … Hopping.'

4   Have the students walk until you say 'stop', and then they must stop immediately. They can continue to move when you provide an instruction such as 'walk', 'run' or 'crawl', but as soon as you say 'stop' then they must immediately stop moving.

5   Play the 'wh' question cube activity while you are all still moving.

6   Take photos of the students moving or have the students draw their own pictures. Put these pictures on the wall with the name and action written underneath.

Ⓟ This page may be photocopied for instructional use only. © Francesca Bierens  Speechmark Ⓢ

7   And/or put the photos in a small photo album with each student's name and action written underneath in a simple sentence structure; for example: 'Poppy is running.' This then becomes your dictionary for additional verbs related directly to your students.

*Examples of 'who, what, where' questions*
❖ Who is jumping?
❖ Who is dancing?
❖ What movements can we do?
❖ What is (name a student) doing?
❖ Where is someone hopping?

Nonverbal responses: The student responds by pointing to the appropriate person.

**What we do during our topic study or field trip**
1   At the beginning of a topic, for example, 'volcanoes', talk about the things you are going to study, using pictures, photos and books to demonstrate these to the students.
2   On the large piece of paper where you wrote the key words around the diagram of the volcano, for example, 'volcanoes' and 'lava', using a different colour pen, add what these things can do; for example: 'Volcanoes **erupt**'; 'Lava can **flow**'; and 'Rocks are **thrown**'.
3   Use the large piece of paper as a big chart 'word list' and put it up on the wall so that it becomes a reference for the students throughout the course of that topic study.
4   When you return from the field trip, for example, a visit to a zoo, go through the photos and assist the students to recall information about what they did, what the animals did and what the zoo staff did; for example: 'The otters were **swimming**. The elephants were **lifting** logs. The zoo staff **fed** the giraffes.'
5   Add this information to the 'word list' that you started before the field trip (see the relevant 'Noun' activity: 'Name the things, people and places in our topic study/field trip'). Use the large piece of paper as a big chart 'word list' and put it up on the wall with the photos of the trip so that it becomes a reference for the students to assist them when talking or writing about the trip.

*Examples of 'who, what, where' questions*
❖ Who is the student (feeding the giraffe)?
❖ What did you do at the zoo?
❖ What animals did we see?
❖ What were they doing?
❖ Where is the (elephant lifting)?
❖ Where is the (otter swimming)?

Nonverbal responses: The student responds by pointing to the photos.

Ⓟ This page may be photocopied for instructional use only. © Francesca Bierens  Speechmark Ⓢ

# Chapter 4
# Add adjectives to put colour into words

| | |
|---|---|
| **What is an adjective?** | An **'adjective'** is a word used to describe a person, place or thing. |
| **Prerequisites:** | • The Preverbal Skills of Language<br>• Nouns. |

## Important points to remember when teaching 'adjectives'

- Adjectives are generally not an essential skill in order for a student to communicate but they are important for their comprehension. Adjectives are frequently included within classroom instructions; for example, 'Get out your **blue** reading books'; 'Please pass me a **big** book'; and 'Don't put your rubbish in the **green** bins'.

- As often as possible, have the students touch, smell and experience the different textures when talking about how various objects feel.

- Many adjectives are very subjective and are dependent on comparisons; a mouse, for example, is **small** in comparison with an elephant but a mouse is **big** in comparison with a flea. So when working on this skill, be aware of what the student perceives. When used as a drawing activity it can highlight what the students are thinking, so they can either be guided appropriately or given clearer instructions.

- Colours are an abstract concept. What exactly are you identifying when you point to a coloured object? It could be the object itself or the texture or shape and this colour green is most certainly not the same colour as that colour green. For some students this is a very difficult and confusing concept, so work on it indirectly to avoid stress and frustration. Some students are interested and motivated by colour; others are not.

Ⓟ This page may be photocopied for instructional use only. © Francesca Bierens Speechmark

# Activities – adjectives put colour into words

## What things look like and feel like

1 Keep the concept of adjectives as simple as possible and focus on just one concept at a time, for example, basic colours, simple shapes or the difference between big and little. If you cook regularly in class with your students, then the adjectives of taste, texture and colour of food are an excellent area to focus on. If art is a frequent subject, then this is also an excellent opportunity to focus on the adjectives of colour, shape and size.

2 Focusing on the one concept, for example, 'big and little', have pairs of items in the same category – such as boxes, books and balls – in which one is big and one is significantly smaller. Introduce one pair at a time and place the items – one big book and one small book, for example – on the table in front of the students.

3 Using the objects and some exaggeration of gesture, show the students the big book and then the little book. Assist the students to point to the big book using gesture to provide any necessary prompts.

4 Once the students demonstrate a clear understanding of this concept with the books, then introduce another pair of objects, for example, boxes.

5 Assist students to take turns drawing a big ball on the board and then a little ball.

6 With colours, identify the colour, for example, 'red', and then identify a small number of items in the classroom that are red, for example, a red coloured pencil and red art paint.

7 When appropriate to the objects and activity, have the students touch, taste and smell the items.

*Examples of 'who, what, where' questions*
- ❖ What is this? (Indicate the big book.)
- ❖ What colour is this pen?
- ❖ Where is the big book?
- ❖ Where is the red pencil?

- Give a student one of the books. Get them to pass it around the class after each question.
  - ❖ Who has the big book?
  - ❖ Who has the little book?

Nonverbal responses: The student responds by pointing.

## What people in our class look like

1 Use the class photos of each student in the classroom and name each student or teacher as you put the photos up on the board.

2 Look at each photo and match it to the student in the class.

3 Identify the main characteristics of each student; for example: 'Lucy has long hair'; 'Kitty has

Ⓟ This page may be photocopied for instructional use only. © Francesca Bierens Speechmark Ⓢ

short hair'; 'Bob has brown hair'; 'Hattie has red hair'; 'Penny has brown eyes'; and 'Mary has blue eyes'.

4   Have each student look at the picture they drew of themselves (see the relevant 'Noun' activity: 'Name the parts of the body') and colour in the additional features.

5   Play the 'wh' question cube activity using the images on the board as prompts for the students to point to and to assist with their verbal responses.

*Examples of 'who, what, where' questions*

❖   Who has red hair?

❖   Who has brown eyes?

❖   What colour hair does (Poppy) have?

❖   Where is someone with long hair?

Nonverbal responses: The student responds by pointing.

**What things in our classroom look and feel like**

1   Place a selection of frequently used classroom items – for example, a pencil, a glue stick and a ruler – on a table in front of the students with their matching photos.

2   Name each object as you show it to the students and demonstrate its function. Then give the objects to the students to touch and assist them to describe how it feels. Model an appropriate adjective to describe the object for the students, for example,' sharp, sticky' or 'long'.

3   Assist the students to recall the adjectives as they identify the object and describe it before passing it to or swapping it with another student, for example, 'a long ruler'.

4   Then return the objects to the front table.

5   Using the photos of the class items (see the relevant 'Noun' activity: 'Name the things we use in the classroom'), give each student one of the photos that they must match to the appropriate object when you provide an adjective; for example, for 'sticky', put the photo of a glue stick beside the actual glue stick and for 'sharp', put the appropriate photo beside a pencil or scissors.

6   Return the photos of each object to the small photo album, with the label and location written underneath. On the opposite or facing page, underneath the function of the object, add one or two adjectives that clearly describe the object; for example, for a pencil write 'long' and 'sharp'.

7   This resource can be used as a classroom dictionary and as a reference for the students to expand their vocabulary.

*Examples of 'who, what, where' questions*

❖   What is long? (eg ruler)

❖   What is red? (eg paints, coloured pencils or coloured blocks)

Ⓟ This page may be photocopied for instructional use only. © Francesca Bierens   Speechmark Ⓢ

❖ What is sticky? (eg glue)
❖ Where is something hard? (eg blocks or a ruler)
❖ Where is something round? (eg globe or shape blocks)

● Give one of the named photos to each student or have each student choose a photo to hold.
    ❖ Who has a photo of something square? (eg a book or a box)
    ❖ Who has a photo of something soft? (eg a cushion from library corner)

Nonverbal responses:  The student responds by pointing.

## What things outside the classroom look like and feel like

1  Have photos or pictures of items you may see outside the classroom, for example, trees, flowers, a playground, some birds, some rubbish bins or nearby houses.
2  Show the students each of the pictures individually, and name each item.
3  Go for a walk outside if possible. Look at the colours, shapes, sizes and textures of things, for example, a red car, a round rubbish bin, a small cat and a shiny gate.
4  Look at the leaves on the trees, paying particular attention to their colour. If it's autumn look at the different colours on the trees. Pick up a fallen leaf and look at the colour and feel its texture. Pick up a bird's feather and look at the colour and feel the smooth 'tickly' texture of the feather. Take these items back to the classroom if possible.
5  Have the students look at the different colours of the objects and feel the different textures. Model the appropriate adjectives to describe each item.
6  Put the objects you found on a large piece of paper and assist the students to provide the appropriate adjective to write beside each item, for example, 'green leaf' and 'small daisy'.
7  Have students draw pictures of one or two of the items they saw and assist them to draw the correct size, colour and shape. Approximations of shapes are of course perfectly acceptable.

*Examples of 'who, what, where' questions*
❖ What is green?
❖ What is wet? (eg a puddle, a water fountain)
❖ What is brown? (eg a leaf, some mud)
❖ Where is something small?
❖ Where is something round?

● Give one of the named pictures or objects to each student or have each student choose a photo to hold.
    ❖ Who has something hard? (eg a rock)
    ❖ Who has something rough? (eg a dead leaf)

Nonverbal responses: The student responds by pointing.

87

Ⓟ This page may be photocopied for instructional use only. © Francesca Bierens

**What things in the different categories look and feel like**

1  Have a selection of common object picture cards from three or four categories – for example, food, clothes, animals and transport – and ask the students to select one category to talk about.

2  Focus on one category at a time, for example, animals. Have pictures of a variety of animals. Encourage the students to bring in photos of their own pets.

3  Look at farm animals, zoo animals and pet animals. Model the appropriate adjective to describe the animals; for example, big animals: elephants and giraffes; small animals: mice and frogs; and soft, furry animals: kittens and rabbits; rough-skinned animals: crocodiles. As you describe the animals, put them into their own categories on a large chart so that you can make comparisons. This helps the students to see and understand the adjectives.

4  Go through these categories of animals again, modelling an appropriate adjective as you write the words on the chart. Then assist the students to take turns to provide one descriptive word for one of the animals. This is also an opportunity to focus on the concepts of: 'same and different', that is, comparing items within the category that look or feel the same or different and opposites, that is, comparing items within a category or comparing items from two categories.

5  When appropriate to the objects and activity, have the students touch, taste and smell the items.

*Examples of 'who, what, where' questions*

❖  What is soft?

❖  What is smooth? (eg an otter)

❖  What has a purple tongue? (eg a giraffe)

❖  What has a long tail?

❖  Where is something long? (eg a snake)

• Give one of the named pictures to each student or have each student choose a picture to hold.

  ❖  Who has a picture of something with big ears? (eg an elephant)

  ❖  Who has a picture of something pink? (eg flamingos)

Nonverbal responses: The student responds by pointing.

**What my favourite singer, music group or actor looks like**

1  Encourage the students to bring in pictures of their favourite singers, music groups or actors.

2  Using pictures from posters, books or the cover of a magazine, assist each student to describe their favourite celebrity by modelling the appropriate adjectives; for example: 'It is a boy with **short**, **straight**, **brown** hair' or 'She wears **black** boots'.

3  After the students have each had a turn to show the pictures and describe their favourite group or singer or actor, assist the other students to recall information about each celebrity

This page may be photocopied for instructional use only. © Francesca Bierens  Speechmark

using one or two appropriate adjectives. Use the pictures to provide the necessary prompts.

4 Make up a poster of the different celebrities and assist the students to provide one or two adjectives that can be written beside the appropriate person or people.

5 Model the appropriate words for the students as necessary, but after having modelled the words a few times, slightly delay your responses or just give an initial sound prompt in order to allow the students to provide the information; for example: 'He has br— … brown hair.' Always repeat the full complete sentence either as a model to provide the information or as a confirmation of the students' response; for example, 'Yes, that's right. He wears a black baseball cap.'

*Examples of 'who, what, where' questions*
- ❖ Who has brown hair?
- ❖ Who wears (a blue jumper)?
- ❖ Who is this? (Show object.)
- ❖ What does (name of celebrity) wear? (Show photo.)

- • Give one of the named photos to each student or have each student choose a photo to hold.
    - ❖ Who has the photo of the person who has (brown hair)?
    - ❖ What does (name of celebrity) look like?

Nonverbal responses: The student responds by pointing.

**What people and animals in stories can look like**
1 Encourage the students to bring in their favourite books (or possibly DVD if absolutely essential) or get them out of the library.
2 Using pictures in the book or on the cover assist each student to describe their favourite characters by modelling the appropriate adjectives, for example, 'black horse with white star on his head'.
3 After the students have each had a turn to share and describe their favourite character then assist them to draw another student's favourite character rather than their own.
4 Use the pictures in the books to provide the necessary prompts. Remember this is not an art activity so as long as the students themselves know what they have drawn, then that is all that matters.
5 When the students have finished their drawings, assist them to describe what they have drawn, modelling the appropriate adjectives and recall which student had chosen it as their favourite character.

*Examples of 'who, what, where' questions*
- ❖ Who wears a red hat?
- ❖ Who is yellow?

This page may be photocopied for instructional use only. © Francesca Bierens Speechmark

❖ Who is this? (Show picture or book.)

❖ Who is (name of student)'s favourite character?

❖ What does (name of character) look like? (Show photo.)

❖ What colour coat does (name of character) wear?

❖ What does he or she look like?

❖ Where is the character with one leg?

Nonverbal responses: The student responds by pointing.

**What things or people or places in our topic study or field trip look and feel like**

1 As you work through your topic, for example, 'volcanoes', continue to expand the students' vocabulary. Using books and pictures read and talk to the students describing various items related to volcanoes.

2 Assist the students to recall these adjectives, add them to the large word list and relate them to the picture of the volcano. Prompt and model the appropriate adjectives as necessary, for example, 'The **boiling hot** lava is flowing down the mountain. The rocks thrown out of the volcano are very rough.'

3 Return the word list to the wall so that it continues to be a reference for the students throughout the course of that topic study.

4 When you return from the field trip, go through the photos and assist the students to recall the information, for example, what the animals and places at the zoo looked like. Adjectives should be used; for example: 'The zebras had black and white stripes' and 'The hippo's enclosure had brown muddy water'.

5 Add this information to the big word chart that you started before the field trip and use it to further increase the students' vocabulary.

6 Put the word chart back up on the wall with the photos of the trip so that it becomes a reference for the students to assist them when talking or writing about the trip.

7 When appropriate to the objects and activity, have the students touch, taste and smell the items.

*Examples of 'who, what, where' questions*

❖ What is very hot?

❖ What animal swims in muddy water?

❖ What do the volcanic rocks feel like?

❖ What colour is the smoke cloud?

❖ What does the elephant look like?

❖ What animals have long tails?

❖ Where is the animal that has stripes?

Nonverbal responses: The student responds by pointing to the photo.

Ⓟ This page may be photocopied for instructional use only. © Francesca Bierens Speechmark Ⓢ

# Chapter 5
# Putting prepositions in their place

| | |
|---|---|
| **What is a preposition?** | A **preposition** is a word used to identify the location of something, for example, 'in', 'on', 'under' and so forth. |
| **Prerequisites:** | • The Preverbal Skills of Language – especially:<br>   ❖ Awareness of sights around them – visual awareness<br>   ❖ Copying actions – motor imitation.<br>• Nouns and verbs. |

## Important points to remember when teaching 'prepositions'

- Prepositions are important in order for students to accurately follow instructions. Prepositions are constantly used in the classroom programme throughout the course of the day.

- Before teaching prepositions have the students copy the simple placement of objects. This will allow you to identify any perceptual difficulties that could impact significantly on a student's ability to understand the concept of prepositions.

- Remember if you include an adjective in the question or instruction, make sure that you have spent time on this concept first and the students understand it; for example: 'What is in the *blue* basket?' Otherwise the student may answer incorrectly because they don't understand the *adjective* (rather than the preposition).

## Activities – putting prepositions in their place

**Where to put things**

1  Have a group of pens or pencils, an open box and a closed box on a table in front of the class so that all the students can see them.
2  Prepare to focus on one preposition at a time. Model an action slowly as you identify the action; for example: 'I'm putting the pen on the box.'
3  Instruct the students to take turns placing a pen **on** the box. Either pass the pen and box around the class or each student can take turns coming up the front to carry out the instruction.

91

Ⓟ This page may be photocopied for instructional use only. © Francesca Bierens Speechmark Ⓢ

4   When the students demonstrate an understanding of this preposition, then move on to another preposition, for example, **in** the box and then another, for example, **under** the box and so forth.

5   Assist the students by using gesture to prompt.

6   When the students are able to consistently carry out these instructions then alternate two prepositions, for example, instructing the students to put the pen **on** the box and **in** the box, gradually reducing the gestural prompt as the students achieve success.

7   Begin with the easier prepositions, that is, '**in**', '**on**', '**under**', and '**beside**'. When the students have acquired an understanding of these basic prepositions, introduce the more difficult prepositions '**in front**', '**behind**', and '**between**'.

8   When students have demonstrated a clear understanding of individual prepositions then teach them as opposites, for example, 'in' and 'out', 'on' and 'off' and 'up' and 'down'.

*Examples of 'who, what, where' questions*

•   Present a choice of two options that you have focused on, for example, pen **on** the box and pen **under** the box.

❖   Where is the pen **on** the box?

❖   Where is the pen **under** the box?

❖   Where is the pen?

•   Have students take turns following simple instructions; for example: 'Put the pen **in** the box.' Use gesture to assist the student as necessary.

❖   What did Penny do? (Response, eg Put pen **in** box.)

❖   Who put the block **in** the box?

Nonverbal responses: The student responds by pointing to object placed.

**Where people are in our class**

1   Assist the students to understand prepositions by having a game positioning them in different places around the classroom. Use gestural prompts as you give each of them the instruction; for example: 'Bob stand **beside** your desk'; 'Penny stand **behind** your chair'; 'Tom stand **beside** Bob'; and 'Poppy stand **in front** of the cupboard'.

2   Assist and prompt the students as necessary. Once students have carried out the instruction, assist them to identify where they are, for example, **between** the desks.

3   Assist the students as much as necessary until they demonstrate an understanding of the concept.

4   Make a simple obstacle course in the classroom using the existing furniture and rearranging the smaller items such as chairs.

5   Give each student an appropriate instruction – such as, 'Go **behind** the bookcase and **under** the chair' – depending on their level of memory and understanding of prepositions.

P This page may be photocopied for instructional use only. © Francesca Bierens   Speechmark

6   Assist the student to repeat the instruction before carrying out the task and then assist them to recall what they did once they have completed the course.

7   Make up photos of this activity to show the students, explaining and using gesture to demonstrate what each student did.

*Examples of 'who, what, where' questions*
Provide gesture and/or the initial sound modelling to prompt as required.

❖   Who is beside Bob?
❖   What did Penny do? (eg went under the table)
❖   What did Fred do? (eg went behind the chair)
❖   Where is Poppy?

Nonverbal responses: The student responds by pointing to person, object or photo of location.

## Where things are in the classroom

1   Put the photos of the objects used or seen in your classroom, for example, pencils, scissors, books, a clock and curtains up on the board so that all the students can see them clearly.

2   Identify each of these items and have the students point to where they can usually be found, for example, books in the bookshelf, pens in the tubs and scrapbooks in the basket.

3   As the students point to the locations, model the specific location using the appropriate preposition; for example: 'That's right, the clock is **on** the wall' or 'The block box is **under** the table'.

4   Go through the photos again and assist the students to give a verbal response by slightly delaying your answer and using gesture to demonstrate the correct response; for example, 'The scissors go … **in** the box' or 'The paints go … **on** the shelf'.

5   Play the 'wh' question cube activity using the pictures on the board as prompts for the students to point to and to assist with their verbal responses.

6   Put the photos of each object back in the small photo album, one photo per page with the label and function written underneath. On the opposite or facing page write the location of this object in the classroom. This then becomes a classroom dictionary identifying where things belong in the classroom that can be referred to regularly.

*Examples of 'who, what, where' questions*

❖   What is in the basket?
❖   What is under the table?
❖   What goes on the back shelf?
❖   Where is the clock?
❖   Where is the glue?
❖   Where do we put the coloured pencils?

Nonverbal responses: The student responds by pointing to object or photo.

Ⓟ This page may be photocopied for instructional use only. © Francesca Bierens  Speechmark Ⓢ

**Where we go to see and buy things**

1   Have a selection of common object picture cards – for example, an ice cream, a shirt and an elephant – and assist the students to name the items and recall their appropriate categories by identifying their function; for example: 'We **eat** an ice cream'; 'We **wear** a shirt'; or 'We can **look** at the elephant'.

2   Have pictures of places where you can see or buy these items, for example, a supermarket, a department store and a zoo. Identify these places with the students.

3   On a large board, have a column of the items placed in categories and another column of the places where you can see or buy these items. Initially, have the appropriate place opposite the category; for example, we buy food at the supermarket so the line connecting the two should go straight across.

4   When the students are able to identify the category and the place to find these items then mix up one of the columns.

5   Assist the students to then match the items to the places where you can see or buy them by drawing lines.

6   Remove the pictures from the board and have the students match the categories in the scrapbook to the places where you can buy or see them.

*Examples of 'who, what, where' questions*

❖  What can we buy at the department store?

❖  What can we buy at the supermarket?

❖  What can I see at the zoo?

❖  Where can you buy ice cream?

❖  Where can you see a monkey?

❖  Where can you buy DVDs?

Nonverbal responses: The student responds by pointing to the photos.

**Where we find things**

1   After the previous activity of identifying items, their categories and the places to buy or see each category, assist students to identify the exact location of these items. Focus on one location at a time, for example, 'supermarket'. Use books or picture cards to prompt the students' responses. On a large board, have a column of the items and another column where these items are located. At the supermarket, for example, ice cream is **in** the freezer section, tins are **on** the shelf and apples are **beside** the other fruit in the fruit section.

2   Initially, have the appropriate place opposite the category, for example, apples opposite baskets of fruit.

3   When the students are consistently able to identify the items and location then mix up one of the columns. Assist the students to match them by drawing a line from the item to the place it is located.

Ⓟ This page may be photocopied for instructional use only. © Francesca Bierens   Speechmark ⚙

4 Play the 'wh' question cube activity using the pictures on the board as prompts for the students to point to and to assist with their verbal responses.

5 If possible make a visit to a supermarket or department store so that the students can see exactly where these items are located.

*Examples of 'who, what, where' questions*

❖ What is in the freezer section?

❖ Where is the milk in the supermarket?

❖ What is beside the bananas?

❖ Where is the bread?

❖ Where are the potatoes?

Nonverbal responses: The student responds by pointing to the photos.

## Where people and animals in stories can go

1 Tell a story, using visual prompts such as finger puppets or cuddly toys.

2 As you tell the story, stress the preposition and demonstrate with the toys; for example: 'The boy ran to the beach and jumped **into** the water. The monkey climbed **up** the tree in the jungle. The rabbit sat **beside** his friend.'

3 At the end of the story, assist the students to identify where the people and animals went, using toys and gesture to prompt their recall.

4 Play the 'wh' question cube activity using the toys and puppets as prompts for the students to point to and to assist with their verbal responses.

*Examples of 'who, what, where' questions*

❖ Who climbed up the tree?

❖ Who ran around the tree?

❖ What went under the ground?

❖ What did (name) do?

❖ Where did (name) go?

❖ Where did (girl) go?

Nonverbal responses: The student responds by pointing to the toys or puppets/or by gesturing.

## Where we find things in our house

1 Have pictures of the various rooms in a house, for example, a bedroom, a kitchen and a bathroom, and assist the student to recall the names of these rooms.

2 Using picture cards or photos or images cut out of supermarket or department store flyers, name the items that students have at home, for example, a television, a bed, some books and some DVDs (see the relevant 'Noun' and 'Verb' activities: 'Name the people and things we have in our house' and 'What we do in our house').

95

This page may be photocopied for instructional use only. © Francesca Bierens  Speechmark

3　On a large board, have a photo column of the items and another column of rooms in the house. Assist the students to match them up by drawing a line from the item, for example, a bar of soap to the appropriate room, for example, a bathroom. Initially, have the items opposite the room in which they would normally be found so the lines go straight across. When the students are able to correctly identify the item and the appropriate room, then mix up one of the columns.

4　Then assist the students to identify the exact location of these items in these rooms, for example, 'clothes **in** the drawers', 'books **on** the bookshelf' and 'slippers **under** the bed'. Use books or picture cards to prompt their responses.

*Examples of 'who, what, where' questions*
❖ What goes on the bookshelf?
❖ What goes under the bed?
❖ Where would you find the fridge?
❖ Where would you find the bed?
❖ Where would you put your clothes?
❖ Where would you put your shoes?

Nonverbal responses: The student responds by pointing to the pictures/photos.

**Where do things go in our topic study or field trip**
1　As you work through your topic, for example, 'volcanoes', talk with the students about where things go.
2　On the large word chart with the simple diagram of the volcano, add the prepositions you all decide on, using a different coloured pen, for example, '**inside** the volcano', 'lava flows **down** the mountain' and 'rocks are thrown **out** of the mountain'.
3　Use the big word chart to increase the students' vocabulary as you expand on your topic. Return it to the wall so that it becomes a reference for the students throughout the course of that topic study.
4　When you return from the field trip, for example, a visit to the zoo, go through the photos and assist the students to recall information about where they went and where the animals were, for example, 'The lions slept **beside** one another'; 'The spiders were **behind** the glass'; and 'We went **into** the giraffe enclosure'.
5　Add this information to the big word chart that you started before the field trip and use it to increase the students' vocabulary.
6　Put the word chart back up on the wall with the photos of the trip so that it becomes a reference for the students to assist them when talking or writing about the trip.

Ⓟ This page may be photocopied for instructional use only. © Francesca Bierens　Speechmark Ⓢ

*Examples of 'who, what, where' questions*
- ❖ What comes out of the mountain?
- ❖ What was beside the zebra?
- ❖ Where did you go to see the ... ?
- ❖ Where does the lava come from?
- ❖ Where does the lava go?
- ❖ Where were the giraffes?

Nonverbal responses: The student responds by pointing to the photos.

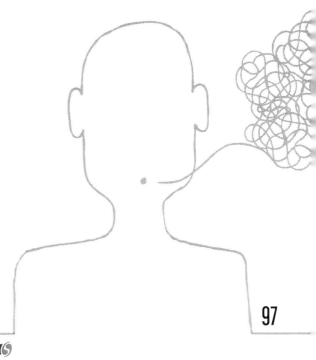

97

This page may be photocopied for instructional use only. © Francesca Bierens Speechmark

Chapter 6

# Making sure negatives are not left out

| | |
|---|---|
| **What is a negative?** | A '**negative**' is a word that expresses denial or refusal' (Collins Gem English Dictionary, 1988, p.355). |
| **Prerequisites**: | • The Preverbal Skills of Language<br>• The Building Bricks of Language – comprehension of the words or concepts included in the question or instruction directed to the student; for example: 'Do not put that **in** the green bucket' (prepositions, adjectives). |

## Important points to remember when teaching 'negatives'

• **Negatives are a much more difficult concept than is often perceived and should be actively taught, including 'yes' and 'no'.** It is often taken for granted that children understand this concept because they can say 'no' but unfortunately that is often not the case and is often the cause of many behaviour issues; for example: the question 'Do you want more ice cream?' may elicit the response, 'No', and so the ice cream is taken away and the child screams because he does want *the rest* of his ice cream!

• Many students understand only the key words in a sentence and have not acquired a clear understanding of the additional concepts that may be included in that sentence such as negatives or time like '**not**' and '**this morning**'; for example: 'You may **not** go outside **this morning**'; 'You may **not** cross the road'; and 'Do **not** leave the group'.

• Other students tend to be 'key word' listeners even though in other situations they demonstrate an understanding of negatives and the more complex concepts. Make sure that these students have listened carefully and understand the direction given; for example: 'Do **not** take your artwork home until tomorrow' or 'Put your hand up if you have **not** finished your maths'.

• Contracted negatives, for example, 'didn't', 'isn't' and 'can't', are easily missed and should always be repeated as a full word 'not' when the instruction or question is important; for

Ⓟ This page may be photocopied for instructional use only. © Francesca Bierens Speechmark Ⓢ

example, 'You can't go – **cannot** go – outside at lunchtime today' and 'We aren't – **are not** – going swimming on Friday'.

- Be sure that the student has acquired adequate knowledge and understanding of all the words or concepts included with the negative. A student must know what something is, before they can understand what it is not; for example: 'Do not cut out the pictures of **unhealthy food**. Just cut out the pictures of **fruit and vegetables**.'

- **Do not react when a student immediately says 'no' to a question or instruction.** They may not in fact mean 'no'; they may just want to finish what they are doing. Wait silently for a few minutes. When they have finished what they are doing they will very possibly be happy to carry out your instruction.

- **Use gesture, body language and facial expression initially when teaching negatives.** Nod and shake your head to assist the students to understand and discriminate between the 'yes and no' concept and the 'not' concept.

## Activities – making sure negatives are not left out

### Who of our classmates and teacher is not here

1 Use the small class photos of each student in the class (see the relevant 'Noun' activity: 'Name our classmates and teacher') or have a class photo board.
2 Regularly identify and greet each student, using the photos to see who is at school that day.
3 Then identify the students who are **not** at school today; for example: 'Is Bob at school today?' **'Yes'** or **'No'**.
4 Slightly exaggerate shaking your head to stress the **'not'** and reinforce the negative.
5 After identifying and greeting each student, make a fun activity of asking students to identify when the correct name is given and when it is not; for example: 'Is this Bob?'; 'Yes'; 'Is this Poppy?'; 'Yes'; 'Is this Penny?'; 'No'; 'Is this Penny?'; 'No'; 'Is this Penny?'; 'Yes'. This also makes a very good listening activity.
6 This activity can be extended after the students have acquired some knowledge of prepositions, for example, 'Who is sitting beside Bob?'; 'Who is **not** beside Bob?'

*Examples of 'who, what, where' questions*
❖ Who is not your teacher?
❖ Who is this? (Indicate a student.)
❖ Who is at school?
❖ Who is your teacher?
❖ Who is not beside Poppy?
❖ Where is (name a student)?

Nonverbal responses: The student responds by pointing.

Ⓟ This page may be photocopied for instructional use only. © Francesca Bierens  Speechmark ⟲

**What people are not doing**

1   Have clear picture cards of people carrying out various activities or use the photos taken of your students involved in various activities, for example, writing; (see the relevant 'Verb' activity: 'What we all do in our classroom'). Look at each picture with the students and review the students' knowledge of the appropriate action; for example: 'The girl is **reading**, reading a book' or 'The man is **eating**, eating an apple'. Demonstrate the action using gesture.

2   Once the students are able to consistently identify the appropriate action then introduce the negative concept; for example: 'Is Bob painting?'; 'Yes'; 'Is Bob eating?'; 'No'; 'Is Bob painting?'; 'Yes'.

3   Present students with a choice of two pictures and request that they identify the negative picture; for example: 'Point to the person who is **not** painting.'

4   Always ensure that the students demonstrate a consistent understanding of what **is** occurring in a picture before introducing the negative.

*Examples of 'who, what, where' questions*
❖ Who is (reading)?
❖ Who is not (reading)?
❖ Who is writing?
❖ Who is not cutting?
❖ Who is talking?
❖ Who is not sitting?

Nonverbal responses: The student responds by pointing.

**The things in the classroom – Yes and No**

1   Review the students' knowledge of things you have in the classroom and assist their recall of label, function and location words (see the relevant 'Noun', 'Verb' and 'Preposition' activities: 'Name the things we use in the classroom', 'What we do with things in the classroom' and 'Where things are in the classroom') by going through a selection of pictures of frequently used classroom items, for example, a pencil, a pair of scissors, a ruler, a computer and some books.

2   When the students demonstrate a consistent knowledge of these items by responding correctly to all questions asked then introduce the negative concept, making this a fun activity. Include the previous concepts as appropriate, for example, the name of the object, its function, its location in the classroom and adjectives; for example: 'Is this a paintbrush?'; 'No'; 'Is this a paintbrush?'; 'Yes'; 'Do we cut with the paintbrush?'; 'No'; 'We cut with the ... scissors'. Play

 This page may be photocopied for instructional use only. © Francesca Bierens **Speechmark**

the 'wh' question cube activity using the pictures on the board as prompts for the students to point to and to assist with their verbal responses.

*Examples of 'who, what, where' questions*
- ❖ What don't we cut with?
- ❖ What do we paint with?
- ❖ What don't we paint with?
- ❖ What is sticky?
- ❖ What is not sticky?
- ❖ Where are the books?
- ❖ Where don't we put the pencils?
- ❖ Where do we keep the scissors?
- ❖ Where don't we keep the scissors?

Nonverbal responses: The student responds by pointing to the photos or pictures.

## What does not belong – categories

1 Review the students' knowledge and assist their recall (see the relevant 'Verb' activity: 'What we do with everyday things (categories)'), by going through a selection of pictures of common objects. Talk about the items that go together and remind them of the categories that the objects belong in, for example, food, clothes, transport or musical instruments.

2 Focus on just one category at a time when introducing the negative concept, for example, 'food'. Put the pictures on the board in a column or line that indicates that they belong in that category.

3 Go through a number of pictures that belong to the selected category assisting the students to name the object and then confirm that it belongs to that category, for example, 'Banana. Can we eat bananas?'; 'Yes'.

4 Then introduce an item that does not belong to the category and proceed with the dialogue; for example: 'Hat. Can we eat a hat?'; 'No, we wear a hat. We can't eat a hat.' Put this picture in a different column.

5 Slightly exaggerate shaking your head to stress the **'not'** and reinforce the negative.

6 Continue to focus on one category at a time until the students can consistently answer 'yes' or 'no' appropriately when placing an object or picture in the category.

7 Then introduce another category so that the students have a choice of two categories – such as food and clothes; for example, 'Can we wear an orange?'; 'No'; 'Can we eat an orange?'; 'Yes'.

*Examples of 'who, what, where' questions*
- ❖ What can we eat?
- ❖ What don't we eat?
- ❖ What category does this belong to? (Show a picture or object.)

Ⓟ This page may be photocopied for instructional use only. © Francesca Bierens

❖ Where is something we can wear?

❖ Where is something we can eat?

❖ Where is something we cannot eat?

• Give each student one of the named photos or have each student choose a photo to hold.

  ❖ Who has something we can wear?

  ❖ Who has something we cannot wear?

Nonverbal responses: The student responds by pointing to the photos.

**The people who are not in the right place in our community**

1 Go through the pictures of various people and places in the community, for example, a librarian, a doctor, a dentist, a hospital and a library with the students. Review their knowledge of the names and/or professions and the places of work (see the relevant 'Noun' and 'Verb' activities: 'Names of people in our community' and 'What people in our community do').

2 When the students demonstrate a consistent knowledge of these people and places by answering all questions correctly then introduce the negative concept, for example, 'What do doctors do? Do doctors put out fires?'; 'Do you call the library if you are sick?'

3 Make this a fun activity by having a photo column of these people and another column of their place of work (see the relevant 'Verb' activity: 'What people in our community do'). Initially, match them up by drawing a line from the person to their correct place of work.

4 When the students have completed this task correctly, mix up one column and assist the students to draw lines from the picture or photo of the person to something that is **not** their profession.

5 When you have completed this task, review the negative column before replacing it with the correct information; for example: 'Dr Wells sells books. No. Dr Wells does **not** sell books; he is the doctor'; 'Miss Blooms is the fire fighter. No. Miss Blooms is **not** the fire fighter. She sells flowers'.

*Examples of 'who, what, where' questions*

❖ Who is not the (librarian)?

❖ Who is the police officer?

❖ Who does not (sell books)?

❖ Who do you visit if you are sick?

❖ Who is this? (Point to a person in the picture, for example, a doctor.)

❖ What does a fire fighter do?

❖ What doesn't a fire fighter do?

❖ Where is the (fire fighter)?

Nonverbal responses: The student responds by pointing to the photos.

Ⓟ This page may be photocopied for instructional use only. © Francesca Bierens Speechmark Ⓢ

**Including the 'nots' of the people, animals and objects in a story**

1   Tell or read a story, using visual prompts such as finger puppets or toys.

2   At the end of the story, assist the students to recall the information acquired by using visual prompts and gesture.

3   Slightly delay your responses in order to provide an opportunity for the students to respond; for example: 'The whole class was in the race. Mary won the … race, but Beth did **not** finish the race. She … fell over.'

4   When the students are able to answer all the questions about the story correctly then introduce the negative concept, using the visual prompts in order to assist their responses.

5   As necessary, provide the students with one or two visual options from the book or by using toys, in order to assist them to respond correctly; for example: 'Who did **not** finish? Beth or Sue?'

6   Always reinforce the student's response by repeating the answer in a confirming manner; for example: 'Yes, **Beth** did **not** finish the race. She fell over.'

*Examples of 'who, what, where' questions*

❖ Who did not (finish the race)?

❖ Who was (in the race)?

❖ Who did **not** (win the race)?

❖ Where is Beth?

❖ Where is Sue?

Nonverbal responses: The student responds by pointing to the toys or puppets.

**The things we do and like in our house and the things we don't**

1   If possible, have photos or talk about each of the student's family, that is, their mum, their dad, their brothers, their sisters, their grandparents, their aunts, their uncles and their pets.

2   Encourage students to recall the information provided about their homes in previous activities (see the relevant 'Noun' and 'Verb' activities: 'Name the people and things we have in our house' and 'What we do in our house'), that is, the people, pets, toys and activities at home.

3   Using pictures or photos as prompts, have students take turns recalling information about their classmates; for example: 'Bob has a brother called Bill and a puppy called Lou and he likes trampolines.'

4   When the students can recall some information about each of their classmates then introduce the negative concept; for example, 'Does Bobby have a sister called Poppy? Who does **not** like swimming?'

5   Assist students to again recall information about their classmates, including one piece of information about something they do not have or do not like.

Ⓟ This page may be photocopied for instructional use only. © Francesca Bierens   Speechmark Ⓢ

*Examples of 'who, what, where' questions*

❖ Who likes riding their bike?

❖ Who does **not** like swimming?

❖ Who has two brothers?

❖ Who does **not** have a brother?

❖ What does Poppy like to do after school?

❖ What doesn't she like to do?

❖ Where does Penny go with her aunt?

❖ Where doesn't Bob go with his puppy?

Nonverbal responses: The student responds by pointing to the pictures or photos.

## The 'nots' of our topic study or field trip

1 Review all of the information presented throughout the topic study, for example, 'volcanoes'.

2 When the students demonstrate a consistent knowledge of the topic by answering all questions correctly, then introduce the negative concept; for example: 'Is lava cold?'; 'What comes out of the volcano?'; and 'What does **not** come out of the volcano?'

3 Use visual prompts such as photos to provide options in order to assist the students to respond correctly.

4 Using the large word list chart with the diagram relating to the field trip, for example, a visit to the zoo, review the students' knowledge of this study.

5 When the students demonstrate a consistent knowledge of the topic by answering all questions correctly then introduce the negative concept; for example: 'What did we see at the zoo?'; 'What **didn't** we see?'; 'Who fed the giraffes?'; and 'Who did **not** feed the giraffes?' Add these phrases to the word list.

6 Return the word list to the wall so that it continues to be a reference for the students throughout the course of that study.

*Examples of 'who, what, where' questions*

❖ Who (fed the lion cubs)?

❖ Who did **not** (feed the lion cubs)?

❖ What animals did we see?

❖ What animals **didn't** we see?

❖ What happens to (the lava)?

❖ What does **not** happen to (the lava)?

❖ Where do the volcanic rocks come from?

❖ Where **don't** the volcanic rocks come from?

Nonverbal responses: The student responds by pointing to the photos.

Ⓟ This page may be photocopied for instructional use only. © Francesca Bierens Speechmark

# Chapter 7
# When we need time

| | |
|---|---|
| **What is time?** | **Time** is a concept of duration, moving from the past to the present and into the future. |
| **Prerequisites:** | • The Preverbal Skills of Language<br>• Not dependent on visual information<br>• Be able to speak in sentences of three or more words. |

## Important points to remember when teaching 'the concept of time'

• The concept of time is a very difficult and confusing concept, however, we use 'time-related' words constantly. What is important is that the students gain some understanding of the meaning, importance and relevance of these words to them.

• Knowledge and the accurate use of the concept of time impacts on the students' ability to use the correct verb tense and is important for comprehension, for example, questioning and understanding if someone is going to go on holiday in the future or has been on holiday in the past.

• A student is often able to answer the question 'What day ...?' but is unable to answer a 'when' question. So use both questions when asking the question; for example: 'When – what day – are we going on our field trip?' Including both methods of asking the 'time' question helps to assist the students' comprehension.

## Activities – When we need time

**When we do things in our classroom**
1   Make up a large weekly timetable and a large daily timetable.
2   Name the days of the week using the weekly timetable as a visual to assist.
3   Go through the large weekly timetable naming the days of the week with the students and modelling the activities that occur throughout the week for the students, for example, swimming on Monday, art on Tuesday and dancing on Thursday.
4   Have photos or pictures of the activities that occur on each day.
5   Introduce the concepts of 'today', 'tomorrow' and 'yesterday'.

Ⓟ This page may be photocopied for instructional use only. © Francesca Bierens  Speechmark Ⓢ

6   Give the students a blank piece of paper and have the students draw the appropriate activity when you identify the day; for example, 'What do we do on Wednesdays?' and 'What do we do on Thursdays?'

7   Discuss the negative; for example: 'What don't we do on a Saturday?'

8   Go through the daily timetable.

9   Focus on the activities to be carried out that day.

10  Introduce the concepts 'before' and 'after', for example, 'before morning tea' and 'after lunch'.

11  Play the 'wh' question cube activity using the calendars and drawings as prompts to assist the students with their verbal responses.

*Examples of 'who, what, where, when' questions*

❖  Who comes to our class on a Tuesday?

❖  What do we do on Tuesdays?

❖  Where do we go on a Friday?

❖  When do we do art? (What day do we do art?)

❖  When do we do reading?

Nonverbal responses: The student responds to the questions asked by pointing to or indicating the response using a chart, pictures or photo.

**When things happen in the year – months of the year**

• Use a 'calendar year' wall chart, that is, January to December, so that all the months of the year are visible at once.

• Go through the months of the year, reciting and clapping the syllables in each month.

• If possible have the months in different colours so that the students have some idea as to the length of each month.

• Identify the month you are currently in.

• Talk about special times of the year, for example, birthdays, Christmas, school holidays and special class and school events.

• Using visual prompts such as pictures, symbols or stickers, identify the months of the year when these special times occur.

• Identify the months when special events are due to take place and months when nothing is planned.

• Play the 'wh' question cube activity using the pictures on the calendar as prompts for the students to point to and to assist with their verbal responses.

*Examples of 'who, what, where, when' questions*

❖  Who has a birthday in May?

❖  Where is the class going in (June)?

❖  What month are we in now?

❖  What month has the most birthdays?

❖  What month doesn't have birthdays?

Ⓟ This page may be photocopied for instructional use only. © Francesca Bierens

❖ When is (insert name or profession) visiting our class?
❖ When is Christmas? What month is it in?
❖ When is Poppy's birthday?
❖ When are we going on the next field trip?

Nonverbal responses: The student responds to the questions asked by pointing to or indicating the response using a chart, calendar, pictures or photo.

**When are the seasons**
- Introduce the four seasons to the students using pictures to characterise the different seasons.
- Focus on one season at a time.
- Make up a wall chart and have the students draw pictures to describe the season, for example, summer – flowers, sun.
- Assist them to think of words to describe that season and write these words on the wall chart. Use books, photos or pictures as prompts to assist the students with their responses.
- Encourage the students to use as many of the concepts as possible; for example: winter – nouns and verbs: 'I **wear** my **coat** and **scarf** and **gloves**'; adjectives: 'I wear my **big warm** coat', 'Winter is **cold** and **wet** and **dark**'; negatives: 'We **can't play** outside'.
- Have a calendar year wall chart and mark in the months of each season. Show the students how the seasons span the months.
- Play the 'wh' question cube activity using the pictures or photos on the calendar as prompts for the students to point to and to assist with their verbal responses.

*Examples of 'who, what, where, when' questions*
❖ What season are we in now?
❖ When is summer?
❖ When is spring?
❖ When is it hot?
❖ When do we see the baby animals?
❖ When is it really cold?
❖ When do the leaves change colour?
❖ When do the daffodils come out?

Nonverbal responses: The student responds to the questions asked by pointing to or indicating the response using a chart, calendar, pictures or photo.

**When do we wear things?**
- From your category of clothes (see the 'Verb' activity: 'What we do with everyday things (categories)') go through the selection of pictures and identify all the pieces of clothing.
- Once the students are able to consistently identify all the things you can wear, have them put the clothes into the different categories of 'when you would wear these clothes'. Include, for

Ⓟ This page may be photocopied for instructional use only. © Francesca Bierens

example, discussion of wearing school uniforms at school, 'best' clothes at church services and 'casual' clothing while playing in the garden.

- Have the students take turns to name an item of clothing either from the selection of pictures or from their own recall and identify when they would or would not wear it.

- Encourage the students to use as many concepts as possible; for example: 'I wear my big woolly coat in winter. I don't wear it in the summer' and 'The blue dress is my best dress; I don't wear that to play at the play park'.

- On the board, put the pictures of the clothes, the students' drawings of the items of clothing and the names of the different clothes so that this information can be used later to assist the students' recall.

- Play the 'wh' question cube activity. Have the pictures of clothing, drawings of items of clothing or written words in categories on the board so that the students can use these to point to and to assist with their verbal responses.

*Examples of 'who, what, where, when' questions*

❖ When do we wear sandals?

❖ When do we wear woolly gloves?

❖ When don't we wear shorts?

❖ When don't we wear a scarf?

❖ What should you wear when it is cold and windy?

❖ What do you wear for a special occasion?

❖ What don't you wear in winter?

❖ When can you wear your bathing costume?

Nonverbal responses: The student responds to the questions asked by pointing to or indicating the response using a chart, calendar, pictures or photo.

**When people in stories do things**

- *Tell* a story or read a story to the students.

- Have a 'calendar', 'days of the week chart' or 'time chart' to provide prompts for the students as the story makes mention of specific months, days or times.

- Focus on just one concept at a time, for example, months, or days of the week.

- When the story mentions a time concept, for example, days of the week, then circle the appropriate chart or put a sticker or symbol on the day to indicate what happened; for example: 'On Monday, Sue went to see her grandfather and then on Tuesday she went with her mother to the zoo.'

- Play the 'wh' question cube activity using the charts as prompts for the students to point to and to assist with their verbal responses.

*Examples of 'who, what, where, when' questions*

❖ What did he do on (Monday)?

℗ This page may be photocopied for instructional use only. © Francesca Bierens **Speechmark**

❖ Where did he go on (Sunday)?

❖ When did (name) go to the (location)?

❖ When didn't (name) go to the (location)?

Nonverbal responses: The student responds to the questions asked by pointing to or indicating the response using a chart, pictures or photo.

**When we do things at home**
- Make up a large weekly timetable and daily timetable.
- Name the days of the week using the weekly timetable as a visual to assist.
- Have the students take turns to share what activities they take part in during the week or weekends.
- Initially focusing on the days of the week, use visual prompts such as pictures, symbols or stickers to identify the day that the students' activities occur, for example, Tuesday is Bob's day for swimming and Thursday is Poppy's day for horse riding.
- Go through the days of the week with the students and model the activities that occur throughout the week for the students.
- When the students demonstrate an understanding of this concept by responding appropriately, provide them with their own weekly timetable with the days of the weeks marked and have them draw their own activities on the appropriate day.
- Play the 'wh' question cube activity using the calendars and drawings as prompts to assist the students with their verbal responses.

*Examples of 'who, what, where, when' questions*

❖ Who doesn't go anywhere on Mondays?

❖ What day is it today?

❖ What does Penny do on Fridays?

❖ Where does your teacher go on Saturdays?

❖ When does Bob go swimming?

❖ When does Poppy go horse riding?

Nonverbal responses: The student responds to the questions asked by pointing to or indicating the response using a chart, pictures or photo.

**When places in the community are open**
- Make up a calendar week with hourly times written in for each day.
- Have pictures of various places in the community and people at work in those locations, for example, a librarian at the library and a doctor at the surgery. (See the relevant 'Noun' and 'Verb' activities: 'Names of people in our community', 'What we can do at fun places in our community' and 'What people in our community do'.)

Ⓟ This page may be photocopied for instructional use only. © Francesca Bierens **Speechmark** Ⓢ

- Go through these pictures with the students and review their knowledge of the person, place and profession (see 'Noun' and 'Verb' activities, 'Names of people in our community' and 'What people in our community do').
- If practical, visit these places in the community and have the students look at the hours that they are open and what time they close. As an alternative, this can be a telephone activity where the students have to look up the telephone number of a business and ring them to ask when they open and close'.
- Mark the day(s) of the week that each business is open and their hours of work, for example, Saturday market – Saturday, 0800 to 1230.
- Play the 'wh' question cube activity using the pictures or photos on the calendar as prompts for the students to point to and to assist with their verbal responses.

*Examples of 'who, what, where, when' questions*
- ❖ What day is it today? Is the bookshop open today?
- ❖ When is the swimming pool open?
- ❖ When is the library closed?

Nonverbal responses: The student responds to the questions asked by pointing to or indicating the response using a chart, pictures or photo.

**When things happen on our field trips or during our topic studies**
- Review all the factual information presented throughout the topic study or field trip. When the students demonstrate a consistent knowledge of the topic by answering all questions correctly then introduce the concept of time.
- Make up the weekly or monthly timetable in order to assist the students to understand the 'time' concept.
- Focus on one concept at a time, for example, days of the week.
- Name the days of the week using the weekly timetable and place the relevant information on the appropriate day; for example: 'We visited the volcano on Wednesday' or 'We went to the zoo on Friday'.
- Review this information when it has been charted on the timetable or calendar.
- Play the 'wh' question cube activity using the calendar or timetable as a prompt for the students to assist with their verbal responses.

*Examples of 'who, what, where, when' questions*
- ❖ What day is it today?
- ❖ What did we do on Wednesday?
- ❖ When did we go to the (place)?
- ❖ When did (name) visit us to talk to us about volcanoes?
- ❖ When didn't we go to the zoo?

Nonverbal responses: The student responds to the questions asked by pointing to or indicating the response using a chart, pictures or photo.

 This page may be photocopied for instructional use only. © Francesca Bierens **Speechmark**

# Chapter 8
# Why the cause must have an effect

| | |
|---|---|
| **What is cause and effect?** | **Cause and effect** is to cause something to happen as the result of an initial action. |
| **Prerequisites:** | <ul><li>The Preverbal Skills of Language</li><li>Not dependent on visual information</li><li>Be able to speak in sentences of three or more words.</li></ul> |

## Important points to remember when teaching 'cause and effect'

- 'Cause and effect' is the concept that teaches students that everything has a consequence, from the simple action to the more complex behaviours.

- 'Cause and effect' is the beginning of problem solving. It therefore requires students to retain previous knowledge and experience in order for them to use this information to work through and find possible solutions to problems presented.

- **Examples of 'wh' questions – nonverbal responses.** Giving a nonverbal response to a 'why' question can be very difficult. Nonverbal responses to 'why' questions can usually be given by gesture, facial expression, miming, signing, indicating 'yes' or 'no' (by nodding or shaking their head or pointing to 'yes' or 'no' symbols) or pointing to an associated picture or object in response to a simple question; for example: 'Why was Toby excited?' Student points to the picture of a puppy. 'Why is she putting on a coat?' The student points to the picture of rain.

- For students who can only give a nonverbal response:
  - ❖ Provide pictures, photos or any other appropriate visuals, such as charts, calendars or objects for the students to point to.
  - ❖ Provide objects, toys or puppets for the students to use in order to demonstrate the response, when appropriate.
  - ❖ Provide answers to more complex questions one at a time to allow the student to give a 'yes' or 'no' response; for example: 'Why was she worried? Was it because her car was broken?' Wait for the student to indicate a 'no' response. 'Was it because she had lost her shoes?' Wait for the student to indicate a 'no' response. 'Was it because Toby was lost?' Wait for the student to indicate a 'yes' response.

- Avoid asking the more complex 'why' questions where a nonverbal response cannot easily be provided.

Ⓟ This page may be photocopied for instructional use only. © Francesca Bierens Speechmark Ⓢ

## Activities – Why the cause must have an effect

**Why do we do things … because …**

1   Present the students with a selection of simple action pictures or photos from previous activities (see the appropriate 'Verb' activities: 'What we all do in our classroom' and 'What we do in our house') and review the students' knowledge and recall of what the people are doing, for example, drinking, eating, sleeping or putting on a coat.

2   Once the students are able to consistently identify the appropriate action, for example, 'eating', then introduce the concept of cause and effect, modelling the response to each question; for example: 'That's right, the girl is eating. Why is the girl eating? She is eating because she is … **hungry**.'

3   Repeat the question, using gesture to assist the students to respond correctly.

4   Repeat the full statement in a confirming manner; for example: 'The girl is eating because she is hungry.'

5   Repeat this procedure using a small number of pictures or photos if necessary; for example:
    'Why is the boy drinking? He is drinking because he is … thirsty.'
    'Why is the girl sleeping? She is sleeping because she is … tired.'
    'Why is she putting on a coat? She is putting on a coat because she is … cold.'

6   Encourage the students to contribute an action and a reason why they do these things. Use the opportunity to include other concepts; for example: 'I ride my brother's bike because mine is too small.'

*Examples of 'who, what, where, when, why' questions*

❖ What is the girl doing?

❖ When is Poppy's mother's birthday?

❖ Why is Poppy drawing a picture?

❖ Why is Bob putting on a pair of boots?

Nonverbal responses: The student responds to the questions asked by pointing to or indicating the response using a chart, pictures or photo.

**Why do we do things in the classroom and school … because …**

• Read through the class rules, reminding the students of what they need to remember and then focus on just two or three of the rules.

• Read one rule at a time; for example: Rule 1: 'We must put things away where they belong.' Then, in the next column, present the students with two or three reasons why this rule is important, using pictures or photos to assist them with their response.

• Have two true statements and one incorrect; for example: Reason 1: 'Because the teacher says so', Reason 2: 'Because it keeps the classroom tidy and safe' and Reason 3: 'Because then we can find things when we need them and they don't get lost'.

 This page may be photocopied for instructional use only. © Francesca Bierens **Speechmark**

- Assist the students to look at all of the reasons and then decide on the best reason or reasons for the rule.
- When they have decided on the best reason(s) for the rule then present the full question to them, that is, 'So, why must we put things away where they belong?' If necessary, either provide prompts in order to assist the students to respond correctly or model the initial response for the students to repeat; for example: 'Because then they don't get lost.'
- Finally, point to the class rules and repeat the full statement in a confirming manner; for example: 'Why must we put things away where they belong? Because then they don't get lost.'

*Examples of 'who, what, where, when, why' questions*

- ❖ Who has to clean the tables this week?
- ❖ Where are the scissors kept?
- ❖ Why do we have class rules?
- ❖ Why do we have to be careful with scissors?
- ❖ When do we have to wear a hat?
- ❖ What is the rule we have to remember when we go on a trip?

Nonverbal responses: The student responds by pointing to the photos or pictures.

## Why we have these people in our community ... because ...

- Review the students' knowledge of the various people in the community and their jobs, for example, the fire fighter, the police officer, the librarian, the doctor, the dentist and the paediatrician and the specialist (if appropriate for any students in your class). (See the relevant 'Noun' and 'Verb' activities: 'Names of people in our community' and 'What people in our community do'.)
- When the students are able to recall this information accurately, introduce the 'cause-and-effect' concept, modelling the response to each question; for example; 'That's right, Dr Tooth is the dentist. Why do we go to the dentist? Because the dentist helps to keep our teeth clean and healthy.'
- Repeat the question, using gesture to assist the students to respond correctly.
- Repeat the full statement in a confirming manner; for example: 'We go to the dentist because the dentist helps to keep our teeth clean and healthy.'
- Using pictures or photos of the people in the community (See the relevant 'Noun' activity: 'Names of people in our community') as a prompt, encourage the students to choose someone and provide a reason for why they are important; for example: 'Mrs Reid is the librarian. She helps me find the information I need when I go to the library.'
- This is also an opportunity to include other concepts such as 'negatives'; for example, 'Do we visit Dr Wells to borrow a book? No. Do we visit Dr Wells to buy flowers? No. So why do we visit Dr Wells?' Delay your response in order to encourage the students to respond, but then repeat the full statement in a confirming manner.

Ⓟ This page may be photocopied for instructional use only. © Francesca Bierens Speechmark

*Examples of 'who, what, where, when, why' questions*

❖ Who helps to keep our teeth healthy?

❖ Who would you go to see if you were sick?

❖ What does Officer Good do?

❖ Where would you go to buy flowers?

❖ Why do we have fire fighters?

❖ Why would you go there?

❖ Why is that important?

Nonverbal responses: The student responds by pointing to the photos.

**Why do people and animals do things in stories ... because ...**

1   Read or *tell* a story using visual prompts such as finger puppets and toys.

2   After relating the story assist the students to recall the important information in the story, for example, who was in the story, where they went and what they did.

3   When the students are able to respond correctly to all questions asked, then introduce the 'cause-and-effect' concept; for example, ask: 'Why did Toby (do something)?'

4   Present the students with two or three reasons for why the character may have behaved in this manner. If necessary use pictures from the book to assist them with their response, or, if telling the story, demonstrate using the finger puppets or toys. Have one true statement as given in the book with the other reasons being obviously wrong.

5   Assist the students to look at all the reasons and then decide on the sole correct answer.

6   When the students have decided on the correct reason for the character's actions, present the full question to them, that is, 'So, why did Toby (do something)?' Then, if necessary, either provide prompts in order to assist the students to respond correctly or model the initial response for the students to repeat; for example, 'Because he ...'

7   Finally, repeat the full statement in a confirming manner; for example, 'Toby (did something) because he (had a particular reason).'

*Examples of 'who, what, where, when, why' questions*

❖ Who climbed up the tree?

❖ Who was very worried?

❖ What did Toby do?

❖ Where is Toby?

❖ Why did he do that?

❖ Why was she worried?

❖ Why was she very pleased to see Toby?

❖ Where was he hiding?

Nonverbal responses: The student responds by pointing to the toys or puppets.

Ⓟ This page may be photocopied for instructional use only. © Francesca Bierens **Speechmark**

## Why we do things at home ... because ...

1   Have the students take turns relating one or two routines or rules that exist for them at home; for example, 'I have to brush my teeth before bed.'

2   Make up a list of the rules on the board for all the students to see.

3   Focus on two or three of the rules or routines and, for each, present two or three options as to why this rule is important; for example, for 'I have to brush my teeth before bed': Reason 1: 'Because mum says so' and Reason 2: 'Because it makes my teeth clean and healthy'.

4   Assist the students to look at all the reasons and then decide on the best reason or reasons for the rule.

5   When they have decided on the best reason for the rule then present the full question to them; that is: 'So, why do you have to brush your teeth before bed?' Then, if necessary, either provide prompts in order to assist the students to respond correctly or model the initial response for the students to repeat; for example, 'Because it makes your teeth clean and healthy.'

6   Finally, point to the home rules and repeat the full statement in a confirming manner; for example: 'Why do you have to brush your teeth before bed? Because it keeps your teeth clean and healthy.'

*Examples of 'who, what, where, when, why' questions*

❖ Who has to brush their teeth before bed?

❖ Who has to walk the dog with Dad?

❖ What does Bob have to remember when playing with his baby brother?

❖ Where do you go walking with Dad and the dog?

❖ Why do you have to brush your teeth before bed?

❖ Why is the park a good place?

Nonverbal responses: The student responds by pointing to the photos.

## The 'why' and 'because' of our topic study or field trip

1   Review all of the information presented throughout the topic study so that the students are able to demonstrate a consistent knowledge of the topic.

2   Focus on the reasons for two or three of these facts.

3   Present one fact at a time; for example: 'Dormant volcanoes can erupt but extinct volcanoes cannot erupt.'

4   Then, in the next column, present the students with two or three reasons for this fact using pictures or photos to assist them with their response.

5   Have two true statements and one incorrect statement.

6   Assist the students to look at all the reasons and when they have decided on the best reason or reasons for the fact, then present the full question to them; that is: 'So, why can dormant volcanoes erupt but extinct volcanoes can't erupt?' Then, if necessary, either provide prompts in order to assist the students to respond correctly or model the initial response for

Ⓟ This page may be photocopied for instructional use only. © Francesca Bierens  Speechmark Ⓢ

the students to repeat; for example: 'Because dormant volcanoes are only asleep but extinct volcanoes are those believed to never erupt again.'

7   Finally, point to the topic fact and repeat the full statement in a confirming manner.

● Follow the same procedure for the field trip topic; for example: 'Why did we go to the zoo? Because … Reason 1: Our teacher made us; Reason 2: To study animals; or Reason 3: To study planets.'

*Examples of 'who, what, where, when, why' questions*
❖ What did you learn about volcanoes?
❖ What did you learn about the animals?
❖ Where can you find some volcanoes?
❖ Where was the tiger enclosure?
❖ Why didn't we walk?
❖ Why do volcanoes erupt?
❖ Why didn't we see the giraffes?
❖ Why was the lioness there?
❖ Why didn't we go to the zoo last week?
❖ When did we go to the zoo?

Nonverbal responses: The student responds to the questions asked by pointing to or indicating the response using pictures or photos.

## What would you do in this situation
● 'Cause and effect' is the beginning of problem solving. Assist students to begin to find solutions to problems by presenting them with simple situations and working through possible responses.

1   Present the students with a common situation, for example, 'finding a toy on the playground' and provide them with two or three options as to what they would do if they found themselves in this situation. Solutions could be, for example: Solution 1 – Keep the toy; Solution 2 – Take it to the school office; and Solution 3 – Give it to a teacher.
2   Assist the students to look at all the solutions and when they have decided on the best solution or solutions to that problem, then present the full situation to them. Either provide prompts in order to assist the students to respond correctly or model the response for the students to repeat; for example: 'Give it to a teacher.'
3   Finally, recall the problem and repeat the full statement in a confirming manner; for example: 'So, if you find something on the playground that is not yours, give it to your teacher.'
4   Do some role playing of the situation as appropriate to your class to assist the students to understand the situation.

Ⓟ This page may be photocopied for instructional use only. © Francesca Bierens **Speechmark** Ⓢ

- This is also an opportunity to include other concepts such as 'emotions' and 'negatives'; for example: Emotions: 'How do you think that person would feel when they lost their toy? How would you feel if you lost your toy?' Negatives: 'Why wouldn't you keep the toy?'

*Examples of 'who, what, where, when, why' questions*
- ❖ Who could you ask for help?
- ❖ What would you do if you were lost in the shopping centre?
- ❖ Where would you go?
- ❖ Why is that your favourite toy?

Nonverbal responses: The student responds to the questions asked by pointing to or indicating the response using pictures or photos.

**Why you would do this**
1 Recall the previous problem and the students' appropriate solution, for example, finding a toy on the playground and giving it to your teacher.
2 Then assist the students to provide two or three reasons for their decision; for example: 'Why is giving the toy to your teacher the best solution? Because … Reason 1: I don't like the toy; Reason 2: It can then be returned to the person who lost it'.
3 Assist the students to look at all the reasons and then decide on the best reason for their decision.
4 When the students have made their decision, present the full situation to them and model the statement in a confirming manner; for example, 'So, if you found something on the playground, you would give it to your teacher because then it could be returned to the person who owns it.'
5 Do some role playing of the situation as appropriate to your class to assist the students to understand the situation.

*Examples of 'who, what, where, when, why' questions*
- ❖ Who could help you decide what to do?
- ❖ What would you do if (something happened)?
- ❖ Why would you do that?
- ❖ Why wouldn't you (take a particular course of action)?

Nonverbal responses: The student responds to the questions asked by pointing to or indicating the response using pictures or photos.

This page may be photocopied for instructional use only. © Francesca Bierens  Speechmark

## Chapter 9

# How to remember the sequence in order

| What is sequencing and sequential memory? | **Sequencing** is an arrangement of things in a successive order. **Sequential memory** is the ability to retain and recall information in the appropriate sequence. |
| --- | --- |
| **Prerequisites:** | • The Preverbal Skills of Language<br>• Not dependent on visual information<br>• Be able to speak in sentences of three or more words. |

**Important points to remember when teaching 'sequential memory' skills**

• Sequencing impacts on all aspects of a student's life and learning, including the sequence of actions that they must carry out when they get up in the morning in order to get ready for school, the sequence of letters they need to know for reading and the sequence of ideas they have to form to communicate in class and in the playground. Sequencing in *all* forms is a skill that should receive a great deal of attention.

• Remember to use all the words that the student will require in order to respond correctly to questions or instructions, for example, 'first', 'before' and 'after'.

## Activities – How to remember the sequence in order

**How we do things in class**

1  Take photos of a daily routine such as getting ready for lunch (the images being, for example, putting books away and washing hands) or getting ready for home time (the images being, for example, packing up bags and sitting on the mat).

2  Using the visuals as prompts, talk about the sequence and assist the students to recall the sequence of tasks by placing the photos in the correct order.

3  Fold a large piece of paper into six sections and assist the students to draw a four- to six-step sequence of a daily routine. (This is not an art activity, so as long as the students know what they have drawn, that is all that matters.)

4  Get each student to tell you in their own words what happened at each step.

Ⓟ This page may be photocopied for instructional use only. © Francesca Bierens Speechmark Ⓢ

5   Write a short, simple sentence beneath each picture, using the student's own word(s) as the basis for your sentence; for example: 'Bag' would be fed back as, 'That's right, you hang up your bag'.

6   If a particular routine is a challenge for some of the students, put the picture sequence of the routine that they have drawn on the wall. When they arrive in the morning, go through the step-by-step sequence of events on the chart; for example: '1. Come into my classroom; 2. Hang up my school bag; 3. Get out a book or toy for free play; and 4. Go to circle time.' The student then carries out these tasks. When they have completed the tasks, review the chart. They should receive a sticker for each step that they have carried out independently.

•   Reduce the steps of this sequence as the student gradually gains independence.

*Examples of 'who, what, where, when, why, how' questions*
❖   What do we do after morning tea?
❖   What do we do before reading?
❖   What do we do first in the morning?
❖   What is the last thing we do at the end of school?
❖   Where do we go after lunch?
❖   How do we get ready for swimming?

Nonverbal responses: The student responds by pointing to the photos or places around the classroom.

**How we make things at school**

1   Take a series of six photos of the sequence of tasks required to complete an activity in class, for example, creating a model of a volcano or creating a model of a zoo.

2   After the activity is completed, show the photos to the students and assist them to recall the series of events as you put the photos into the correct sequence; for example: 'To make fruit salad, first we washed the fruit, and then we cut it up and then we put the pieces in a bowl, and then we mixed it all together.'

3   Once the photos are in the correct sequence, assist the students to recall the sequence of tasks, using the photos as prompts.

4   Once the students are able to recall the information correctly, turn one or two of the photos over so that they cannot be seen and assist the students to recall the sequence correctly without seeing all of the photographs. Eventually, turn all the photos over, so that the students need to recall the information without any visual prompts.

5   Put the photos in a sequence on the wall.

6   Later put the photographs in a photo album to be used as a 'sequence' activity when required.

Ⓟ This page may be photocopied for instructional use only. © Francesca Bierens  Speechmark Ⓢ

*Examples of 'who, what, where, when, why, how' questions*

❖ Who cut up the oranges?

❖ What did we do first?

❖ What did we do before we put the fruit in the bowl?

❖ What did we do after we washed the fruit?

❖ Why did we use (baking soda)?

❖ How did we make the fruit salad?

❖ How did we make the volcano?

❖ How did we make the elephant enclosure?

Nonverbal responses: The student responds by pointing to the photos or people.

## How we get to people, and places and things at school

1   Make up a little map of the school and use it to give directions to the students.

2   Have the students take turns to follow the directions given in order to take a message to the office or to another classroom. Draw lines on the map as you give the instruction in order to assist the students to follow the directions; for example: 'First, go out of our classroom door and turn left. Walk past three classrooms …'

3   Have the students then use the *directions drawn on* the map *as a prompt* to repeat the instruction given before carrying out the task. When they return, they must recall where they went in the correct sequence.

4   This activity can also be used to encourage students to initiate information. For example, ask one or two students to deliver a message to a familiar place, such as the office. They must then draw a line on the map to indicate the direction they would go in order to deliver a message. Model the directions as the student draws the line in order to help them to recall the directions; for example: 'Very good. Yes, you go past the library …'

*Examples of 'who, what, where, when, why, how' questions*

❖ What is beside the library?

❖ What is behind the hall?

❖ What is the best way to get to the …?

❖ Where is the front office?

❖ Where is the sick bay?

❖ Where is the principal's office?

❖ How do we get to the library?

Nonverbal responses: The student responds by pointing to the map.

Ⓟ This page may be photocopied for instructional use only. © Francesca Bierens  Speechmark

**How we go shopping at the supermarket**

1   Using the pictures from supermarket pamphlets, pictures or photos, have the students take turns selecting one or two things that they would like to buy at a supermarket. (See the relevant Noun activity: 'Name the things we buy when we go shopping'.) Put the remaining pictures of things you are *not* going to buy in a different column.

2   After making a list, assist the students to explain the sequence of events required to obtain these items. Draw the sequence as it is explained on a large piece of paper; for example: 'First we select a shopping trolley or basket, and then we walk through the supermarket and find the items on our list, and then we wait in the line and pay for our items.'

3   Cut the paper into individual steps and assist the students to put the pieces into the correct sequence as they recall the sequence of events.

4   The students then retell the sequence themselves using the sequence pictures as a prompt.

5   Turn the pictures over so that they cannot be seen and assist the students to recall the sequence without the visual prompts. Turn each picture over to assist as required. Include the concepts of **'first'**, **'next'**, and **'last'** in your sequences.

6   If possible make a visit to a supermarket and use the sequence drawn on the paper to recall the sequence of events that was carried out with the students.

*Examples of 'who, what, where, when, why, how' questions*

❖   Who wanted to buy chocolate?
❖   What did we do first?
❖   What three things did we do?
❖   What didn't we buy?
❖   Where did we go after buying the fruit?
❖   Why do we go to the supermarket?
❖   When did we go to the supermarket?
❖   How do we go shopping at the supermarket?

Nonverbal responses: The student responds by pointing to the pictures.

**How we do things at home**

1   Read a book or *tell* a story to the students about a child's morning or evening routine that explains the usual sequence of events that occurs at home in the morning.

2   Assist the students to explain what their sequence of events is at home; for example: 'First, I have my breakfast, and then I brush my teeth and then I have a wash.' As the students explain the sequence of events, draw the sequence on a large piece of paper or have a series of picture cards that you can place in the sequence that the students explain. Each student is likely to have a different routine, and some may have a different routine depending on which day of the week it is.

3   Using the visuals (that is, the drawing or the sequence cards) assist the students to draw a

This page may be photocopied for instructional use only. © Francesca Bierens

four- to six-step picture sequence of their morning routine. The students can then tell you what happened at each step, in their own words. You can then write a short, simple sentence beneath each picture, using the students' own words as the basis for the sentence; for example: to the student's response, 'Eat toast' the teacher's verbal response may be, 'You eat toast for breakfast – excellent' and the sentence written will be along the lines of, 'I eat toast for breakfast.' (If the student is able to write a basic phrase then that is even better.)

4    Cut the paper into individual steps and assist the students to put the pieces into the correct sequence as they retell the sequence.

5    Turn the pictures over so that they cannot be seen and assist the students to recall the sequence without the visual prompts. Turn each picture over to assist as required.

*Examples of 'who, what, where, when, why, how' questions*

❖ Who looks at their books before school?

❖ What do you do after washing your face?

❖ What does Bob do first in the morning?

❖ What do you do after breakfast?

❖ What do you have for breakfast?

❖ When do you brush your teeth?

❖ How do you get home from school?

❖ How do you get ready for school?

Nonverbal responses: The student responds by pointing to person or object or picture or by gesturing.

**How things happened to people and animals in the story**

1    Read the story to the students, using visuals, for example, puppets, toys or Fuzzy-Felts.

2    Retell the story focusing on the key details, using the visuals.

3    Fold a large piece of paper into six sections, with enough room for the students to draw a picture in each section.

4    Using the visuals as prompts, assist the students to draw a four- to six-step picture in the sequence of the story.

5    Have each student tell you in their own words what happened at each step.

6    Write a short, simple sentence beneath the picture, using the student's own words as the basis for your sentence; for example, if the student says, 'Boy swim' then you may say, 'That's right, the boy is swimming' and write, 'The boy is swimming.' (If the student can write a basic phrase then that is even better.)

7    Remember that this is not an art activity, so as long as the students themselves know what they have drawn, that is all that matters.

8    Cut the paper into individual steps and assist the students to put the pieces into the correct sequence as they retell the story. Include the concepts of **'first'**, **'next'**, and **'last'**.

Ⓟ This page may be photocopied for instructional use only. © Francesca Bierens Speechmark Ⓢ

9   The students then retell the story looking at the pictures. Turn the pictures over so that they cannot be seen and assist the students to recall the story without the visual prompts. Turn the pictures over to assist as required.

*Examples of 'who, what, where, when, why, how' questions*
❖  Who got lost?
❖  What happened first?
❖  What happened last?
❖  What happened at the end?
❖  What happened at the beginning of the story?
❖  Where did she find the dog?
❖  Why didn't the girl go to school?
❖  When did she go to the airport?
❖  How did the story end?
❖  How did she get to …?

Nonverbal responses: The student responds by pointing to the toys or puppets.

**How to give instructions to the other students**
1   Make a fun activity of having the students take turns to give instructions to one another regarding conducting a short sequence of events, for example, completing an obstacle course.
2   Assist each student to give a short three-step sequence of instructions to another student or to the rest of the class. Naturally assist the students to give instructions appropriate to the ability of the students; for example: 'Walk to the back of the classroom. Clap three times. Sit in the library corner.'
3   Once the student has told you what they want to say, it may be necessary for you to model the sequence for them in order to ensure that the other students clearly understand the instructions. Once they have given their sequence of instructions, repeat it back to the class in a confirming manner to ensure that all of the students have clearly heard and understood what is required.
4   Include the concepts of '**first**', '**next**' and '**last**' in your sequences.
5   Assist each student to have a turn at recalling the sequence of instructions that they have just carried out.

*Examples of 'who, what, where, when, why, how' questions*
❖  Who went first?
❖  Who went after you?
❖  Whose turn was it before you?
❖  What did you have to do first?
❖  What was the last thing you did?

This page may be photocopied for instructional use only. © Francesca Bierens

❖ Where did you go last?

❖ Where did you go after (you put the books on the shelf)?

❖ Why didn't Poppy clap three times? (for example, broken arm)

Nonverbal responses: The student responds by pointing to person or object or picture or by gesturing.

**The sequence of events in our topic studies or field trip**

1  When you have worked through the series of events with your topic (for example, 'volcanoes') make up a series of photographs or pictures that the students have drawn and have the students relate what happens as you put the drawings into the correct sequence of events on the board; for example: 'First, the volcano erupts, and then lava flows …'

2  Have students recall the complete sequence of events using the pictures as visual prompts. Then turn the pictures over so that they cannot be seen and assist the students to recall the events without the prompts.

3  Take a series of photographs during the field trip. Back in the classroom, put approximately six key photos up on the board. Have the students retell what they did as you put the photos into the correct sequence; for example: 'First, we all got in the van to go to the zoo. Next, we paid the entry fee. Then we visited the tigers. Then we …' Include the concepts of 'first', 'next' and 'last' in your sequences.

4  Have the students recall the complete sequence of events using the photos as visual prompts. Turn the photos over so that they cannot be seen, and help the students to recall the events without the prompts.

5  Put the photos in sequence on the wall and later put them in a photo album to be used as a 'sequence' activity when required.

*Examples of 'who, what, where, when, why, how' questions*

❖ Who drove the van?

❖ What did we do first?

❖ What happened after the volcano erupted?

❖ What happened first?

❖ What did we do last?

❖ When did we have lunch?

❖ Why did we go to the zoo?

❖ How did the volcano erupt?

❖ How did we get to the zoo?

Nonverbal responses: The student responds by pointing to or selecting the pictures or photos.

Ⓟ This page may be photocopied for instructional use only. © Francesca Bierens Speechmark

# Chapter 10
# Emotions put feelings into words

**What is an emotion?** An **emotion** is something that brings about an intense state of feeling.

**Prerequisites:**
- The Preverbal Skills of Language
- Not dependent on visual information.

## Important points to remember when teaching 'emotions'

- Simple emotions – for example, happiness, sadness and anger – can be introduced earlier, but the student needs to have acquired more complex language skills in order to fully understand and effectively express their emotions.

- Emotions can be a very difficult concept to teach. It is important for the students to be:
  - ❖ aware of the different emotions
  - ❖ able to recognise and identify the different emotions so that they can express themselves
  - ❖ able to know how to react appropriately to the different emotions that they may be feeling
  - ❖ aware that all people have emotions and thus that the feelings of others must be taken into consideration
  - ❖ aware that we can all feel different emotions about the same thing and that is all right.

## Activities – Emotions put feelings into words

**How we can feel**
1 Have a simple emotions chart of the basic facial expressions to show the students. Identify and talk about the different feelings.
2 Look at all of the different emotions on the chart, but just focus on the five basic emotions at this initial stage, that is, happiness, sadness, fear, anger and excitement (unless it is appropriate to focus on more).
3 Have students imitate the different facial expressions and identify the emotion.
4 Have the students draw their own facial expressions when you identify an emotion.

Ⓟ This page may be photocopied for instructional use only. © Francesca Bierens Speechmark Ⓢ

*Examples of 'who, what, where, when, why, how' questions*
❖ Who is happy?
❖ Who is sad?

• How do I feel? (Demonstrate an emotion. Have students take turns demonstrating an emotion.)
   ❖ How does Penny feel?
   ❖ How does Bob feel?

Nonverbal responses: The student responds by pointing to the picture, emotion chart or person.

**How people in our class feel**
1  Have a simple emotions chart or pictures, and focus on the five basic emotions at this initial stage, that is, happiness, sadness, fear, anger and excitement.
2  Use visuals (such as pictures) of situations – such as receiving a present or a favourite toy breaking – and ask the students to identify how they would feel in that situation.
3  Talk about the different emotions, and assist the students to identify what other situations make them happy, sad, angry, excited or scared.
4  Have the students draw the situations that make them happy, sad or excited. Explain and demonstrate how we all feel things differently; for example, some students love art but others don't like art. Talk also about how the same situation can make one student happy but another scared; for example, if someone brought a dog to school and some of the students loved dogs but others were afraid of them.
5  This can be included in the morning news time. Using the emotion cards or chart as a prompt, ask the students how they feel today and the reason. Make up your own wall chart of emotions.

*Examples of 'who, what, where, when, why, how' questions*
❖ Who is angry?
❖ Who is excited?
❖ What makes (Poppy) happy but (Penny) scared?
❖ What makes (Bob) excited?
❖ Why is (Penny) tired?
❖ How does your teacher feel when you are all working well together?
❖ How do you all feel when it is time for (music)?

Nonverbal responses: The student responds by pointing to the picture.

Ⓟ This page may be photocopied for instructional use only. © Francesca Bierens **Speechmark**

## How people in our school feel

1   Go through the simple emotions chart or cards briefly to remind the students of the different emotions. Gradually start including one or two of the other – more complex – emotions as appropriate to your class.

2   Talk with the students about how other people may feel in various situations and how their own behaviour can impact on other people's feelings.

3   Do some 'role playing' if appropriate, to assist students to 'experience' and understand a situation. For example:
    *How your teacher feels when:*
    Students are helpful and kind to one another.
    *How the librarian feels when:*
    Students lose books.
    *How the head teacher and caretaker feel when:*
    Students break things or leave a mess.

*Examples of 'who, what, where, when, why, how' questions*
❖ Who would be sad if no one was listening?
❖ What would make Miss (Keys) happy?
❖ What would make me excited?
❖ Why is Mrs (King ) disappointed?
❖ How would Mrs (Booker) feel if you…?
❖ How would I feel if …?
❖ How would Mrs (King) feel if …?

Nonverbal responses: The student responds by pointing to the emotion pictures or chart.

## What people and animals in stories feel when …

1   Go through the emotions chart or cards briefly to remind the students of the different emotions, incorporating one or two of the other – more complex – emotions as appropriate to your class.
2   Talk briefly about how other people may feel in various situations.
3   *Tell* or read a story to the students using puppets.
4   At appropriate parts of the story, demonstrate the emotion using your own facial expression and voice, and use the puppet to show the students how the character would be feeling.
5   At the end of the story, using the puppet and the emotion pictures or chart, talk about how the characters may have felt when, for example:
    a.  They were lost.
    b.  They discovered some treasure.
6   Give the students a situation from a story and have them draw how they would feel.

Ⓟ This page may be photocopied for instructional use only. © Francesca Bierens  Speechmark Ⓢ

*Examples of 'who, what, where, when, why, how' questions*
- ❖ Who was excited?
- ❖ What made (story character) scared?
- ❖ How did Poppy feel when …?
- ❖ How did (story character) feel when …?

Nonverbal responses: The student responds by pointing to the emotion cards.

**How I feel at home when …**

1   Go through the emotions chart or cards briefly to remind the students of the different emotions, incorporating one or two of the other more – complex emotions – as appropriate to your class.

2   Talk about the people at home and the things the students like to do at home. If you have photos of the students' families ( See the appropriate 'Noun' and 'Verb' activities: 'Name the people and things we have in our house' and 'What we do in our house'), these can be used to prompt responses.
   - • Have students talk about **How I feel at home when …**
   - • I play with my puppy or cat.
   - • my brother takes my toys.
   - • my friend is allowed to come over to play.
   - • Mum makes my favourite dinner.
   - • I have to clean my room.

3   Do some 'role playing' if appropriate, to assist students to 'experience' and understand a situation.

4   Give the students a situation that may occur at their home and have them draw how they would feel.

*Examples of 'who, what, where, when, why, how' questions*
- ❖ Who gets excited when …?
- ❖ Who is sad when …?
- ❖ What makes (Penny) happy and laugh?
- ❖ What makes (Penny) laugh?
- ❖ What makes (Poppy) sad?
- ❖ How does (Bob) feel when …?

Nonverbal responses: The student responds by pointing to the picture, photo or person.

Ⓟ This page may be photocopied for instructional use only. © Francesca Bierens  Speechmark

## How my family at home feel when …

1  Go through the simple emotions chart or cards briefly to remind the students of the different emotions. Gradually start including one or two of the other – more complex – emotions as appropriate to your class.

2  Talk about the people at home and the things the students like to do at home. If you have photos of the students' families (See the relevant 'Noun' and 'Verb' activities: 'Name the people and things we have in our house' and 'What we do in our house'), then these can be used to prompt responses.

3  Talk about how the other people at home may feel in various situations and how the student's behaviour can impact on other people's feelings.

4  Do some 'role playing' if appropriate, to assist students to 'experience' and understand a situation; for example:

*How my brother feels when:*
❖  I let him share my toys.

*How my grandmother feels when:*
❖  I find her glasses.

*How my cat or dog feels when:*
❖  I forget to feed her.


*Examples of 'who, what, where, when, why, how' questions*
❖  Who would be happy if you …?
❖  What would make your grandfather excited?
❖  What would make your Mum sad?
❖  How would your Dad feel if …?
❖  How would my dog feel if …?
❖  How would my sister feel if …?
❖  How would your aunt feel if you bought her a present?


Nonverbal responses: The student responds by pointing to the emotion pictures or chart.

## How people in 'pictures' and 'photos' are feeling

1  Go through the emotions chart or cards briefly to remind the students of the different emotions, incorporating more of the complex emotions as appropriate to your class.

2  Show the students pictures of people in books or photos demonstrating a range of emotions.

3  Go through each of these pictures individually and ask the students how they think the people may be feeling. Draw the students' attention to the facial expressions and hand positions.

4  Assist the students to give possible reasons for these emotions.

5  Use the emotions chart to help the students find the appropriate emotion to explain the expression.

Ⓟ This page may be photocopied for instructional use only. © Francesca Bierens  Speechmark Ⓢ

*Examples of 'who, what, where, when, why, how' questions*

❖ Who feels tired?
❖ Who feels worried?
❖ Why is that lady …?
❖ How does this girl feel?
❖ How does this man feel?

Nonverbal responses: The student responds by pointing to the emotion pictures or chart.

**How we felt during our topic study or field trip**

1 Go through the emotions chart or cards briefly to remind the students of the different emotions, incorporating more of the complex emotions as appropriate to your class.

2 Talk about the different situations experienced by the students during the topic study (for example, 'volcanoes') or field trip, for example, 'visit to the zoo'.

3 Help the students to recall how they felt in the different situations, such as looking at books about volcanoes, watching a movie of a volcano erupting or making a model of a volcano.

4 Add these words to the large word list related to the diagram on the chart. Explain and demonstrate how we all feel things differently, and how the same situation – for example, watching the movie of a volcano erupting – can make one student excited but another scared.

5 Return the word list to the wall so that it continues to be a reference for the students throughout the course of that topic study.

*Examples of 'who, what, where, when, why, how' questions*

❖ Who got excited when …?
❖ Who was happy when …?
❖ What made (Bob) worried?
❖ What made you scared?
❖ What did you enjoy most about volcanoes?
❖ What did you enjoy most about the zoo?
❖ How did you all feel when you watched the volcano erupt?
❖ How did Poppy feel when …?
❖ How do you think the lions felt when …?

Nonverbal responses: The student responds by pointing to the picture.

Ⓟ This page may be photocopied for instructional use only. © Francesca Bierens  Speechmark Ⓢ

# Chapter 11

# Asking questions to gain some answers

| | |
|---|---|
| **What is asking questions?** | **'Asking questions'** is the ability to seek information from another person. |
| **Prerequisites:** | • The Preverbal Skills of Language<br>• The Building Bricks of Language – an appropriate level of vocabulary and concepts required to ask the question and recall the information. |

## Important points to remember when teaching students to ask questions

- Asking a question requires the student to:
  - ❖ invert their statement; for example: 'Is it a book?' (statement, 'It is a book.')
  - ❖ use a question word; for example: 'Why?'
  - ❖ and/or include a question word and invert their statement; for example: 'What is it?'

- The students must be able to listen, understand and accurately recall the responses given to their question.

- Using visual prompts such as question cards (for 'what', 'who', 'where', 'why', 'when' and 'how') and modelling the question structure for the student and then with the student are extremely useful tools for teaching this skill.

## Activities – asking questions to gain some answers

**The students need to ask: 'Is it ...' questions**
*Activity: 'Proper noun, noun and verb' level*
Visuals required: for example, photos, pictures and objects

1   Choose four to six pictures from your pictures of classroom objects and the photos of the students and teacher in the class. Go through and name each of the pictures chosen with the students, for example, 'book', 'table', 'pencil', 'scissors', 'Poppy' and 'Toby'.

131

Ⓟ This page may be photocopied for instructional use only. © Francesca Bierens  Speechmark Ⓢ

2 Choose one picture from the pile that the students cannot see. Tell them that they have to ask an 'is it' question in order to find out what picture it is.

3 Model the initial question for them; for example: **'Is it the book?** No.' Put that picture down so that the students can see it. **'Is it Toby?** No.' Put that photo down so that the students can see it.

4 Ask each student in turn, allowing them initially to ask the question in their own way; for example: **'It is a** …' Then model and stress the correct question structure, that is, **'Is it …?'** before answering yes or no.

5 Repeat the student's question in a confirming manner so that all the students can hear; for example: **'Is it** a pencil? No' followed by, **'Is it** Poppy? Yes.'

6 As the students achieve success with this activity, then:
   ❖ Increase the number of pictures.
   ❖ Limit it to five questions each.

**The students need to ask: 'Who' questions**
*Activity: 'Proper noun and verb' level*
Visuals required: for example, photos, pictures and objects

1 Use the photos of each student in your class participating in a simple activity.

2 Choose a good-quality photo and model the question first, reminding the students of the importance of using the other student's name when asking them a question; for example: 'Bob, who is this?' while showing Bob a photo.

3 Have each student take turns choosing one clear photo and showing it to another student, asking, 'Who is this?' or 'Who is (verb)?'

4 Allow the student to ask their question in their own way, for example, 'Penny, who drawing?' and then model the correct question structure in a confirming manner, that is, **'Penny, who is drawing?'**

5 When the student has replied to the question, ask the first student to recall the response given to the question he asked; for example: **'Bob.'** Then repeat the response, modelling the correct sentence structure; for example: **'Bob** is drawing.'

6 Some prompts and repetitions may be required. As the students achieve success with this activity, reduce the frequency of modelling and repeating responses.

**The students need to ask: 'What' questions**
*Activity: 'Verb' level*
Visuals required: for example, photos, pictures and objects

1 Have photos of recent class events or activities.

2 Choose a good-quality photo and model the question first, reminding the students of the

Ⓟ This page may be photocopied for instructional use only. © Francesca Bierens Speechmark Ⓢ

importance of using the other student's name when asking them a question; for example: 'Toby, what are you doing (in this photo)?' as you show him the photo.

3 Listen to the student's answer and then repeat it to the class in order to model the desired response; for example: 'Toby is drawing the giraffe he saw at the zoo.'

4 Have each student take turns choosing one clear photo from a class photo book and show it to the relevant student who is in the photo, asking, 'What are you doing?'

5 Allow the student to ask their question, for example, 'What you do, Penny?' and then model the correct question structure in a confirming manner, that is, 'What are you doing, Penny?'

6 When the student has replied to the question, ask the first student to recall the response given to the question he asked; for example: 'Write story.' Then repeat it, modelling the correct sentence structure; for example: 'Penny is writing her story?'

7 Some prompts and repetitions may be required.

8 As the students achieve success with this activity, reduce the frequency of modelling and repeating responses.

**The students need to ask: 'Who' , 'what' questions**

*Activity: 'Adjectives' level*

Visuals required: for example, photos, pictures or objects

1 Gather photos of recent class events or activities.

2 Choose a good-quality photo and show it to the students. Model the question first, reminding the students of the importance of using the other student's name when asking them a question; for example: 'Tammy, who is wearing a red hat?'

3 Listen to the student's answer and then repeat it to the class in order to model the desired response; for example: 'That's right. Toby is wearing a red hat.'

4 Have each student take turns choosing one clear photo from a class photo book and showing it to another student, asking questions such as: 'What colour is Bob's T-shirt?' and 'Who is reading the *big* book?'

5 Allow the student to ask their question; for example: 'Poppy, who big book?' Then model the correct question structure in a confirming manner, that is, 'Poppy, who is reading the big book?'

6 When 'Poppy' has replied to the question, ask the student to recall her response to the question; for example: 'Bob.' Then repeat it, modelling the correct sentence structure; for example: 'That's right. Bob is reading the big book.'

7 Provide as much assistance with this activity as required. However, as the students achieve success, gradually reduce the frequency of modelling and repeating responses.

**The students need to ask: 'who' , 'what' ,'where' questions**

*Activity: 'Prepositions' level*

Visuals required: for example, photos, pictures and objects

This page may be photocopied for instructional use only. © Francesca Bierens  Speechmark

1   Gather photos of recent class events or activities.

2   Choose a clear photo and show it to the students. Model the question first, reminding the students of the importance of using the other student's name when asking them a question; for example: 'Toby, where is Penny?'

3   Listen to the student's answer and then repeat it to the class in order to model the desired response; for example: 'That's right, Penny is **in** the police car.'

4   Have each student take turns choosing one clear photo from a class photo book and showing it to another student, asking questions such as: 'Where is …?', 'Who is beside the …?' and 'What is under the …?'

5   Allow the student to ask their question; for example: 'Tammy, who 'side Bob?' Then model the correct question structure in a confirming manner, that is, '**Tammy, who is beside Bob**?'

6   When 'Tammy' has replied to the question, then ask the student to recall the response given; for example: '**Poppy**.' Then repeat it, modelling the correct sentence structure; for example: '**Poppy** is **beside** Bob.'

7   Provide as much assistance with this activity as required. However, as the students achieve success, gradually reduce the frequency of modelling and repeating responses.

**The students need to ask: 'who' , 'what' 'where' questions**

*Activity: 'Negatives' level*

Visuals required: for example, photos, pictures and objects

1   Have photos of recent class events or activities.

2   Choose a clear photo and show it to the students. Model the question first, reminding the students of the importance of using the other student's name when asking them a question; for example: 'Bob, who is **not** in the photo?' Listen to the student's answer and then repeat it to the class in order to model the desired response; for example: 'That's right, **Penny** is **not** in the photo.'

3   Have each student take turns choosing one clear photo from a class photo book and showing it to another student, asking questions such as: 'Who is not …?', 'What is not in the …?' and 'Where didn't we …?'

4   Allow the student to ask their question; for example: 'Bob, where we not go?' Then model the correct question structure in a confirming manner, that is, 'Bob, where didn't we go?' It may be necessary to prompt the reply; for example: 'We did not go to the …?'

5   When 'Bob' has replied to the question, ask the student to recall the response given; for example: 'Slide.' Then repeat it, modelling the correct sentence structure; for example: 'That's right. We did **not** go to the **slides**, at the playground.'

6   Provide as much assistance with this activity as required. However, as the students achieve success, gradually reduce the frequency of modelling and repeating responses.

℗ This page may be photocopied for instructional use only. © Francesca Bierens   Speechmark ⑤

**The students need to ask : 'who' , 'what' 'where' 'when' questions**

*Activity: 'Time' level*

1  After talking about class timetables, model the question first, reminding the students of the importance of using the other student's name when asking them a question; for example: 'Bob, when, what day, do we do cooking?' Listen to the student's answer and then repeat it to the class in order to model the desired response; for example: 'That's right. We do cooking on a Friday.'

2  Have each student take turns asking a question of another student. Possible questions: '**Who** visits our class on a …?', '**What** do we do after lunch?', '**Where** do we go on a Thursday?' and '**When** do we go to …?'

3  Allow the student to ask their question; for example: 'Bob, when go assembly?' Then model the correct question structure in a confirming manner, that is, 'Bob, when do we go to assembly?'

4  The students only need to ask one question of another student. Prompts may be required.

5  When 'Bob' has replied to the question, have the student who asked the question recall the response given; for example: 'Monday.' Then repeat it, modelling the correct sentence structure; for example: 'That's right. We go to assembly on Monday.'

6  Provide as much assistance with this activity as required. However, as the students achieve success, gradually reduce the frequency of modelling and repeating responses.

**The students need to ask: 'why' questions**

*Activity: 'Cause and effect' level*

1  After talking about recent class activities or home events, model the question first, reminding the students of the importance of using the other student's name when asking them a question; for example, 'Bob, why did you go to your aunt's house during the weekend?' Listen to the student's answer and then repeat it to the class in order to model the desired response; for example: 'Because it was her birthday.'

2  Have each student take turns asking a 'Why' question of another student. Allow the student to ask their question; for example: 'Toby, why away?' Then model the correct question structure in a confirming manner, that is, 'Toby, why were you away (from school) yesterday?' Prompts may be required.

3  When 'Toby' has replied to the question, have the student who asked the question recall the response given; for example, 'Sick.' Repeat the answer to the class, modelling the correct sentence structure; for example: 'Toby was away yesterday because he was sick.'

4  Provide as much assistance with this activity as required. However, as the students achieve success, gradually reduce the frequency of modelling and repeating responses.

This page may be photocopied for instructional use only. © Francesca Bierens  Speechmark

**The students need to ask: 'How' questions**

*Activity: 'Sequencing' level*

1  After talking about recent class activities or home events, model the question first, reminding the students of the importance of using the other student's name when asking them a question; for example: 'Tammy, how did we make the sandwich?' Listen to the student's answer and then repeat it to the class in order to model the desired response.

2  Have each student take turns asking a 'How' question of another student. Prompts may be required but as much as possible allow the student to ask their question in their own way; for example: 'Poppy, how you get school?' Then model the correct question structure in a confirming manner, that is, 'Poppy, how do you get to school?'

3  When 'Poppy' has replied to the question, have the student who asked the question recall the response given; for example: 'Walk, bus, school.' Then repeat it, modelling the correct sentence structure; for example: 'Poppy walks to the bus stop, and then she gets on the school bus that takes her to school.'

4  Provide as much assistance with this activity as required. However, as the students achieve success, gradually reduce the frequency of modelling and repeating responses.

**The students need to ask: 'who' , 'what', 'when' and 'how' questions**

*Activity: 'Emotions' level*

1  After talking about recent class activities or home events, model one or two questions first, reminding the students of the importance of using the other student's name; for example: 'Penny, how did you feel when we went to see the snakes at the zoo?' Listen to the student's answer and then repeat it to the class in order to model the desired response; for example: 'You felt scared.'

2  Have each student take turns asking a question of another student about how they felt. Possible questions could be: 'What did you like best at the …?', 'Who didn't like the …?', and 'When (something happened) … how did you feel?'

3  Prompts may be required but as much as possible allow the student to ask their question in their own way; for example: 'Bob, how you feel, firemen?' Then model the correct question structure in a confirming manner, that is, 'Bob, how did you feel when the firefighters visited the school?'

4  When 'Bob' has replied to the question, have the student who asked the question recall the response given; for example: ''cited.' Repeat the answer to the class, modelling the correct sentence structure; for example: 'Bob felt excited when the firefighters visited the school.'

5  Provide as much assistance with this activity as required. However, as the students achieve success, gradually reduce the frequency of modelling and repeating responses.

Ⓟ This page may be photocopied for instructional use only. © Francesca Bierens    Speechmark Ⓢ

# Chapter 12

# Making 'The Building Bricks of Language' activity box

1. Asking questions to gain some answers

2. Emotions put feelings into words

3. How to remember the sequence in order

4. Why the cause must have an effect

5. When we need time

6. Making sure negatives are not left out

7. Putting prepositions in their place

8. Add adjectives to put colour into words

9. Putting verbs into action

10. Putting a name to the noun

## Box Two

### ACTIVITIES TO TEACH THE BUILDING BRICKS OF LANGUAGE
The words required for communication to develop

P This page may be photocopied for instructional use only. © Francesca Bierens. Speechmark S

Creating a 'Building Bricks of Language' activity box gives you immediate access to the skills and activities required. It also makes it easier for the students to access the activity cards when necessary.

## Procedure

1   Buy or make a box that can fit a standard photo-sized card.

2   Make up the 'The Building Bricks of Language' headings and use as dividers in the box.

3   Colour-code the skill headings for quick and easy recognition by both teacher and students.

4   Copy and paste each activity on to a card and place it in the appropriate skill section.

5   Place the 'Building Bricks of Language' activity box in a very visible and readily accessible location in the classroom.

This page may be photocopied for instructional use only. © Francesca Bierens  Speechmark

# Chapter 13

# Making 'The Building Bricks of Language' activity cubes

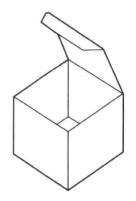

## Three 'wh' questions cubes – for encouraging students to respond to or ask questions

The student or teacher rolls the dice and the student must respond by pointing or by verbally answering the appropriate question related to the visual information presented.

- One cube: Three questions only on the cube – 'who', 'what' ,'where'.

  - ❖ Questions from 'proper noun', 'noun', 'verb', 'adjectives', 'prepositions' and 'negatives' levels only.

- Use this cube initially for students to answer questions only. Later, as their skills develop, use the cube for students to both answer and ask the questions, as appropriate to the level of the student.

Ⓟ This page may be photocopied for instructional use only. © Francesca Bierens  Speechmark Ⓢ

## 'The Building Bricks of Language' activity cubes

**Cube template**

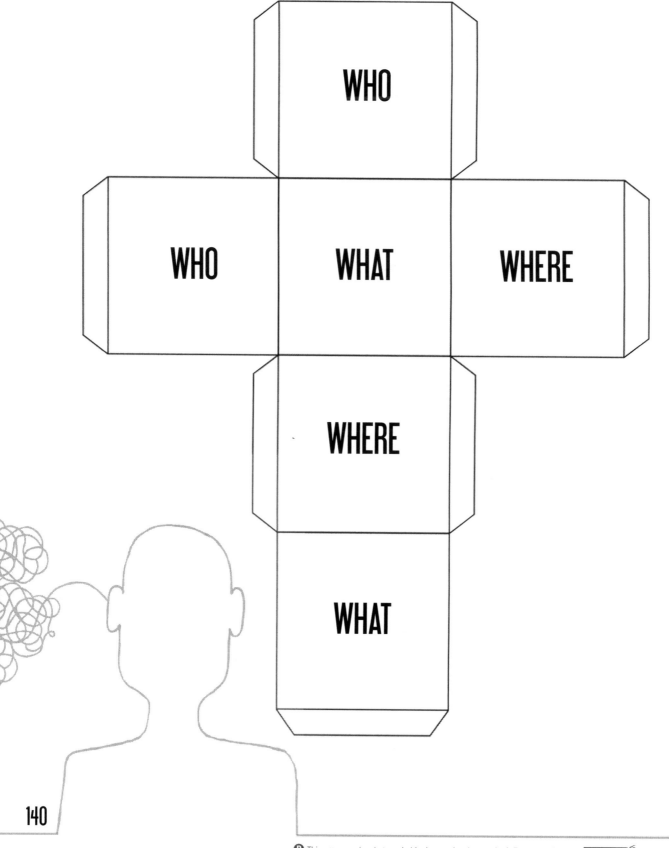

This page may be photocopied for instructional use only. © Francesca Bierens Speechmark

# 'The Building Bricks of Language' activity cubes

- Two cubes: All six questions on the cube – 'who', 'what' ,'where', 'when', 'why' and 'how'.
  - ❖ Questions from all levels of 'The Building Bricks of Language'.
- One cube for students to **answer** the question.

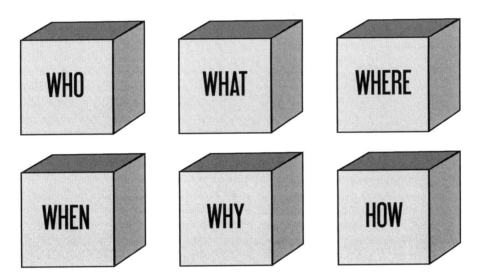

**One cube for students to *answer* questions.**

# 'The Building Bricks of Language' activity cubes

- Two cubes: All six questions on the cube – 'who', 'what' ,'where', 'when', 'why' and 'how'.
  - ❖ Questions from all levels of 'The Building Bricks of Language'.
- One cube for students to **ask** the question.

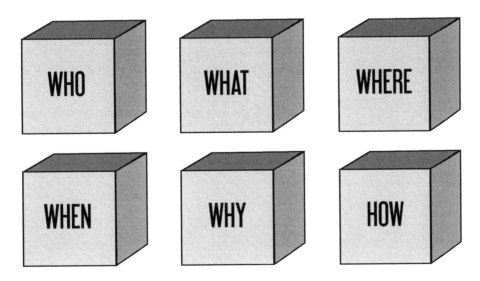

**One cube for students to *ask* questions.**

ⓟ This page may be photocopied for instructional use only. © Francesca Bierens Speechmark Ⓢ

## 'The Building Bricks of Language' activity cubes

**Cube templates**

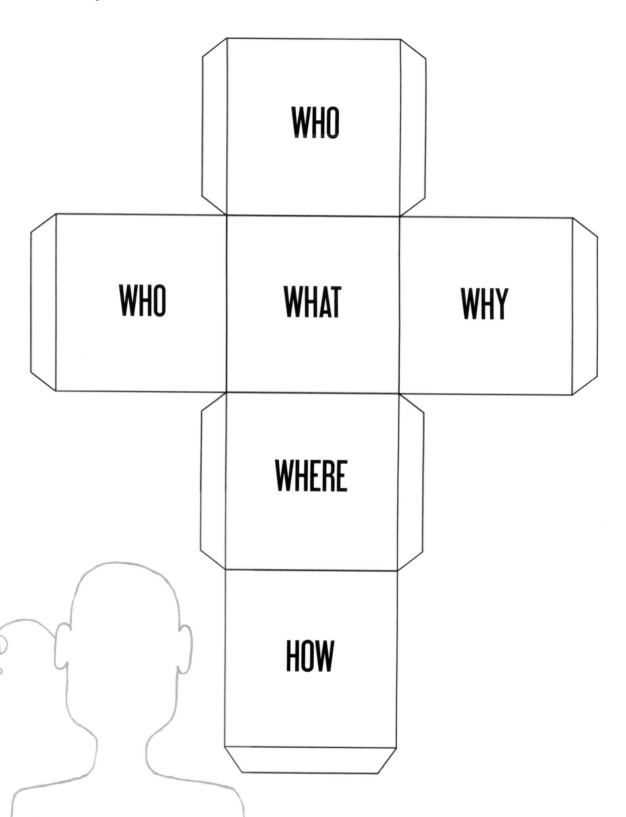

One cube for students to *answer* questions.

℗ This page may be photocopied for instructional use only. © Francesca Bierens  Speechmark

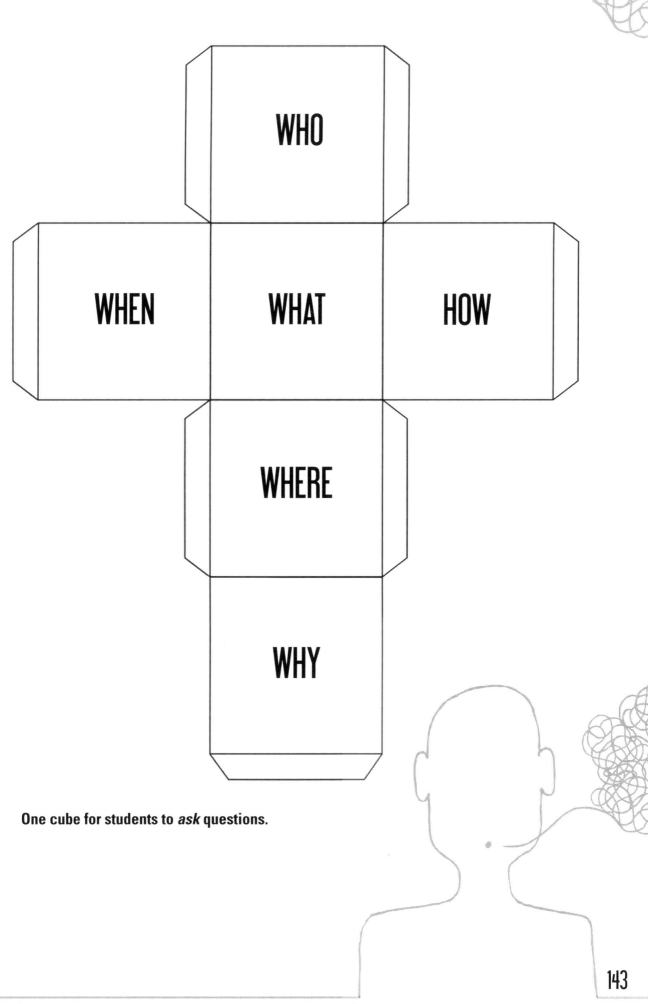

**One cube for students to *ask* questions.**

This page may be photocopied for instructional use only. © Francesca Bierens Speechmark

# Part 4

## Assisting students with language delays in the classroom to acquire 'The Skills of Conversation'

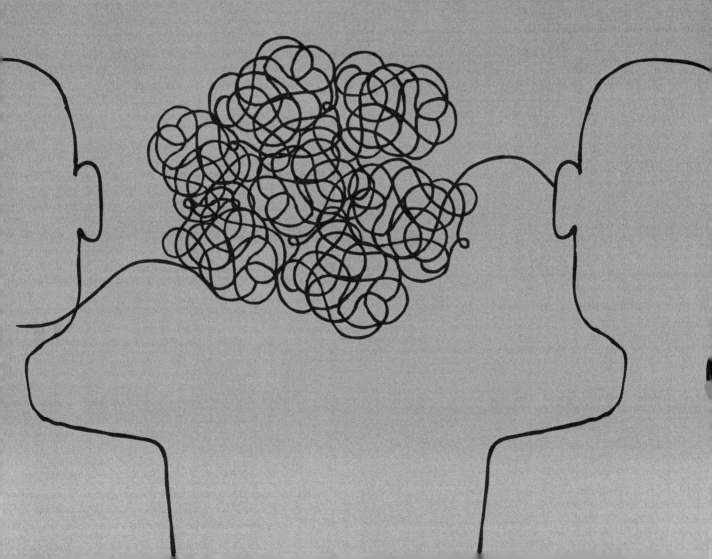

# Introduction

**The Skills of Conversation** are extremely important as they determine how successfully we interact with others. They are necessary at the early developmental level in order for children to establish friendships and maintain play with other children. They are also required at the highest level of adult interaction, personally and professionally.

In order for a student to acquire even the basic skills of conversation, they must first have acquired the preverbal skills of language and must have developed adequate knowledge and use of verbal language. To acquire the more complex skills of conversation (that is, asking and answering interactive questions), the student must develop excellent and immediate comprehension and effective verbal language using longer, more complex sentences (see 'Language development at a glance' – Figure 2: 'Verbal language development summary').

This programme focuses on the pragmatic skills or social skills of language that impact most on school-aged students.

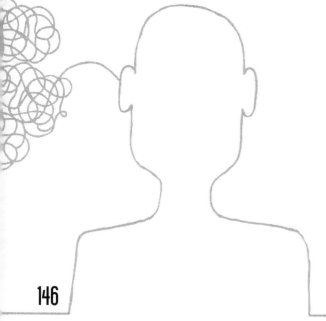

P This page may be photocopied for instructional use only. © Francesca Bierens  Speechmark

# Chapter 1

# Looking politely at people and standing at an appropriate distance

| | |
|---|---|
| **What is it?** | **Looking politely at people and standing at an appropriate distance** is the student's ability to look at a person or group of people both spontaneously when speaking to them and wh en requested (that is, when their name is called), and to stand at a comfortable distance when speaking to another person. |
| **Why is it important?** | It is necessary for a student to look at a person (or people) when speaking to them in order to acquire and maintain their attention and as an indication that they are addressing them specifically. Standing at an appropriate distance from another person is important for establishing and maintaining comfortable interaction. |
| **Prerequisites:** | • Adequate vision<br>• The Preverbal Skills of Language – especially<br>   ❖ looking at people – facial regard<br>   ❖ awareness of sights around them – visual awareness. |

## Recommendations for encouraging 'Looking politely at people and standing at an appropriate distance'

| | |
|---|---|
| **Ideal response:** | The student spontaneously establishes and maintains comfortable facial regard with the relevant person or people throughout the interaction while standing at an appropriate distance. |
| **Acceptable response:** | The student establishes brief facial regard with the relevant person or people as the information is presented while standing at an appropriate distance. |

Ⓟ This page may be photocopied for instructional use only. © Francesca Bierens Speechmark Ⓢ

## Activities for 'Looking politely at people and standing at an appropriate distance'

The students need to:

- Look at the teacher and stand at an appropriate distance.

- Look at their classmates and teacher when greeting them.

- Look at each student when giving items to classmates.

- Look at their classmates when giving morning news.

- Look at the person and stand at an appropriate distance when greeting visitors to the class.

- Look at the person when giving messages to the secretary at the office or to another teacher and stand at an appropriate distance.

## Activities – Looking politely at people and standing at an appropriate distance

**1   The students need to:   Look at the teacher and stand at an appropriate distance.**

**Activity:**

1   Ask a student to get a required item for you.

2   The student must look at you (the teacher) – even if it is only briefly – when giving the item.

3   Direct the student to stand at an appropriate distance from you if they tend to stand too far away or too close.

4   Have the students take turns to routinely get an item required every morning for circle time (such as the class roll or a photo book) from the place where it is kept and give it to the teacher.

The focus must be on the student looking at you when handing over the item.

Ⓟ This page may be photocopied for instructional use only. © Francesca Bierens   Speechmark

**2  The students need to: Look at the classmate or teacher they are greeting.**

**Activity:**

1   Ask a student to greet each of their classmates and teacher by name and say, 'Good morning.'

2   The student must look at each student and the teacher – even if only briefly – when saying their name.

3   If appropriate for your class, have the students take turns to routinely greet each of their classmates and teacher in the morning.

The focus must be on the student looking at the person – even if only briefly – when saying the student's or teacher's name.

**3  The students need to: Look at the person when giving items to classmates.**

**Activity:**

1   Ask a student to give out items such as books to their classmates.

2   The student must identify each of their classmates by name and look at them – even if only briefly – as they *give* them the required item.

3   If appropriate for your class, have the students take turns to routinely give out a required item to each of their classmates for a particular subject.

The focus must be on the student looking at the person when giving the item to their classmates.

**4  The students need to: Look at their classmates when giving morning news.**

**Activity:**

1   When giving morning news, remind the students to look around the class and look at their classmates.

2   At the end of their news, the student must then look at and name the student who has their hand up in the hope of asking a question about the news; for example: 'Yes, Bob?'

3   They must then look at that student as they respond to the question.

The focus must be on the student looking at the students as they speak to their classmates.

Ⓟ This page may be photocopied for instructional use only. © Francesca Bierens  Speechmark Ⓢ

**5   The students need to: Look at the person when greeting visitors to the class.**

**Activity:**

1   When a visitor enters the classroom, a named student must look at the visitor as they are greeted and welcomed to the class.

2   Remind the student to stand at an appropriate distance from the visitor so that they are neither too far away nor too close to them.

3   If appropriate for your class, have the students take turns to greet and welcome visitors to the class.

**6   The students need to: Look at the person when giving messages to another teacher or person in the office.**

**Activity:**

1   Ask a student to take a message to the secretary at the office or to another teacher.

2   The student must look at the secretary or teacher – even if only briefly – as they either pass them the written message or give a verbal message.

3   Remind the student to stand at an appropriate distance from the teacher when giving the message so that they are neither too far away nor too close to them.

4   If appropriate for your class, have the students take turns to take a message to another person at the school.

The focus must be on the student looking at the person to whom they are giving the message.

Ⓟ This page may be photocopied for instructional use only. © Francesca Bierens  Speechmark Ⓢ

# Chapter 2

# Looking carefully in order to see important things

| | |
|---|---|
| **What is it?** | **The skill of looking carefully in order to see important things** is the student's ability to maintain an interest and understanding of the visual information that is either around them or presented to them. |
| **Why is it important?** | This skill is essential in order for the student to acquire an awareness or consciousness of the subtle as well as the obvious things occurring around them. |
| **Prerequisites:** | • Adequate vision<br>• Preverbal Skills of Language – especially<br>  ❖ looking at people – facial regard<br>  ❖ awareness of sights around them – visual awareness<br>  ❖ attention and concentration.<br>• The Building Bricks of Language – comprehension of the language and information being presented. |

## Recommendations for encouraging the skill of 'Looking carefully in order to see important things'

**Required response:** The student remains attentive and responsive, actively showing an interest and understanding of the visual information presented or to which they are directed.

Ⓟ This page may be photocopied for instructional use only. © Francesca Bierens Speechmark Ⓢ

## Activities for 'Looking carefully in order to see important things'

The students need to:

- Look and identify facial expression.

- Look at the pictures or objects and 'spot the difference'.

- Look and recall what is missing.

- Look, find and identify objects by their description.

- Look, find and identify objects that are out of place.

- Look, find and identify objects that are 'not'.

## Activities – looking carefully in order to see important things

### 1   The students need to: Look and identify facial expression.

**Activity:**

1   Review the 'Emotions' activities ('How we can feel') from 'The Building Bricks of Language' section so that the students are able to consistently recognise the different emotions.

2   Do some role playing and have the students take turns demonstrating an emotion that the other students have to identify.

3   Then say a few phrases for the students that include an emotion, for example, 'I feel so happy today' and 'Yes, I'll go', and have the students identify how you feel when you say those phrases.

4   Then have the students listen to what you are saying but while looking at your facial expression. For example, using a sad expression, repeat the comment, 'I feel so happy today.'

5   Ask the students how you really feel. Is what you are saying matching your expression? What tells you how the person is feeling: the words or the expression? What should you be saying to match your expression?

6   Have the students take turns to make up a sentence that does not match what they are saying and have the other students identify how that person is really feeling and what they really should be saying.

Ⓟ This page may be photocopied for instructional use only. © Francesca Bierens   Speechmark Ⓢ

## 2 The students need to: Look at the pictures or objects and 'spot the difference'

### Activity:

1   Review the 'categories' activities from 'The Building Bricks of Language' (see the relevant Verbs activity: 'What we do with everyday things (categories)') so that the students are reminded of the simple categories and are able to identify some of the items that belong together.

2   Have a selection of objects or pictures that belong to one of the reviewed categories and have the students identify the category.

3   Put the pictures on the board where they can clearly be seen by all of the students.

4   Include one or two pictures that do not belong to that category, for example, 'shoe' in the 'food' category.

5   Have the students look at the selection of pictures and identify the picture that does not belong and why; for example: 'What is not in the category? Can we eat a shoe? No.'

6   Have the students take turns to add one or two 'odd' pictures to a category that the other students must identify.


## 3 The students need to: Look and recall what is missing.

### Activity:

1   Have the students choose six small objects – such as a pen and a block – from around the classroom.

2   Identify each of the objects with the students naming each item.

3   When the students have demonstrated a consistent knowledge of these objects then place them on a tray and show them again to all of the students.

4   Then remove one or two of the objects out of sight of the students by either turning away from the students or by covering the tray with a cloth as you remove the items.

5   Then show the students the tray and have them identify the object that has been removed.

6   As they achieve success with this activity, gradually remove more of the objects or cover the tray completely so that they have to recall all of the items.

7   Also gradually increase the number of objects on the tray.

153

**4   The students need to: Look, find and identify objects by their description.**

**Activity:**

1   Review the 'Adjectives' activities from 'The Building Bricks of Language' section ('What things look like and feel like' and 'What things in our classroom look and feel like') so that the students are able to recognise simple adjectives and can describe objects around the classroom.

2   Describe a common item in the class; for example: 'It is round and yellow.' Have the students look around the room and name the items that match that description until they have identified the correct object, that is, a clock.

3   Have the students take turns to describe a common item in the class, being careful not to identify it.

4   Have the students look around the room and name the items that match that description until they have identified the correct object.

5   Encourage the students to look around the classroom rather than just choosing items that are in front of them.

**5   The students need to: Look, find and identify objects that are out of place.**

**Activity:**

1   Review the 'Nouns' and 'Prepositions' activities from 'The Building Bricks of Language' section ('Name the things we use in the classroom' and 'Where things are in the classroom') so that the students are able to recognise and identify objects and their location around the classroom.

2   Make sure that the students can demonstrate a consistent knowledge of the names of objects and can identify where they belong.

3   Then, out of sight of the students (have them cover their eyes), move some of the objects around the room so that they are obviously in the wrong place, for example, the maths blocks in the library corner.

4   Have the students look around the room and find the things that are out of place and then identify where they should be.

5   Have the students take turns (out of sight of the other students), to move one or two common items to a place they do not belong in the classroom, and have the other students look around the room and find them.

Ⓟ This page may be photocopied for instructional use only. © Francesca Bierens  Speechmark

**6   The students need to: Look, find and identify objects that are *'not'*.**

**Activity:**

1   Review the 'Negatives' activities from 'The Building Bricks of Language' section ('What people are not doing', 'The things in the classroom – Yes and No' and 'What does not belong (categories)').

2   When the students have demonstrated a consistent knowledge of negatives then have them identify the appropriate object around the room when described; for example: 'This object is *not* big and *not* in the library corner' and 'This person is *not* sitting'.

3   Have the students look around the room and name the items that match that description until they have identified the correct object. For example, possible responses could be, 'Small maths block in the maths corner' and, 'Teacher'.

4   Make sure the object or person is clearly within vision.

5   Initially, it may be necessary to provide a specific area of attention within the classroom so that the students have a clear limitation of objects and locations.

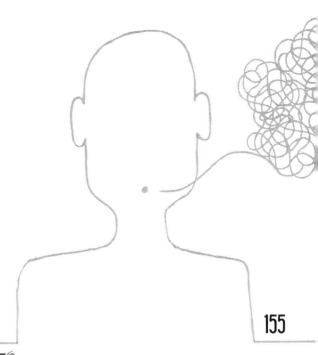

Ⓟ This page may be photocopied for instructional use only. © Francesca Bierens  Speechmark Ⓢ

## Chapter 3

# Listening attentively and remembering what has been heard

| | |
|---|---|
| **What is it?** | **Listening attentively and remembering what has been heard** is the student's ability to maintain an interest and awareness of the information they are hearing and/or what is being said. |
| **Why is it important?** | This skill is essential in order for the student to acquire an alertness of the subtle as well as the obvious things they hear and/or what is being said. |
| **Prerequisites:** | • Adequate hearing<br>• The Preverbal Skills of Language – especially<br>   ❖ attention and concentration<br>   ❖ awareness of sounds around them – auditory awareness<br>• The Building Bricks of Language – comprehension of the language and information being presented. |

## Recommendations for encouraging 'Listening attentively and remembering what has been heard'

**Required response:** The student remains on task and responsive, showing an active interest and understanding in what they are hearing and/or what is being said.

## Activities for 'Listening attentively and remembering what has been heard'

The students need to:

• Identify and discriminate environmental and animal sounds.

• Listen and identify a key word.

• Listen and identify speech sounds.

Ⓟ This page may be photocopied for instructional use only. © Francesca Bierens Speechmark ⑤

- Listen and repeat a short sentence.

- Listen and repeat a short clapping rhythm.

- Listen and match rhyming words.

If the students have difficulty with these activities, keep the activity as simple as possible and provide them with as much assistance as necessary in order for them to achieve success.

## Activities – Listening attentively and remembering what has been heard

### 1 The students need to: Identify and discriminate environmental and animal sounds.

### Activity:

1  Create a game of 'sound lotto' – either your own created version or one of the commercial varieties.

2  Have a variety of sounds, such as household sounds (like a telephone ringing and a bath running), environmental sounds (like the sea crashing on to the beach and the sounds of a thunderstorm), transport sounds and animal sounds.

3  Have the students listen carefully to the sounds and match the sounds to the selection of pictures in front of them.

4  Play the game in small groups or as a class activity.

### 2 The students need to: Listen and identify a key word.

### Activity:

1  Give the students a key word such as a common object in the classroom (for example, 'book').

2  Initially, if necessary, have a book as a visual prompt on the table in front of the students to assist them for the first trial.

3  Give the students a piece of paper and pen or stamp and every time they hear the key word, they make a mark on the paper.

4  Begin by slowly just giving the key word (for example, 'Book – book – book') with the students marking the paper each time.

5  Then add in another 1 or 2 words for example, table – pencil – book.

6  Initially, stress the key word, point to the book on the desk and wait for the students to recognise it as the key word, and mark their paper.

7  As the students achieve success with this activity, remove the visual prompt and add more words to the list so that the students have to listen carefully for the key word.

157

This page may be photocopied for instructional use only. © Francesca Bierens  Speechmark

**3  The students need to: Listen and identify speech sounds.**

**Activity:**

1  Identify one speech sound, for example, 'm'. Write it on the board, make the sound and have the students imitate the sound.

2  Use the sound, that is, 'm' as a key sound that the students have to identify when they hear it.

3  Give the students a piece of paper and pen or stamp and every time they hear the key sound, they make a mark on the paper.

4  Begin by slowly just giving the key sound (for example, 'M – m – m') with the students marking the paper each time.

5  Then add in another one or two sounds that do *not* sound like the key sound (for example, 'l' and'k').

6  Initially, include one or two sounds, stress the key sound and wait for the students to recognise it as the key sound and mark their paper.

7  As the students achieve success with this activity, add more dissimilar sounds to the list so that the students have to listen very carefully for the key sound.


**4  The students need to: Listen and repeat a short sentence.**

**Activity:**

1  Begin with a short phrase or sentence of three words; for example: 'I like apples.'

2  Say the sentence clearly and at a slower speed.

3  Have the students take turns to repeat the sentence.

4  When the students are able to accurately repeat the sentence, then increase the length by one word; for example: 'I like crunchy apples.'

5  Introduce new sentences and as the students are able to repeat them correctly, gradually increase their length and complexity.

6  If the student is unable to repeat the sentence, then go back to a sentence that they are able to repeat successfully. It is always important to finish the activity with the student achieving success.

℗ This page may be photocopied for instructional use only. © Francesca Bierens  Speechmark

**5 The students need to: Listen and repeat a short clapping rhythm.**

**Activity:**

1 Begin with a short, even-timed clapping rhythm of two claps.

2 When the students are able to accurately repeat the rhythm, gradually increase the length and complexity, for example, three claps – loud – short – short.

3 Have the students take turns to repeat the sequence.

4 As the students are able to repeat the rhythm correctly, continue to increase the length and complexity of the clapping rhythm, for example, short – short – loud – loud – short – short.

5 If the student is unable to repeat the sequence, go back to a sequence that he was able to repeat successfully.

6 It is always important to finish the activity with the student achieving success.

**6 The students need to: Listen and match rhyming words.**

**Activity:**

1 Start with simple words, for example, the 'at' words, and write them on the board, for example, 'hat', 'cat' and 'mat'. Say the words on the board as you write them, underlining the 'at' so that the students see the pattern.

2 Go through the list of words slowly so that the students have time to contribute and then prompt the next word with just the initial sound, for example, 'S … sat.'

3 Often the students are more successful at adding the rhyming words after a number of words have been provided rather than just one.

4 As the students gain success with one group of sounds then introduce another family of sounds, for example, 'op' – 'top', 'mop' and 'pop'.

5 When the students consistently demonstrate an understanding of simple rhyming words, introduce a rhyming poem where the students must finish the last word of the phrase. Assist them when necessary by providing them with an initial sound prompt.

6 If the students have difficulty with this activity, provide them with as much assistance as necessary in order for them to achieve success.

P This page may be photocopied for instructional use only. © Francesca Bierens Speechmark

## Chapter 4

# Waiting, listening to others and recalling information given

| | |
|---|---|
| **What is it?** | **Waiting, listening to others and recalling information given** is the student's ability to establish and maintain awareness as well as interest and active participation in what is being said by another person or other people. |
| **Why is it important?** | This skill is essential in order for interactive conversation to occur. |
| **Prerequisites:** | • The Preverbal Skills of Language<br>• The Building Bricks of Language – an understanding and functional use of the words and concepts being presented. |

## Recommendations for encouraging the skill of 'Waiting, listening to others, and recalling information given'

**Required response:** The student is able to actively wait and listen to another person speaking and understand and retain what they are saying and contribute appropriately in a turn-taking manner.

## Activities for 'Waiting, listening to others, and recalling information given'

The students need to:

- Listen to their classmates, repeat their sentence and then take their turn.
- Wait and listen to their classmates telling information about themselves and then recall it.
- Wait and listen to their classmates telling information about a picture card and then recall it.
- Wait and listen to their classmates telling information from a photo and then recall it.
- Wait and listen to their classmates giving news and then recall it.
- Wait and listen to their classmates recalling a sequence of information from a single class event and then recall it.
- Wait and listen to their classmates recalling a single event with emotion and then recall it.

Ⓟ This page may be photocopied for instructional use only. © Francesca Bierens  Speechmark

- Wait and listen to their classmates make up part of a sentence, which they must then add to.

# Activities – Waiting, listening to others and recalling information given

**1   The students need to:   Listen to their classmates, repeat their sentence and then take their turn.**

**Activity:**

1   Have the students take turns to make up one simple sentence.

2   Each sentence must include four concepts: one of time, one proper noun, one verb and one noun. For example, 'On Monday, Tammy eats bananas.'

3   Use visual prompts of each concept to be included if necessary.

4   The teacher can give the first sentence in order to model what is required.

5   The other students must listen to the person giving the sentence.

6   When the sentence is finished, the student will call the name of one of their classmates. The student named must then repeat the sentence given and make up one of their own.


**2   The students need to:   Wait and listen to their classmates telling information about themselves and then recall it.**

**Activity:**

1   Have each student take turns to tell three pieces of information about themselves, for example, their name, their age and their interests.

2   Have the students listen and, when named, they recall at least two facts from the information given by one or two of the other students.

The focus is on good listening, so the recalled facts must be accurate without the inclusion of any additional information.


**3   The students need to:   Wait and listen to their classmates telling information about a picture card and then recall it.**

**Activity:**

1   Give each student a clear picture card of people participating in a familiar activity.

2   Have each student take turns telling five pieces of information about a picture card: who is in it, what they are doing, where they are and so forth. The information must be given in sentences of at least three words.

This page may be photocopied for instructional use only. © Francesca Bierens  Speechmark

3 Have the students listen and, when named, recall at least three facts from the information given by one or two of the other students. The recalled information must be given in phrases or sentences.

The focus is on good listening, so the recalled facts must be accurate without the inclusion of any additional information.

**4 The students need to: Wait and listen to their classmates telling information from a photo and then recall it.**

**Activity:**

1 Have each student take turns telling five pieces of information from a photo of a recent class activity or event, for example, where we went, what we saw, who we met and so forth. The information must be given in sentences of at least three words.

2 Have the students listen and, when named, recall at least four facts from the information given by two or three of the other students. The recalled information must be given in phrases or sentences.

The focus is on good listening, so the recalled facts must be accurate without the inclusion of any additional information.

**5 The students need to: Wait and listen to their classmates giving news and then recall it.**

**Activity:**

1 Have each student take turns giving news.

2 The news must be given in clear sentences of at least three words and must contain at least three pieces of information, for example, what you did, why you went and who you went with.

Have the students listen and, when named, recall at least two facts from the news of two or three of the other students.

4 The recalled information must be given in phrases or sentences.

The focus is on good listening, so the recalled facts must be accurate without the inclusion of any additional information.

**6 The students need to: Wait and listen to their classmates explaining the sequence of information from a single class event and then recall it.**

**Activity:**

1 Have the students take turns recalling a three-step sequence of information related to recent

P This page may be photocopied for instructional use only. © Francesca Bierens  Speechmark

class activities or events in which they have all participated, for example, making a model volcano.

2   The sequence of information must be given in clear sentences of at least three words.

3   Have the students listen and, when named, recall the three facts from the sequence of information given by the student. The recalled information must be given in the appropriate sequence in phrases or sentences.

The focus is on good listening, so the recalled facts must be accurate without the inclusion of any additional information.

## 7   The students need to:   Wait and listen to their classmates explaining a single event including an emotion and then recall it.

### Activity:

1   Have the students take turns recalling a single event involving a sequence of relevant information that consists of at least four facts, including at least one emotion, that is, where they went, what they did, how they got there, how they felt and so forth. This can be class-related or home information. The sequence of information must be given in clear sentences of at least three words.

2   Have the students listen and, when named, recall at least three of the facts from the sequence of information given by the student, including the emotion. The recalled information must be given in phrases or sentences, be accurate and be provided in the appropriate sequence.

## 8   The students need to:   Wait and listen to their classmates make up part of a sentence that they must then add to.

### Activity:

1   Begin by modelling one sentence that must include a person, a verb (action) and a noun (object). This may be true or made up; for example: 'I paint pictures.'

2   The next student must repeat the first sentence and then add on another sentence that is related to the first sentence; for example: 'I paint pictures. I paint cats.'

3   The next student must repeat the first *and* second sentences and then add on another sentence that is related to the previous information in order to form a story; for example: 'I paint pictures. I paint cats. My sister paints dogs.'

4   Continue the sequence with each student having a turn to add a sentence, until there is an obvious change in topic. Then have one student recall the full story.

5   Then begin another story with the sentences gradually including one or more complex concepts, that is,  adjectives, negatives, emotions, or time; for example: 'I like green jellybeans. I don't like black jellybeans. I only eat jellybeans on my birthday.'

This page may be photocopied for instructional use only. © Francesca Bierens  Speechmark

## Chapter 5

# Speaking clearly

| | |
|---|---|
| **What is it?** | **Speaking clearly** is the student's ability to make themselves clearly understood when speaking to other people. |
| | This includes: |

- intelligible speech, that is, being able to say all age-appropriate speech sounds and use these sounds correctly in words when speaking
- speaking at an appropriate speed, volume and pitch.

| | |
|---|---|
| **Why is it important?** | This skill is essential in order for the student to interact comfortably with others. Poor intelligibility of speech often leads to frustration for the student when people are unable to understand what they are saying. |
| **Prerequisites:** | |

- Adequate hearing skills
- The Preverbal Skills of Language – especially
  - ❖ awareness and control of the face and mouth muscles
- Adequate health
  - ❖ The body is wonderful and looks after us well. It uses its resources depending on its priorities. If the child has a heart condition or weak lungs, the body's priority will be to support the breathing first, so speaking in lengthy sentences with good voice projection is not the main priority.

## Recommendations for 'Speaking clearly'

| | |
|---|---|
| **Ideal response:** | The student is able to use all age-appropriate speech sounds when speaking and can make themselves clearly understood in all situations. |
| **Acceptable response:** | The student is able to make themselves understood in all situations even if they are not using all age-apropriate speech sounds. |

Ⓟ This page may be photocopied for instructional use only. © Francesca Bierens  Speechmark Ⓢ

### Recommended sequence when focusing on speech sounds

*This is a general guideline only. Your speech and language therapist may have different recommendations depending on the specific needs of your students.*

1  Lip sounds: – 'p', 'b', 'm'.

2  Tongue sounds: – 't' , 'd', 'n'.

3  'f' 'v' 'w'

4  Back sounds: – 'k', 'g', 'h'

5  'sh', 'ch', 's', 'z', 'j'

6  Tongue tip sound: – 'l'

7  'r', 'th'

## Activities for 'Speaking clearly'

### The students need to:

- Improve breath control and inflection.

  - ❖ Encourage imitation of inflection. This requires sustained breath control, so is a very good exercise.

  - ❖ Say a slow 'uuuuuuup' with rising inflection followed by 'dooooown' with a falling inflection.

  - ❖ If possible and appropriate for your students have them gently and slowly rise up on to the balls of their feet as they g ive a rising inflection while lifting their arms up, and then down again with the falling inflection as they lower their arms.

- Say single vowel and consonant sounds.

  - ❖ Sequence of consonants:

    - 'p', 'b', 'm'
    - 't', 'd', 'n'
    - 'k', 'g', 'h', 'f', 'v', 'w'
    - 'sh', 'ch', 's', 'z', 'j'
    - 'l'
    - v'r', 'th'

- Combine consonants with simple vowel sounds.

  - ❖ Simple vowels: 'ah', 'ee' and 'oo'

165

❖ Sound combinations: for example, 'ma – ma' five times

❖ Sound combinations: for example, 'ma – mee – moo'. Only combine these sounds when the student is able to correctly say the sounds individually.

- Imitate sounds in single words.

- Imitate sounds in words of two or more syllables.

- Use simple consonant and vowel syllables in silly sentences.

- Use simple consonant and vowel syllables in Janet's rhymes:

    ❖ Children generally enjoy fun rhymes. When they *first* recite the rhyme, let them enjoy the silliness of the words and don't worry about how they say the sounds.

    ❖ Focus on using the consonant and vowel syllables correctly in the rhyme when the rhyme is repeated. It is not necessary for the student to say all of the words in the rhyme correctly.

    ❖ When students have achieved success with the key syllables, introduce one additional word to be said correctly, for example, 'bird'. If appropriate, gradually increase the number of additional words that need to be said correctly. Make sure to only focus on the simple words.

    ❖ Focus on using the correct consonants and vowel syllables spontaneously when answering questions about the rhymes.

## Activities – Speaking clearly

**1 The students need to: Improve breath control and inflection.**

**Exercises:**

- Breathing exercises:

    ❖ Have students stand as straight and upright as possible with their hands relaxed by their sides (not in pockets).

    ❖ With the mouth closed (lips gently together), breathe in through the nose slowly to a count of five.

    ❖ Hold the breath for a count of two.

    ❖ *Slowly* breathe out through the mouth to a count of five blowing very slightly.

    ❖ Keep shoulders down when breathing in.

    ❖ Do this five times.

 This page may be photocopied for instructional use only. © Francesca Bierens  Speechmark

- Rising and falling inflection:

  ❖ Have students say a slow and controlled 'uuuuuuup' with rising inflection followed by 'dooooown' with a falling inflection.

  ❖ Do this five times.

**2  The students need to: Say single vowel and consonant sounds.**

**Exercises:**

1  Review the vowel exercises in the 'Preverbal skills – Lip exercises' and have the students practise correctly forming the simple vowels 'ah – ee – oo'.

2  Model each consonant sound on its own and then have the students imitate these sounds. Focus on one sound at a time, for example, 'p'. Do this five times, for example, 'p … p … p … p … p'.

3  Model and have the students imitate these sounds in a three-sound sequence, for example, 'p, p, p', 'p, p, p', 'p, p, p'.

**General sequence in which speech sounds should be focused on:**

- 'p', 'b', 'm', 't', 'd', 'n'

- 'k', 'g', 'h', 'f', 'v', 'w'

- 'sh', 'ch', 's', 'z', 'j'

- 'l'

- 'r', 'th'

**3  The students need to: Combine consonants with simple vowel sounds.**

**Exercise:**

1  Model and have the students imitate combining simple speech sounds with the three simple vowels 'ah – ee – oo'.

2  Begin with the lip and tongue sounds, that is, 'p', 'b', 'm', 't', 'd'.

3  Have students imitate one syllable at a time, for example, 'baa', 'bee', 'boo'.

4  When the students are able to imitate these individual syllables correctly, then slowly model the three consonant–vowel sequence and assist them to imitate; for example: 'baa – baa – baa', 'mee – mee – mee', 'too – too – too'.

Ⓟ This page may be photocopied for instructional use only. © Francesca Bierens  Speechmark Ⓢ

5   Focus on just one consonant-vowel combination at a time.

6   When the students are able to imitate these syllables correctly, then slowly model the three vowel sequence and assist them to imitate; for example: 'baa – bee – boo', 'maa – mee – moo', 'taa – tee – too'.

7   Focus on just one consonant sound at a time.

8   Make sure that the sounds are said correctly, that is, lips together for 'b' and 'm', and that there is good vowel variation.

   •   'baa – bee – boo', 'baa – bee – boo', 'baa – bee – boo', 'baa – bee – boo'

   •   'maa – mee – moo', 'maa – mee – moo', 'maa – mee – moo'

9   Do each of these exercises five times, using a variety of different volumes and speeds.


**4   The students need to: Imitate sounds in words.**

**Exercise:**

1   Sit on the floor with the students sitting a short distance away.

2   Roll a ball to each of the students and have them imitate individual speech sounds, for example, 'p', 't', 'k'.

3   Model and tap out on the ball the *initial sound* in simple single-syllable words, for example, '**b**all' and '**p**en'. Model the word and then roll the ball to a student who has to imitate the word, focusing on the *initial sound* in the word, and then roll the ball back to you.

4   Model and tap out on the ball the *final sounds* in simple single-syllable words. Focus on words used frequently throughout the day, for example, 'cu**t**' and 'boo**k**'.

5   Model the word and then roll the ball to a student who has to imitate the word, focusing on the *final sound*, then roll the ball back to you.


**5   The students need to: Imitate words of two or more syllables.**

**Exercise:**

1   Sit on the floor with the students sitting a short distance away.

2   Roll the ball to each of the students and as students achieve success with the previous exercise, introduce words of two or more syllables focusing on words used frequently throughout the day, for example, 'table' and 'computer'.

3   Model the word as you tap out the number of syllables on the ball, for example, 'com … pu … ter'.

Ⓟ This page may be photocopied for instructional use only. © Francesca Bierens  Speechmark Ⓢ

4   Roll the ball to a student who has to imitate the word as they tap it out on the ball and then roll the ball back to you.

**6   The students need to: Use simple consonant and vowel syllables in silly sentences.**

**Exercise: Sentences:**

- **baa – bee – boo** is a big, bouncing bumblebee.

- **moo – maa – mee** is a mighty, musical moose.

- **tee  – taa – too** is a teeny, tiny turtle.

- **kah  – kee – koo** is a cute, cuddly cow.

- **soo  – see – saa** is a small, smooth, seal.

- **lee – loo – laa** is a likeable, lazy lion.

The focus of the activity is to use the consonant and vowel syllables correctly, for example, '**moo maa mee**', in the sentence. It is not necessary for the student to say all the words in the sentence correctly.

1   Read the sentences to the students so that they hear them first.

2   Write the sentences on the board or make up a chart.

3   Then say the sentences slowly together to make sure the students are saying the sounds correctly.

4   Recite these sentences at different volumes, for example, the first verse in a whisper, the second verse in an 'inside voice' and the third verse in a loud voice.

5   After learning and reciting the sentences a few times, ask simple questions of the students related to the sentences.

6   Initially, keep the sentences written up on the board so that the students have a visual prompt in order to answer the questions correctly.

7   The focus of the activity is to use the correct consonant and vowel syllables spontaneously when answering the questions. It is therefore not necessary for the student to say all of the words in the sentence correctly if additional questions are asked; for example: 'What is **moo maa mee**?' (A mighty musical moose.)

8   Encourage and assist the students to make up their own silly sentences with variations on the consonant and vowel syllables.

**Question examples:**

- Who is a mighty musical mooose?     Answer: **moo – maa – mee**

- Who is a teeny, tiny turtle?     Answer: **tee  – taa – too**

- Who is a likeable, lazy lion?     Answer: **lee – loo – laa**

This page may be photocopied for instructional use only. © Francesca Bierens   Speechmark

**7   The students need to: Use simple consonants and vowel syllables in rhymes.**

**Activity: Janet's rhymes:**

1   When the students have achieved success with sentences, introduce Janet's fun rhymes.

2   Read the rhyme to the students so that they hear it first.

3   Write the rhyme on the board or make up a chart and say it together.

4   The rhyme is repetitive, so many of the students will be able to remember it after it has been recited a few times.

5   When they first recite the rhyme, let them enjoy the silliness of the words and don't worry about how they say the sounds.

6   Repeat the rhyme together slowly, this time making sure that the students are saying the key syllables correctly, that is, '**baa – bee – boo**' and '**lee – lah – loo**'. Recite these rhymes at different volumes, for example, the first verse in a whisper, the second verse in an 'inside voice' and the third verse in a loud voice. The focus of the activity is to use the consonant and vowel syllables correctly in the rhyme. It is not necessary for the students to say all of the words in the sentence correctly.

7   When students have achieved success with the key syllables, introduce one additional word to be said correctly, for example, '**bird**' or '**bear**'. If appropriate, gradually increase the number of additional words that need to be said correctly, but make sure to only focus on the simple words.

Please feel free to adapt these rhymes as appropriate.

**8   The students need to: Correctly use consonant and vowel syllables when answering questions about the rhymes.**

**Activity: Janet's rhymes:**

1   After learning and reciting the rhymes a few times, ask simple questions of the students related to the rhymes.

2   Initially, keep the rhyme written up on the board so that the students have a visual prompt in order to answer the questions correctly. The focus of the activity is to use the correct sounds spontaneously when answering the questions, rather than having to think of the answer to the questions.

3   The focus of the activity is to use the correct consonant and vowel syllables spontaneously when answering the questions. It is therefore not necessary for the student to say all of the words in the sentence correctly if additional questions are asked; for example: 'What is **baa bee boo**?' ('A busy bear'.)

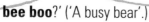 This page may be photocopied for instructional use only. © Francesca Bierens

## Question examples:

- Who is a kiwi bird?                       Answer: **kee – kaa – koo**

- Who is a talented tortoise?               Answer: **too – taa – tee**

- Who bakes his bread in a bucket?          Answer: **baa – bee – boo**

- Who lives in a lettuce leaf in London?    Answer: **laa – lee – loo**

- Who likes lime lollipops and liquorice?   Answer: **loo – laa – lee**

# Janet's rhyme

**Baa bee boo's** a busy bear
**Baa bee boo's** a busy bear
**Baa bee boo's** a busy bear
He bakes his bread in a bucket

**Mee moo maa's** a marmoset
**Mee moo maa's** a marmoset
**Mee moo maa's** a marmoset
He marches up mountains on Mondays

**Too taa tee's** a talented tortoise
**Too taa tee's** a talented tortoise
**Too taa tee's** a talented tortoise
He tap dances on trampolines in Tripoli

**Kee kaa koo's** a kiwi bird
**Kee kaa koo's** a kiwi bird
**Kee kaa koo's** a kiwi bird
He's kind to kangaroos and corgis.

**Saa see soo's** a silly salmon
**Saa see soo's** a silly salmon
**Saa see soo's** a silly salmon
He sings instead of swims, in the Southern Seas

*Written by Janet Marshall.*

Ⓟ This page may be photocopied for instructional use only. © Francesca Bierens.  **Speechmark** Ⓢ

## Janet's rhyme

Ⓟ This page may be photocopied for instructional use only. © Francesca Bierens

**Laa lee loo's** a ladybird
**Laa lee loo's** a ladybird
**Laa lee loo's** a ladybird
She lives in a lettuce leaf in London

**Lee loo laa's** a lonely lion
**Lee loo laa's** a lonely lion
**Lee loo laa's** a lonely lion
He listens to lyrics in the laundry

**Loo laa lee's** a little lamb
**Loo laa lee's** a little lamb
**Loo laa lee's** a little lamb
She likes lime lollipops and liquorice

**Lee laa loo's** a lucky leopard
**Lee laa loo's** a lucky leopard
**Lee laa loo's** a lucky leopard
He leaps in the lavenders and lilacs.

*Written by Janet Marshall.*

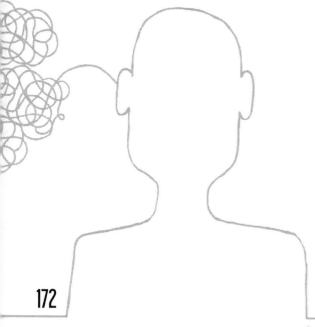

Ⓟ This page may be photocopied for instructional use only. © Francesca Bierens  Speechmark Ⓢ

# Chapter 6
# Asking and answering conversational questions

| | |
|---|---|
| **What is it?** | **Asking and answering conversational questions** is the ability to establish and maintain a conversation. |
| **Why is it important?** | This skill is essential for interactive situations such as play and for establishing and maintaining friendships. |
| **Prerequisites:** | • The Preverbal Skills of Language<br>• The Building Bricks of Language – all previous language skills and vocabulary.<br>The reason that this activity is at the end of the language programme is because the student requires all of the previous skills and knowledge in order to carry out this skill successfully. Before attempting this activity, make sure that the student has achieved all previous skills in order to avoid frustration. |

## Recommendations for encouraging ability to ask and answer conversational questions

| | |
|---|---|
| **Ideal response:** | The student is able to ask a sequence of relevant, correctly structured questions of another person, peer or adult, with appropriate use of all conversational skills and be able to respond appropriately to their questions. |
| **Acceptable response:** | The student is able to ask a sequence of two to three relevant questions of another person, peer or adult, using a clear question structure, with appropriate use of all conversational skills and be able to respond appropriately to their questions. |

Ⓟ This page may be photocopied for instructional use only. © Francesca Bierens Speechmark Ⓢ

# Activities for asking and answering conversational questions

**The students need to:**

- **Ask the question: 'Is it a … ?'**

  ❖ The focus of this activity is for the students to listen carefully to *all* answers given. For example, if one student asks, 'Is it a fruit?' and receives a 'no' response, then the next student should know not to ask, 'Is it an apple?'

  ❖ To assist the students with this, put pictures related to each category on the board and turn them over as that category is eliminated.

  ❖ Limiting the number of questions helps the students to remain focused throughout the activity.

- **Ask the questions and recall the response about a photo.**

  ❖ The focus of this activity is for the students to be able to accurately structure the questions and ask them in an interactive sequence, listening attentively to the responses given.

- **Ask and answer questions with a partner.**

  ❖ The focus of this activity is for the students to be able to accurately structure the questions, ask them in an interactive sequence and recall the responses given in an informative manner.

- **Ask the interactive questions at news time.**

  ❖ The focus of this activity is for the students to be able to listen attentively to information given to the group rather than individually and be able to construct relevant questions related to what they have heard.

- **Ask three interactive questions.**

  ❖ The focus of this activity is for the students to be able to accurately structure the questions, listen to the response given and then determine and ask the most appropriate question in an interactive sequence.

- **Ask questions about playing.**

  ❖ The focus of this activity is for the students to learn how to interact appropriately with others in a play situation.

- **Ask interactive questions to create a play.**

  ❖ The focus of this activity is for the students to interact and cooperate within a small group by using their skills of asking questions, listening to responses and answering questions in order to create an appropriate role play.

- **Ask questions to clarify information:**

  ❖ The focus of this activity is for the students to:

Ⓟ This page may be photocopied for instructional use only. © Francesca Bierens  Speechmark

- be aware that they require more specific information in order to carry out the activity correctly

- listen to the answers given to all questions asked and follow them carefully, rather than just draw what they assume.

  ❖ Try to make the instructions different to what the students may automatically assume that they are going to be, for example, 'boy *beside* the skateboard' rather than 'boy *on* the skateboard'.

  ❖ This is not an art test, so it doesn't matter if the items are unrecognisable to anyone other than the student.

  ❖ Make this a more difficult activity by adding in coloured pencils.

  ❖ Gradually make the pictures more complex.

## Activities – Asking and answering conversational questions

**The students need to ask the question: 'Is it a …?'**

**Activity:**

1 Review the categories activities from 'The Building Bricks of Language' (see the 'Verbs' activity: 'What we do with everyday things (categories)'). Choose **two pictures** from **four categories** only and go through and name each of these **eight pictures** with the students, for example, 'food', 'animals', 'clothes' and 'furniture', so that they can identify all of the pictures.

2 Choose one picture from this group, out of sight of the students, and have the students guess the chosen picture.

3 Model the initial question for them; for example: **'Is it something we can eat?'**

4 Each student then has a turn to ask. Allow them to form their own question; for example: 'It is a … ?' Then model and stress the *correct* question structure for the students, that is, **'Is it a … ?' before answering 'Yes' or 'No'**. Repeat the student's question in a confirming manner so that all the students can hear; for example: 'Is it an animal?'

5 When the picture has been guessed, have each student take a turn to select a picture and respond to the questions asked by the other students.

6 As the students achieve success with this activity:

  ❖ Increase the number of pictures in each category and reduce the need to go through and name the list of pictures.

  ❖ Limit it to five questions each or have teams. This encourages them to listen more carefully to the answers given as they don't want to waste a question.

℗ This page may be photocopied for instructional use only. © Francesca Bierens  Speechmark

**The students need to ask the questions and recall the response about a photo**

**Activity:**

1  Have photos of class events or activities ('see The Building Bricks of Language activities: 'How we make things at school' and 'The sequence of events in our topic studies or field trip') – or use the students' photo books of photos taken throughout the year.

2  Have each student take turns choosing one clear photo from a class photo book and showing it to another student who is in the photo, asking initially, 'What are you doing?' and then, after receiving a response, asking the second question, 'Who is this?' pointing to another person in the photo, or 'Who is with you?'

3  Allow the students to ask the two questions and listen to the responses.

4  When the second student has replied to the two questions, ask the first student to recall the responses given.

5  When the students have asked and answered the questions, model the correct question sequence in a confirming manner, and repeat the response in a full sentence. Allow enough time for the students to respond; for example: 'What are you doing, Penny? Penny … is counting the maths blocks. Who is with you, Penny? … Bob is with Penny.'

6  As the students achieve success with this activity, reduce the frequency of modelling and repeating.

**The students need to ask and answer questions with a partner**

**Activity:**

1  Initially, model the questions with one or two students, listening and recalling their responses.

2  Then put the students together in twos, and have them take turns asking each other the three questions related to a recent weekend or holiday activity, that is, 'What did you do?', 'Who did you go with?' and 'Where did you go?'

3  The students need to be able to: ask the three questions; recall each response; and answer the questions when they are asked.

4  It may be necessary to move around the groups and model the questions for some of the students to ensure that the meaning is clear.

5  Have the students then report back to the class and recall the three responses given to their questions. Some prompts and repetitions may be required; for example: 'Poppy shopping with aunty. Shoe shops.'

6  Wait until the students have recalled the information before repeating their responses in a full sentence structure in a confirming manner. 'Very good, that's right. Poppy went shopping with her aunty. They went to the shoe shops.'

Ⓟ This page may be photocopied for instructional use only. © Francesca Bierens  Speechmark Ⓢ

**The students need to ask interactive questions at news time**

**Activity:**

1   At news-time have the students take turns to give three pieces of information to the class.

2   The other students must listen, and then they must ask questions relevant to the news given in order to acquire further or more specific information.

3   The students need to be able to: listen to the news; think about and form a relevant question related to the information given; and recall the response.

4   It may be necessary to repeat and model the question for some of the students to ensure that the meaning is clear.

5   When the students have given their news and responded to the questions, then ask one of the other students to recall 'two or more things you learned about (student's) news'. Some prompts, repetitions and clarification may be required.

6   When the student has replied, repeat the response in a confirming manner, modelling the correct sentence structure.

7   As the students achieve success with this activity, reduce the frequency of modelling and repeating.


**The students need to ask three interactive questions**

**Activity:**

1   Initially, model the questions with one or two students.

2   Then have each student choose a friend and ask them three related questions about their weekend, from a choice of: 'What?', 'Who?', 'Where?', 'When?', 'Why?' and 'How?'

3   Provide them with 'wh' prompt cards on the board so that they are reminded of what they can ask. The students need to be able to: ask a question, listen to the response and then ask the next question related to the answer given to the previous question; for example, to the first answer, 'I went to the movies' the next question may be, 'What movie did you see?'

4   They must also ask one 'emotion' question related to the responses; for example: 'Did you like the movie?'

5   The student chosen to answer the questions must then ask three questions of their partner.

6   Have the students recall the four responses (including the emotion question) given to their questions when asked, 'What did you learn about Bob's weekend?' Some prompts, repetitions and clarification may be required.

7   Wait until the students have recalled the information before repeating their responses in full sentences in a confirming manner.

This page may be photocopied for instructional use only. © Francesca Bierens  Speechmark

**The students need to ask questions when playing with others**

**Activity:**

1  Select a number of interactive activities, for example, blocks and games, and give them to a small number of students to set up and start playing.

2  Ask each of the other students which activity they would like to play with.

3  Direct the students to the appropriate activities and model the question they need to ask the student who is currently playing with that activity – 'May I play with you?'

4  When the answer is 'yes' (as of course it will be) then the students can join in and participate in the activity.

5  Throughout this activity, model the questions and responses needed in order to establish and maintain successful interactive play with one or more other students; for example, 'Can I have the …?' and 'Is it my turn?'

6  Some guidance may be required for this activity. As the students achieve success, gradually reduce the frequency of adult involvement.

**The students need to ask interactive questions to create a play**

**Activity:**

1  Talk to the students about the current topic of interest (for example, 'Safety') and discuss the different situations, for example, lost in the shopping centre and smell smoke.

2  Put the students into groups of four and have them make up a short play related to your current class topic of interest.

3  The students have to decide among themselves who plays what part; what they are going to do and say; where they going to be and why; and how they are going to look, move, and feel.

4  Provide them with 'wh' prompt cards on the board so that they are reminded of what they have to ask one another and decide on.

5  This situation provides the students with an immediate opportunity to respond to questions asked; for example: responding to 'Who wants to be the police officer?' with 'I do; I'll stand up straight and walk slowly' and responding to 'Who wants to be lost?' with 'Me – I'll look scared because I don't know where I am'.

6  Then have the students take turns putting on their play for the class.

Some guidance may be required for this activity in order to assist the students to ask the right questions; however, as the students achieve success gradually reduce your level of involvement.

This page may be photocopied for instructional use only. © Francesca Bierens Speechmark

**The students need to ask questions to clarify information**

**Activity:**

1   Give each student a blank piece of paper and a pencil.

2   Have a very simple picture of items on a page, (for example, a skateboard, a boy, a bird and a tree), which you do not show to the students.

3   The students must listen to the very simple instructions given, and then they need to ask questions in order to gain specific information about the picture and then draw the picture.

4   Model the activity to the students first by giving them basic information about the picture, giving one or two instructions at a time, for example, 'Draw a skateboard. Draw a boy.'

5   Students need to ask questions to gain further information; for example: 'Where is the boy?'

6   Give a full answer to the questions asked; for example: 'The boy is standing beside the skateboard.'

7   When the students have finished the first instruction, add the next; for example: 'Draw a tree and a bird.' Wait for them to ask the necessary questions; for example: 'Is it a big or little tree? Where is the bird?' Your response may be, for example, 'It is a big apple tree. The bird is flying above the tree.'

8   If the students have asked the right questions and listened to the answers given, then their picture should be similar to the original picture.

9   Have the students take turns 'being the teacher', giving the basic instructions about a simple picture and then answering the questions asked by the other students.

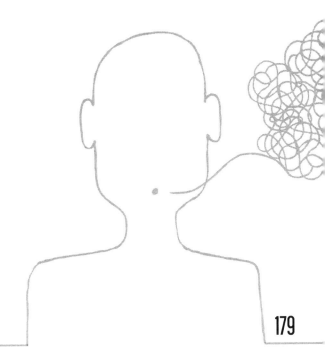

This page may be photocopied for instructional use only. © Francesca Bierens  Speechmark

Chapter 7

# Making 'The Skills of Conversation' activity box

1. Asking and answering conversational questions

2. Speaking clearly

3. Waiting, listening to others and recalling information given

4. Listening attentively and remembering what has been heard

5. Looking carefully in order to see important things

6. Looking politely at people and standing at an appropriate distance

## Box Three

### ACTIVITIES TO TEACH THE SKILLS OF CONVERSATION
The skills that turn communication into interaction

Creating a 'The Skills of Conversation' activity box gives you immediate access to the skill and activities required. It also makes it easier for the students to access the activity cards when necessary.

**Procedure:**

1   Buy or make a box that can fit a standard photo-sized card.

2   Make up the 'The Skills of Conversation' headings and use as dividers in the box.

3   Colour-code the Skill Headings for quick and easy recognition by both teacher and students.

Ⓟ This page may be photocopied for instructional use only. © Francesca Bierens   Speechmark

4   Copy each activity on to a card and place it in the appropriate skill section.

5   Place the 'The Skills of Conversation' activity box in a very visible and readily accessible location in the classroom.

Ⓟ This page may be photocopied for instructional use only. © Francesca Bierens   Speechmark Ⓢ

## Chapter 8

# Making 'The Skills of Conversation' activity cube

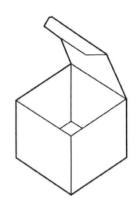

## Six-sided cube with a skill either written or illustrated on each side

'The Skills of Conversation' cube has a skill either written or illustrated on each side. This cube can be used as a dice to select a skill. The teacher rolls the dice or the students take turns to roll the dice to determine which skill they are going to practise. The teacher or a student then selects an activity from the appropriate section of 'The Skills of Conversation' activity box:

- Looking politely at people and standing at an appropriate distance

- Looking carefully in order to see important things

- Listening attentively and remembering what has been heard

- Waiting, listening to others and recalling information given

- Speaking clearly

- Asking and answering conversational questions

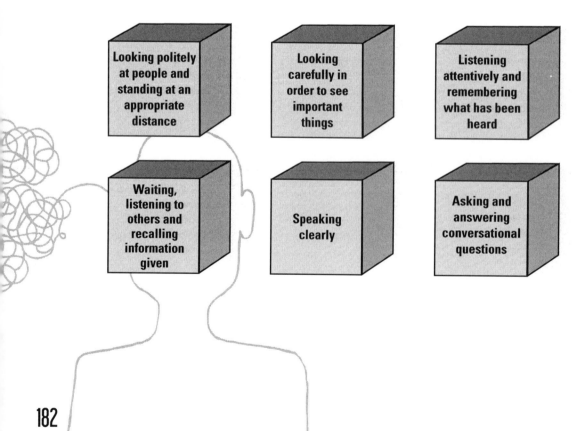

Ⓟ This page may be photocopied for instructional use only. © Francesca Bierens **Speechmark** Ⓢ

# The 'Skills of Conversation' activity cube

Ⓟ This page may be photocopied for instructional use only. © Francesca Bierens

**Cube template**

|  |  |  |
|---|---|---|
|  | **Looking politely at people and standing at an appropriate distance** |  |
| **Looking carefully in order to see important things** | **Listening attentively and remembering what has been heard** | **Waiting, listening to others and recalling information given** |
|  | **Speaking clearly** |  |
|  | **Asking and answering conversational questions** |  |

Ⓟ This page may be photocopied for instructional use only. © Francesca Bierens  Speechmark

# References

**Collins Gem English Dictionary** (1988) New Edition – Pocket Dictionary, Collins Sons & Co. Ltd, Great Britain.

**Crystal A, Fletcher P & Garman M** (1979) *Working with LARSP,* Edward Arnold, London.

**Gleason J** (1996) Semantic development: learning the meaning of words (Chapter 4). In: *The Development of Language,* Fourth Edition. Allyn and Bacon, Boston, MA.

This page may be photocopied for instructional use only. © Francesca Bierens  Speechmark